Managing People in Sport Organizations

Managing People in Sport Organizations provides a comprehensive overview of the theory and practice of managing people within a strategic framework. This revised and updated second edition examines a range of strategic human resource management approaches that can be used by sport organizations to respond to contemporary challenges and to develop a sustainable performance culture. Drawing on well-established conceptual frameworks and current empirical research, the book systematically covers every key area of HRM theory and practice, including:

- recruitment
- training and development
- performance management and appraisal
- motivation and reward
- organizational culture
- employee relations
- diversity
- managing change.

This new edition also includes expanded coverage of social media, volunteers, and individuals within organizations, and is supported with a new companion website carrying additional resources for students and instructors, including PowerPoint slides, exam questions and useful web links. No other book offers such an up-to-date introduction to core concepts and key professional skills in HRM in sport, and therefore *Managing People in Sport Organizations* is essential reading for any sport management student or any HR professional working in sport.

Tracy Taylor is a Professor of Sport Management and Business School Deputy Dean at the University of Technology, Sydney, Australia. Tracy's research focus is human resource management, cultural diversity management in sport, and sport and security. Tracy leads the HR module of the Executive Masters in Sport Organisations Management which is supported by the International Olympic Committee, Olympic Solidarity and the European Olympic Committees. Tracy is the incoming Editor of *European Sport Management Quarterly* and immediate past Editor of *Sport Management Review*.

Alison Doherty is a Professor in the Sport Management program at Western University, Canada. Her research focuses broadly on the management of non-profit and community sport, and particularly sport and event volunteerism, governance, organizational capacity and innovation. Alison is a Research Fellow of the North American Society for Sport Management and was the 2012 Zeigler Lecture Award honouree. She is the Editor of *Sport Management Review*.

Peter McGraw is an Associate Professor in the Department of Marketing and Management at Macquarie University, Australia, where he teaches subjects in human resource management and leadership. He researches and publishes in a variety of areas concerned with management, human resource management and employee relations, and is the author of over 60 academic articles and book chapters as well as two HR textbooks.

Sport Management Series

Series Editor: Russell Hoye, La Trobe University, Australia

This Sport Management Series has been providing a range of texts for core subjects in undergraduate sport business and management courses around the world for more than 10 years. These textbooks are considered essential resources for academics, students and managers seeking an international perspective on the management of the complex world of sport.

Many millions of people around the globe are employed in sport organizations in areas as diverse as event management, broadcasting, venue management, marketing, professional sport, community and collegiate sport, and coaching as well as in allied industries such as sporting equipment manufacturing, sporting footwear and apparel, and retail.

At the elite level, sport has moved from being an amateur pastime to one of the world's most significant industries. The growth and professionalization of sport has driven changes in the consumption and production of sport and in the management of sporting organizations at all levels.

Managing sport organizations at the start of the twenty-first century involves the application of techniques and strategies evident in leading business, government and non-profit organizations. This series explains these concepts and applies them to the diverse global sport industry.

To support their use by academics, each text is supported by current case studies, targeted study questions, further reading lists, links to relevant web-based resources, and supplementary online materials such as case study questions and classroom presentation aids.

Available in this series:

Managing People in Sport Organizations

A strategic human resource management perspective

SECOND EDITION

Tracy Taylor, Alison Doherty and Peter McGraw

Routledge
Taylor & Francis Group

LONDON AND NEW YORK

First published 2007
by Routledge

This edition published 2015
by Routledge
2 Park Square, Milton Park, Abingdon, Oxon OX14 4RN

and by Routledge
711 Third Avenue, New York, NY 10017

Routledge is an imprint of the Taylor & Francis Group, an informa business

British Library Cataloguing-in-Publication Data
A catalogue record for this book is available from the British Library

Library of Congress Cataloging in Publication Data
Taylor, Tracy.
Managing people in sport organizations : a strategic human resource
management perspective / Tracy Taylor, Alison Doherty and Peter McGraw.
– Second Edition.
    pages cm – (Sport Management)
    Includes bibliographical references and index.
    1. Sports administration. 2. Personnel management. 3. Associations,
institutions, etc. – Management. I. Doherty, Alison. II. McGraw, Peter.
III. Title.
    GV713.T39 2015
    796.06´9–dc23   2014024533

ISBN: 978-0-415-71532-4 (hbk)
ISBN: 978-0-415-71534-8 (pbk)
ISBN: 978-1-315-88188-1 (ebk)

Typeset in Berling and Futura
by HWA Text and Data Management, London

Contents

Figures

Tables

Boxes

Preface

The strategic management of human resources in contemporary sport organizations is a challenging task in the context of changing technologies, workforce composition, job roles and work patterns, stakeholder expectations, methods of employee recruitment and selection, worker and volunteer attitudes and values, employment legislation and the impact of a global workforce and global competition. Effective strategic human resource management is not only about facilitating short-term performance but also assisting a sport organization to build sustainable longer-term performance. We examine different approaches to strategic human resource management that can be used by sport organizations to respond to contemporary challenges and to develop a sustainable performance culture. These approaches are located within relevant theoretical and regulatory contexts. At the operational level, approaches, practices and frameworks for thinking about the day-to-day activities of front line managers and supervisors in hiring, motivating, rewarding and retaining both employees and volunteers are outlined.

Strategic human resource management (SHRM) is about the overall process of managing people in organizations so that they are motivated and able to perform to their potential. A robust and well-designed SHRM process will maximise the overall effectiveness of the organization in meeting its goals. SHRM provides an integrated framework for planning and making decisions about the people in an organization, who to appoint, how to reward good performance, what motivates people to perform to their full capacity, how to determine training and development needs, and if and when to let people go. This book introduces the basics of SHRM and how the SHRM approach conceptualizes the fundamentals of workforce planning, hiring, performance appraisal, compensation systems and other HR functions. Human resource functions have shifted from the traditional personnel function being more about people and performance, and we present the implications of this shift in focus for sport organizations.

The book discusses the contemporary sport organization and how a SHRM perspective can help it to attain its goals. In parallel with this, we consider how contemporary people management challenges and opportunities impact on SHRM. The effective management of individuals who work and volunteer in sport organizations are addressed through examining aspects such as their competencies, personality, needs, values and beliefs. The nature and attributes of workgroups in which individuals find themselves is also considered, as this is a fundamental part of the context of HRM in sport organizations.

The second edition of the book further reinforces the importance of the strategic alignment of systems and processes that sport organizations can deploy to make good decisions about managing people. The book has been revised to incorporate the latest research and thinking about SHRM in sport organizations. The new content reflects the rapid increase and impact of technologies on HRM, including the rise of social media and the expanding use of big data. We have also integrated new examples and 'dilemmas' to demonstrate key HRM issues, and incorporated complementary illustrative case studies from around the world. End-of-chapter discussion questions and exercises are included to facilitate discussion and reinforce key concepts covered in the chapter.

Acknowledgments

We would like to acknowledge all the people who helped to make the production of this book possible. Simon Whitmore, Senior Commissioning Editor, Sport and Leisure, for his encouragement and support in developing a second edition of the book and, most notably, Ashlee Morgan for her dedicated work in sourcing new material and painstakingly performing the final manuscript checks and editing. We are also grateful to the following individuals for providing examples and cases that have enriched the book:

- Eric MacIntosh, Associate Professor, University of Ottawa (Chapter 5, GoodLife Fitness Clubs Inc.)
- Robert Jefferies, Volunteer Support Officer, British Cycling Manchester (Chapter 6, From the Field –Training Officials in British Cycling)
- Katie Misener, Assistant Professor, University of Waterloo (Chapter 8, Camp Pinnacle)

CHAPTER 1

Introduction

LEARNING OBJECTIVES

After reading this chapter you will be able to:

- Identify the unique challenge of managing people in contemporary sport organizations
- Identify the key human resource (HR) issues that affect sport organizations
- Explain how the human resource management (HRM) perspective affects HR policies and practices
- Describe how effective HRM contributes to the sustainability of sport organizations

CHAPTER OVERVIEW

In this chapter the concept of HRM is introduced in the context of a short historical overview of its evolution from personnel management. The case is made that contemporary HRM techniques are the most effective methods of increasing performance in modern organizations, particularly in the service sector. We overview some key issues relating to the effective management of personnel in sport organizations. In the context of this book volunteers are defined as individuals who provide their services free of charge to sport organizations for the benefit of those organizations. As is highlighted throughout the book, the prevalence, cultural context and meaning of 'volunteering' varies quite significantly from country to country.

The chapter concludes with a discussion of various elements of HRM and where these are covered in the remaining chapters of this book. We also acknowledge the themes that are integrated throughout the book that are related to the management of individuals and workgroups, staff and volunteers, and in geographically and culturally different contexts.

MANAGING SPORT ORGANIZATIONS

There has been much written about the unique nature of sport and the organizations associated with its delivery. The premise underpinning the inimitability of sport relates to its ability to engender irrational passions and emotional attachments, despite the often variable quality of the product. This is evidenced in the devoted fans who continue to support their favorite team through product purchases and spectator attendance even though the team is in the bottom half of the competition ladder, the organization is financially mismanaged or there are questionable ethics employed in player transfers. There is also the example of the wealthy team owner who continues to sustain massive losses year after year, but is alternatively rewarded by the associated status and sense of benevolence of his or her actions in financially propping up the team! This passion for sport may also be reflected in the individuals who choose to work in the sport industry where, except for some professional athletes, the salaries and earning potential tends to be below what similarly qualified individuals could earn in jobs unrelated to sport (Parks & Parra, 1994). It is also reflected in the vast legions of volunteers who congregate to help stage mega-sport events such as the Olympic Games, and who constitute the majority of coaches, managers and administrators running community sport clubs and associations (Cuskelly, Hoye & Auld, 2006).

The sport industry's distinctiveness is further exemplified by the features of intangibility, heterogeneity and inseparability of production and consumption (Buswell, 2004). By way of illustration, a consumer's valuation of, for example, a professional sports match or a personal training session with a coach or fitness consultant cannot be determined until that person has watched the match or engaged in the training session. This underscores the importance, and organizational challenge, of offering what will be seen as a quality product or service. These distinguishing characteristics of sport combine to create a unique management environment for sport organizations, of which the effective management of people who are working and volunteering for the organization is the most critical. In the same way that getting the best out of their players is the hallmark of a good coach, getting the best out of employees and volunteers is the hallmark of a good manager acting within an effective HR system.

As with many industry sectors there is extensive variability in the scope and size of sport organizations. Organizations dealing with sport range from small locally based volunteer run sport clubs that have no paid employees, to medium-sized organizations with a mixture of paid staff and volunteers, to multinational corporations that are staffed by a large global workforce. In delineating the sport industry, Hoye, Smith, Westerbeek, Stewart and Nicholson (2005) classified sport into three sectors: the public sector, the non-profit or voluntary sector and the professional or commercial sector. Sport organizations in the public sector include the sport and recreation branches of local, state/provincial and national governments (e.g., city recreation department, or provincial or federal ministry of sport), as well as government-funded specialist agencies that support such areas as high performance athlete or coaching development (e.g., a national sports institute). The non-profit or voluntary sector includes such organizations as community-based sport clubs (e.g., local swimming or football club), regional and national sport governing bodies (e.g., state or national athletic association) and international sport governing bodies (e.g., International Olympic Committee). The professional or commercial sector includes organizations such as professional sport teams and their governing leagues (e.g., Boston Celtics and the National Basketball Association (NBA), sport apparel and equipment manufacturers and retailers (e.g., Nike or Li-Ning, China), and sport stadia and facilities (e.g., Estadio Azteca, Mexico; Wembley Stadium, UK; Estadio Do Maracana Stadium, Brazil).

People management issues, processes and practices are inexorably linked to the orientations of these sport organizations. Some examples of sport organizations, their missions and their staffing requirements are presented in Table 1.1 using the Hoye et al. (2005) industry sectors framework.

TABLE 1.1 Sport organization sectors and staffing

Sector	Organization	Mission	Typical staffing profile
Public	National sport institute	A national basis with a particular focus on success at the Olympic Games and World Championships	Executive Director, Technical and administrative support staff, Nutritionist, Sport psychologist Board of Directors – appointed by government
Voluntary	Youth sport club	To provide an appropriate supportive environment for youth to enjoy sport in an atmosphere of fun, sportsmanship, democracy, and peace	Volunteers – large numbers in a range of roles. Coach, Manager, Event organizer, Fund raising, Promotion, Maintenance, Legal, Accounting, Risk management Paid administrative staff – limited number (e.g., Executive Director) Volunteer Board of Directors
Non-profit Membership	Local golf club	To be financially self-sustaining while providing a quality experience to members and guests with a commitment to exceptional perceived value through loyalty, growth, leadership and community citizenship	Paid staff – Chief Executive Officer (CEO), Golf-based Professional, Green Keeper, Catering staff, Administration. Volunteer Board of Directors
Commercial	Sport and fitness centre	To inspire our members to achieve their fitness goals with the finest fitness equipment, knowledgeable instructors and a safe, fun and friendly atmosphere	Paid staff – Administration, Aquatics, Dance and Fitness Instructors, Management, Operations, Personal Training, Reception, Sales
Professional	Sports franchise	Dedicated to winning Championships, growing new fans, and providing superior entertainment, value and service.	Paid staff – CEO, Vice President, management, Marketing and Broadcasting, Legal and Financial, Administrative and support staff Head Coach, training and sport operations staff Medical Staff Stadium staff Interns Community and event day volunteers Governance – Chair, Board members

HRM considerations are shaped by the environment in which the sport organization is located. The environment includes not only the sector but also the geographical location and cultural context. This operating context presents both opportunities and challenges for sport organizations.

In the public sector, government policy and legislation can support, regulate or dictate activities. At the general level this can impact sport organizations through the financial resources available from government sources for employing staff, to more specific operational implications, such as mandatory police checks of all employees and volunteers who work with children under child protection legislation. Non-profit and voluntary organizations inevitably have to grapple with volunteer management challenges. Organizations with a workforce consisting of both paid employees and volunteers require an approach to managing people that recognizes the different perspectives, motivations and capacity that each group brings to the organization. A volunteer workforce can provide sport organizations with the resources to perform such vital roles as officials, umpires, coaches, team managers, administrators, facility and grounds managers, registration and accreditation officers, fundraisers and event managers, to name just a few. The challenge is to recruit sufficient volunteers, maintain their motivation and to retain their services. The importance of volunteers to the sport sector has been well recognized and there are now many well-developed volunteer management programs and initiatives in countries such as Australia, Canada, New Zealand, the USA and across Europe.

Professional and commercial sport organizations have challenges such as meeting customer expectations and stakeholder demands via an effective workforce. Contemporary sport businesses have to make decisions about where to invest in HR and what types of HR activities will bring long-term, strategic benefit to the organization. Professional sport organizations have to deal with complex HR matters related to player trades and acquisitions, salary caps, team contract negotiations, player welfare and increasing scrutiny of integrity matters. In many sport-specific organizations there are also dilemmas about whether to recruit staff for their technical expertise or skills irrespective of their sporting background or their knowledge of the sport.

Regardless of sector, location or size, successful sport organizations require an approach to managing people, both on and off the field, which ensures that each individual realizes his/her potential and one that leverages capabilities across groups and that provides a rewarding work environment.

Throughout this book we present cases for discussion, ask you to think about questions related to the content, and present you with some 'dilemmas' to promote discussion and debate about different perspectives on HRM issues.

After reading the introduction, discuss/debate the following situation:

Your sport club/team has always operated with a small number of professional staff but a recent government grant has provided the funds to make an additional senior management appointment. The top two candidates are a degree-qualified management specialist with five years business experience but no association with the sport, and a recently retired former captain of your first grade/tier team with 15 years' experience with the club including having held a board role. How might you differentiate between these two candidates? What 'weight' would you give to these considerations?

CONTEMPORARY SPORT ORGANIZATIONS

Increased globalization, commercialization and accountability in the sports industry over the past few decades have led sport organizations to adopt more sophisticated management systems and become more 'business' orientated. These forces have shaped the scale and delivery of sporting competitions, the ways in which sports are organized, managed and governed, and the multidirectional flow of athletes, coaches, managers and executives across local, national and international locations. Significant change can be found in sport organizations in countries where fundamental political and ideological shifts have occurred (e.g., China, Russia) or where government funding in the provision of sport has been tied to restructured sport delivery systems and increased accountability for that funding (e.g., Canada, Australia, New Zealand). In the past few decades we have seen sports assume professional status (e.g., Rugby Union, Triathlon, Snowboarding) and long-established professional clubs achieve significant global exposure and build their brand equity (e.g., Manchester United, Barcelona, Bayern Munich). The transnational movement of athletes and coaches in professional sport has intensified, and global companies are involved in the management of these personnel (e.g., IMG, Octagon). We have seen the growth and increasing sophistication of chain organizations (e.g., Fitness First with over 1 million reported members in 2013), and in organizations that deliver major sport events (e.g., Organizing Committees for the Olympic Games, the FIFA World Cup, Formula One). A vast array of specialist providers associated with sport spectatorship has emerged (e.g., Global Spectrum – facility management; Nevco – sport scoreboards/displays) together with companies providing security for sport events and an ever expanding array of sport technologies.

The shift in the way sport has been traditionally organized may be most evident in bodies such as provincial/state and national level representative sport organizations where a growing number of paid employees have been appointed in roles traditionally held by volunteers (Ferkins, Shilbury & McDonald, 2005; Skirstad & Chelladurai, 2011). The classic examples of this are national sport organizations (NSO). These organizations were traditionally managed by former athletes and sport enthusiasts with a passion for the sport and the NSOs' measures of success were tied to on-field success and participant numbers rather than operational effectiveness. Changes to the sport environment have meant that increasingly NSO employees are selected for their technical or professional expertise in managing a business irrespective of their knowledge of the sport, and board members are recruited for their business acumen and not just their sporting knowledge or prowess.

As a sport develops, it is important to remain cognizant of how sport organizations have evolved, their cultural contexts, origins and core values, who the stakeholders are, and how staffing and HR policies can be used to meet their missions and goals for the future.

THE PEOPLE MANAGEMENT CHALLENGE IN SPORT ORGANIZATIONS

Human resources are of critical importance, alongside other valuable intangibles of a sport organization such as brand value and customer relationships. Attracting, developing and retaining talented people can provide a sport organization with the resources it needs to prosper, grow and, ultimately, gain competitive advantage. For example, the right coach or manager, a dynamic CEO or a new key player can transform the fortunes of sport organizations in a short period of time from the bottom of the pile into league or world champions.

The attraction, retention and development of high-caliber people is a major source of competitive advantage for sport organizations and should therefore be a high strategic priority. Creating competitive advantage through people means being able to identify the best mix of technical, team and leadership skills and abilities required for the organization. The 'best mix' is the combination that will allow the organization to meet its strategic objectives now and into the future. Recruiting the right people into the organization can provide the basis for improved efficiency, increased productivity and high morale in the workforce. Such people are likely to be motivated to give their best and will deliver the flexibility and commitment that most sport organizations seek.

Retention of talented employees and volunteers is one of the most important challenges for sport organizations today. Retention is often linked to issues of motivation, satisfaction, positive morale and appropriate rewards and recognition. Therefore, it is important to find out what creates motivated, committed and contributing employees and volunteers. Structuring a reward and recognition system that is aligned with the organization's strategic direction can contribute to positive employee and volunteer motivation, morale and retention. Training and developing employees and volunteers can create a more positive organizational culture by adding value to its key resources, and underpins a commitment to organizational learning and its associated benefits. Training and development of individuals will also assist the sport organization to satisfy current and future HR needs.

Retaining good employees and volunteers also contributes to customer satisfaction and facilitates greater sport consumption. Effective succession planning and talent management will also be of increasing importance, as over the next few years the Baby Boomers (born 1946–1964) will retire, and the much smaller cohort of upcoming Generation Xers (1965 to 1976–1982) will mean that there are significantly fewer people available to work.

How well sport organizations cope with the future challenges facing them will depend to a large degree on how well they can manage people to succeed in new ways of working and how successful they are at negotiating associated changes. Irrespective of the nature and degree of current and future people management challenges, the importance of attracting, developing, motivating, retaining, rewarding and managing the 'right' people needed to optimize the sport organization's performance is central to effective HRM and organizational performance.

WHAT IS HRM?

Human Resource Management is broadly defined as the policies, practices, procedures and systems that influence the behavior, attitudes, values and performance of people who work for the organization. An organization's HRM system at its most basic level administers people management systems which support broader organizational activities. In other words the HRM system follows strategic decisions taken in the mainstream business and ensures that such decisions can be implemented effectively by coordinating the people-related aspects of them. To be effective the HRM system must be both aligned with the strategic direction of the organization and be internally consistent. Strategic HRM (SHRM) takes this idea one step further by integrating HRM decisions into the strategic decision-making process so that it no longer just implements strategy, but actually helps to define and enable it in the first instance. The concept of SHRM is discussed in detail in Chapter 2 of this book.

The HRM system within an organization can be shaped by many factors depending on the type of organization (e.g., public or private sector), the external environment in which the organization operates (e.g., the nature of the labor market), and the choices made by the organization about how work is organized (e.g., the extent to which rewards are equally shared within the organization). As a result of these factors and choices there will be different human resource configurations within different organizations.

Before we consider a model of HRM it is useful to briefly outline the evolution of the concept from personnel management. This brief history is useful for three reasons. First, it helps us to understand how HRM is conceptually different from personnel management. Second, it helps us to understand how different HR functions have evolved historically at different times and as a result of different external pressures. Third, it helps us to understand that personnel and HR practices have been shaped by key theoretical advances which are to this day important underpinnings of practice and which will be referred to again in the various chapters of this book outlining different HR practices.

THE EVOLUTION OF THE HRM CONCEPT

HRM in practice varies greatly between sport organizations, from those with modern HRM techniques that are integrated and strategic to others that are still implementing an older style personnel model. In a study of Australian non-profit sport organizations, Taylor and McGraw (2006) found that only a minority had formal HRM systems in place and few organizations took a truly strategic approach. Similarly, at the community sport level, Cuskelly, Taylor, Hoye and Darcy (2006) reported that the use of HRM practices with volunteers varied significantly across community sport organizations. In order to better understand the continuum along which HRM is located, the following section will briefly outline the history of the two concepts.

Personnel management has existed in some form or other since large groups of people began to be organized to work for a common purpose. The first formal personnel practices were implemented during the late Victorian period in the UK with the emergence of welfare workers in larger industrial factories with generally poor working conditions. Welfare workers typically administered practices such as sick pay schemes, subsidized canteens and worker education programs. The earliest innovators in the welfare movement were philanthropists such as Robert Owen, who built a model industrial community at New Lanark, Scotland in the early nineteenth century. Later innovators were the highly religious Victorian entrepreneurs such as Rowntree, Cadbury, Lever, Salt, and Boot (Watson, 1977). The social reformist orientation of this group was based on a Christian concern for the well-being of the workers coupled with recognition that improved welfare for employees would also enhance the performance of the business. Cadbury explicitly made this connection describing welfare and efficiency as 'two sides of the same coin' (Legge, 1995: 11). These early initiatives led eventually to the establishment, in 1913, of the Institute of Welfare Officers in the UK (now the Institute of Personnel and Development) and employee welfare continues to be a part of the HR in contemporary organizations.

New elements were added to the personnel role around the time of the First World War with the widespread introduction of scientific management (Legge, 1995). Scientific management was associated with the ideas of the American Fredrick Taylor whose lifework revolved around scientifically studying the way that work was performed and how it could be made more efficient by finding the 'one best way' to complete a task. Taylor's work led to the advent of highly efficient standardized production techniques into factories with a pronounced division of labor, so that jobs became simple and could be easily learned by relatively unskilled workers. Although Taylor's ideas were widely criticized as leading to 'dehumanization' of work, because jobs became so simple, repetitive and boring, the efficiency gains from scientific management were so great that it was adopted in industrial countries around the world and laid the foundation for job design for the remainder of the century. Working with the principles of scientific management, personnel specialists became involved with the analysis, design, evaluation, and classification of jobs on the one hand and the use of this information in the administration of wages and salaries, particularly piecework bonus schemes which were also advocated by Taylor, on the other. Involvement with job design and compensation is a major part of the HR role in modern organizations.

Also evident from around the time of the First World War, and the consequent need for greater efficiencies in armament and munitions factories, was a greater focus on environmental factors such as lighting, heating, and ventilation, and their relationship with worker productivity. The focus on these factors and others associated with finding the best match between workers and jobs saw the emergence of the industrial psychology profession and also laid the foundation for the ongoing involvement of HR staff in occupational health and safety matters.

The next major movement to influence the practice of personnel management was the human relations movement which was associated with the motivation theories of the Harvard Professor, Elton Mayo. Human relations focused on the importance of building the social identification of workers with each other and with the organization as a whole as a way of stimulating higher levels of motivation and hence productivity. Human relations work involved initiatives designed to foster better cooperation within and between groups, and stronger identification of employees with the overall goals of the organization. Human relations quickly became popular and a strong influence on the practice of personnel management because it provided a strong counter-force against the alienating side effects of scientific management, and many elements of human relations are still practiced by the HR staff today, particularly those associated with building organizational identity and high performance teams.

The period following the Second World War saw the growth of legal, administrative and industrial relations components of the personnel function. This occurred in the tight, highly unionized labor markets associated with the long post-war boom which existed in developed countries around the globe. Legge (1995) identified three key developments in the overall role of personnel departments (from the 1960s onwards). First, the emergence of a role concerned with organizational efficiency. The emphasis was on creating clear objectives in jobs and fostering wider organizational commitment. Legge (1995) has suggested that the aim was the development of an open, flexible work culture that could fit more easily with the demands of a changing business environment. Involvement in organizational development and attempts to build cultures high on trust were characteristics of this period.

Second, the emergence of a role dealing with the increasingly complex employment law. This has been termed as a 'legal wrangling' role by Torrington (1989). Personnel managers often became experts in interpreting the rights of employers, employees and trade unions during this era of high union membership and influence. The third role, 'manpower analyst', was concerned with achieving the tightest fit between resources and organizational needs, and encompassed forecasting and implementing plans associated with future needs for staff (Torrington, 1989). These developments overlapped, and in some cases complemented, the emergence of the HRM movement.

EARLY APPROACHES TO HRM

Increasing levels of global competition in the 1980s focused attention on HRM in North America (Guest, 1987; Legge, 1995). In particular growing competitive pressure from Japan stimulated a response from organizations in the USA (Beer, Spector, Lawrence, Quinn & Walton, 1985; Fombrum, Tichy & Devanna, 1984; Tichy, Fombrum & Devanna, 1982), which focused on ways of replacing adversarial labor relations with more collaborative relationships. The patterns of collaboration between management and labor developed in Japan were admired by many American managers, at least in terms of outcomes, and inspired in the USA a call for improvements in management–union–employee relations. Alongside this change in management thinking was pressure from workers with higher levels of education to be more involved in their organizations (Guest, 1987).

In response to these developments, a new course was developed in HRM at the Harvard Business School which reflected the view that employees were a resource to be developed, not merely exploited, and that managers required new skills to best motivate their staff to cope with future organizational challenges. The authors have described the ideas presented as a 'broad causal mapping of the determinants and consequences of HRM policies' (Beer et al., 1985: 15). The projected outcomes of staff commitment, competence, congruity, and cost effectiveness at the organizational level, it was argued, would generate long-term benefits for individuals, organizations, and society, provided there was wholehearted commitment to the effort (Beer et al., 1985).

This theoretical development ushered in the use of the term 'human resources management' which defines the area today as well as a conceptual model which has been highly influential in defining the practice of HRM as something very different to old style personnel management. The Harvard model, as depicted in Figure 1.1, provides a useful holistic framework for understanding and analyzing HRM within the broad societal context and as well as in relation to specific choices that organizations can make about the way that HR is managed depending on their overall purpose and strategy. Thus, the Harvard model also established the foundation for later approaches to strategic HRM that are discussed in Chapter 2.

THE HARVARD MODEL OF HRM

The Harvard model shows how HRM policy decisions within organizations as well as their outcomes and consequences are influenced by a variety of interdependent stakeholder interests and situational factors. For example, the extent to which labor markets are regulated by government intervention is a situational factor that will have a major effect on HRM decisions with regard to wage rates, hours of work, equal employment practices and so forth. Managing HRM effectively means that sport organizations need to maintain their strategic direction while responding to changes in situational factors and balancing the

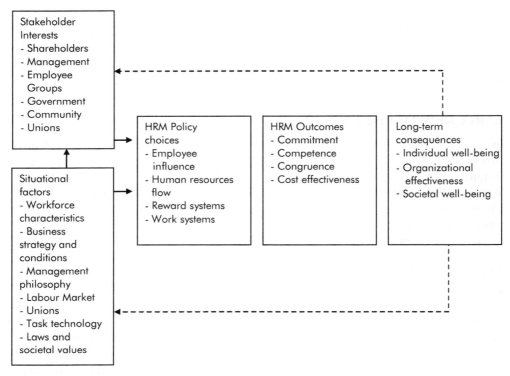

FIGURE 1.1 The Harvard model (Source: Beer et al., 1985)

varying stakeholder interests. The policy choices are what results from the balancing of these interests and factors. Within this model a balance is struck between organizational goals and societal norms, so while organizational strategy has a major influence on organizational practice, other factors, such as community expectations, the characteristics of the workforce and the presence, or absence, of unions are also relevant. The model is dynamic because the balance of interests and factors changes over time and for different organizations.

The model first outlines the various stakeholders of an organization. The influence of respective stakeholders may vary enormously, depending on the type of organization. For example, in community sport organizations, the most important stakeholders are the community sport participants. By contrast, a professional sport franchise has to first and foremost satisfy the interests of shareholders who own the business. In the vast majority of organizations the interests of different stakeholders are contested and subject to subtle shifts which represent changing points of balance in the interests of the various stakeholders.

The model then focuses on macro-level situational factors influencing the organization, including the workforce characteristics, business strategy and conditions, philosophy of management, the state of the labor market, influence of unions, level of technology employed, and societal laws, norms and values. These too will change over time and influence a dynamic process of HR change and adaptation to shifts in the external environment. Next, broad HR policy choices are considered. These relate to, for example, the level of employee and volunteer involvement as well as policy choices about reward systems and the way work is structured within the organization. According to the framework these policy choices will result in various HR outcomes such as the level of employee or volunteer commitment, the organization's HR capability, and the overall cost effectiveness of HR within the organization. These outcomes, in turn, have long-term consequences for the individuals who work for the organization, the overall organizational effectiveness and hence its long-term survival, and the contribution of the organization to the community. Finally, a feedback loop is incorporated into the model which can operate both ways. Thus, situational factors can not only influence and constrain policy choices but can also be influenced by long-term outputs from the employment process.

HRM has traditionally been focused almost exclusively around employees, but has more recently been broadened to include all people who contribute to the work of an organization as reflected in the Harvard model. This is particularly important for sport organizations where a significant number of people who contribute to the organization may be, for example, volunteers, interns, short-term contractors or consultants. Another key feature of HRM is that it incorporates, implicitly or explicitly, the idea that the way that people are managed makes a difference to the bottom line of the organization. In other words organizations that manage their people effectively are more likely to be successful in the marketplace because their HR system confers a competitive advantage. This will lead to superior performance relative to competitor organizations through, for example, faster speed of execution, higher quality of service, and/or more flexibility of response to customer specifications.

The purpose of HRM is to attract the best people to an organization, allocate them to appropriate roles on the basis of their skills and attitudes, manage them so that they can maximize their contribution to the organization, and retain them for an appropriate length of time so as to maximize the contribution from the 'resource'. In this way HRM makes a critical contribution to both the effectiveness and competitiveness of the organization. A meta-analysis of over 100 research studies (Jiang, Lepak, Hu, Kia & Baer, 2012) confirms the positive impact of effective HRM. Consistently across this collection of investigations, systematic recruitment, selection and training ('skill-enhancing HR practices') were found to be associated with the development of human capital, while performance appraisal, compensation and promotion ('motivation-enhancing practices') and job design and employee involvement ('opportunity-enhancing practices') were associated with employee motivation. Both human capital and motivation inversely predicted (reduced the likelihood of) employee turnover and directly predicted (enhanced) operational outcomes, both of which impacted on organizations' financial outcomes (Jiang et al., 2012). The findings provide evidence-based encouragement for organizations to invest in these HRM practices.

It is important to note at the outset that the work of HRM is not undertaken solely by staff employed in the HR department. Most of the people management in any organization is done on a day-to-day basis by general or line managers. So, for example, whereas HR staff may establish hiring procedures for an organization they should not necessarily be the only ones involved in hiring decisions. Similarly, whereas the performance management system in an organization may be set up and monitored by HR staff, the actual appraisals should be conducted by line managers. In this sense it is useful to view the 'HR function' as a broadly dispersed people management competence in an organization rather than just the activities carried out by specialists in the HR department. It is quite possible to have good HR procedures, but if these are poorly implemented by general managers then the net outcome is poor HRM. Therefore, when looking at HRM effectiveness in an organization the effectiveness of line managers in managing people must also be considered. This is particularly critical in small organizations where there are often limited or no dedicated HR staff.

At its simplest level HRM involves recruiting and selecting the best available staff, getting high productivity from these employees through high commitment management practices, retaining them for longer, maintaining high levels of staff satisfaction and morale through providing them with interesting work, and managing them in a way that generates commitment to the organization and low levels of grievances and associated 'maintenance' costs. Another way of thinking about this is to envisage the most desirable outcomes that organizations want from their staff policies and practices. Effective HRM systems should produce staff who are creative, loyal to the organization, committed to its long-term survival, can work independently without extensive supervision, produce high-quality outputs, are flexible in their work practices and prepared to embrace change.

In synthesizing the work of a number of writers, Guest (1987) summarized the conceptual model of HRM as comprising the following four propositions. First, 'if human resources can be integrated into strategic plans, if HR policies cohere, if line managers have internalized the importance of human resources and this is reflected in their behavior, and if employees identify with the company then the company's strategic plans are likely to be more successfully implemented' (Guest, 1987: 512). Second, 'organizational commitment, combined with job-related behavioural commitment, will result in high employee satisfaction, high performance longer tenure and a willingness to accept change' (Guest, 1987: 514). Third, 'flexible organization structures together with flexible job content and flexible employees will result in a capacity to respond swiftly and effectively to changes and ensure the continuing high utilization of human and other resources' (Guest, 1987: 515). Finally, 'that the pursuit of policies designed to ensure the recruitment and retention of high-quality staff to undertake demanding jobs, supported by competent management will result in high performance levels' (Guest, 1987: 515).

Effective HRM requires each strand of the suite of HRM policies and practices to work together in an integrative form and to complement and reinforce one another. For example, an effective recruitment and selection system should dovetail with well-developed orientation and training processes to help employees adjust to and learn organizational systems and procedures, and acquire further skills as necessary.

OVERVIEW OF BOOK CONTENT

The requirement for integration between different elements of HR provides a useful framework for overviewing the contents of this book. The book outlines the different HR activities in a similar sequential order to that taken by an organization looking to build its HR practices from the ground up.

Chapter 2 outlines *the concept of SHRM*, its links to overall business strategy as well as some key strategic planning tools for establishing a broad framework of policies, principles and practices in a sport organization. A model of SHRM and key elements of SHRM good practice are discussed within the context of sport organization performance.

Chapter 3 covers *human resource planning and strategy*, the fundamental building blocks for ensuring that the organization has the right human resources in place to meet the organization's strategic goals. This involves the assessment of the organization's internal and external environment, forecasting a sport organization's future demand and supply for employees and volunteers, based on its organizational requirements, and developing associated strategies. We outline how HR planning is used to identify the organization's HR management goals and expected results, identifying strategies and activities to achieve those goals, and measuring organizational progress towards their achievement. A process for selecting HR management practices that will enable the sport organization to meet its strategic goals is presented.

Recruitment and selection for sport organizations are presented in Chapter 4. Recruiting and selecting the right people for the right job is crucial to an organization's success. The recruitment and selection challenge is to ensure that each individual brought into the organization has the appropriate mix of skills, expertise and knowledge to assist the organization to meet its goals. Ways to achieve an effective recruitment process that will generate a suitable pool of people from which an appointment can be made are presented, along with elements of a good selection process that can be used to increase the likelihood that the best candidate is appointed for the position.

Chapter 5 covers *orientation and organizational culture*. The stages of organizational socialization are described along with a variety of orientation strategies and practices. The importance and process of orientating sport volunteers and the role of organizational culture and in newcomer orientation are also elaborated upon.

Chapter 6 is about *training and development in sport organizations* and the establishment of training priorities and outcomes that are aligned with strategic objectives. Training and development processes to ensure that the organization's workforce has the skills, knowledge, abilities and performance to meet current and future needs and objectives are discussed.

Chapter 7 looks at how *performance management* systems can be used as a means to recognize and reward good performance, to manage under-performance and to maintain and improve the performance of individuals, teams, and organizations. Approaches to identify and define the performance expectations for individuals and teams are presented. It should be noted that in sport, 'high performance' is a term used to describe the support given to elite athletes to achieve international success both as individuals and as a team. This could include training programs, direct athlete support, employment of coaches or associated support staff, talent identification and support for elite squad members. These types of programs, while important for athletes, are outside the scope of this book.

Motivation and rewards management in sport organizations are outlined in Chapter 8. This includes the role of rewards in employee and volunteer motivation, different types of intrinsic and extrinsic rewards, and components of a financial compensation plan. The importance of volunteer recognition is also highlighted in this chapter.

Sport organizations and employee relations are covered in Chapter 9. What does employee relations means in sport organizations? The role of the psychological contract in employee–management relations and different forms of organizational justice in the workplace, the bases and process of workplace grievance are presented. The concept of trade unions and the collective bargaining process is outlined. The nature of volunteer relations in sport organizations is also discussed.

Diversity management is covered in Chapter 10. People differ in many ways and this has implications for workplace interactions. Diversity management refers to the management of differences to capitalize on the benefits of diversity and to minimize its potentially negative consequences. Sport organizations can use diversity management to enhance their competitive edge and deliver increased value for stakeholders. Diversity management also addresses demands for equity, equality, and fairness in an era of growing demographic diversification.

The chapter on *managing change and future challenges* is presented in Chapter 11. It is a major HRM challenge to successfully plan, implement and communicate organizational change. As discussed earlier in this chapter the sport industry has undergone dramatic changes over the past 20 or so years. Change in sport organizations has been needed to deal with a range of issues including: problems with board governance, tension between paid staff and volunteers, movement from amateur to professional status, declines in skilled and committed volunteers, and demand for greater accountability, higher performance and quality programs and services from a whole range of stakeholders. Effective change management processes are reviewed and a number of workforce challenges and opportunities associated with the changing nature of society and work are presented.

Throughout the book the reader will find reference to (and should also consider on his or her own) the implications of the management of both individuals and workgroups in sport organizations. Individuals have particular competencies, values, personalities and needs that determine 'how [they] perceive what goes on around them, and how they react' in an organization (Doherty, 1998: 4). These characteristics may distinguish individuals within an organization, and explain important differences in their attitudes and behavior. As such, individual characteristics (and differences) are fundamental considerations in many HRM practices, including recruitment, selection, training and performance management.

Individuals may also be members of workgroups, which have further implications for effective HRM. Workgroups are formal collections of personnel established for the purpose of accomplishing a specific task or function (e.g., a volunteer board of a community sport organization, a road race organizing committee). Group members have a common goal and there is an expected degree of interaction among them for the purpose of achieving that goal. The notion of formal workgroups as *teams* is increasingly popular, and the two terms may be used interchangeably (Langton, Robbins & Judge, 2010). Workgroups or teams are intended to be more efficient and effective than individuals working on their own, with the opportunity for multiple perspectives and the division of tasks to group members with perhaps specialized skills working towards the same goal. However, the performance of the group will be dependent on its composition of members with their own particular characteristics, the norms or shared standards for acceptable behavior that develop within the group, and other dynamics such as trust, cohesion, conflict and groupthink (where members tend towards conformity rather than allowing multiple perspectives). Thus, the nature of workgroups is also a fundamental consideration in HRM practices, such as personnel selection, motivation and rewards, and diversity management. It is also important here to acknowledge and distinguish the presence of informal groups in the workplace. These tend to be socially based units that form, independent of any strategic effort on the part of the organization, around common interests – for example, a particular group of sport camp counsellors eat lunch together because they all attend the same university or play the same sport. While such groups have no formal role in the organization, they may be a source of support and motivation to their members and a critical means of communication within the organization.

Another theme woven throughout the chapters is the consideration of volunteers. In the context of this book volunteers are defined as individuals who provide their services free of charge to sport organizations for the benefit of those organizations. Remuneration for services is the main feature distinguishing volunteers and paid staff, and there certainly are important implications for rewards as a motivating tool for these different personnel. However, many of the HRM practices addressed in the book are just as meaningful for staff and volunteers. Volunteers play a critical role in the sport industry (Cuskelly et al., 2006), from sport club fundraisers, board members and coaches, to game day and mega sport event delivery. As with paid staff, the effective deployment, performance and retention of these invaluable human resources also relies on strategic HR planning, recruitment, orientation, training, motivation and recognition, and volunteer relations. As is also noted throughout the book, however, the prevalence, cultural context and meaning of 'volunteering' varies quite significantly from country to country.

Through the reference to geographically diverse situations, some insights are provided into the way in which sport organizations operate in different national contexts. This is accomplished by drawing on theoretical and conceptual developments from around the world and through discussions of culturally distinct people management issues.

Finally, given the ever-increasing globalization that continues to connect people, cultures and economies across nations, we have included throughout the book geographically diverse situations and case studies to provide insights into the way in which sport organizations operate in and across different national contexts. This is highlighted by presenting theoretical and conceptual developments that can be applied to issues facing the strategic management of culturally distinct people.

SUMMARY

This chapter identified some of the key challenges of managing people in sport organizations. The chapter also described the nature of contemporary sport organizations. The general concepts of HRM and SHRM were introduced and explained, and the ideal outcomes of an effective HR system were outlined. Finally, the key areas of HRM were overviewed as they relate to sport organizations and the case was argued that effective HRM is essential to the sustainability of sport organizations.

DISCUSSION QUESTIONS

1   Describe the different categories of individuals that typically work in sport organizations and outline some of the challenges of managing them side by side.

2   Name three key theoretical developments in the evolution of personnel management.

3   What are the key conceptual features of HRM?

4   Think of a sport organization that you are familiar with. Is it practicing HRM or personnel management? Think of examples to justify your answer.

5   Identify three examples of challenges facing sport organizations in different areas of HR practice.

CHAPTER 2

Strategic human resource management

LEARNING OBJECTIVES

After reading this chapter you will be able to:

- Identify the origins of strategic human resource management (SHRM) and how it relates to broader developments in the practice of management
- Understand developments in theories of strategy and how these emphasize the importance of efficient internal processes such as SHRM within sport organizations
- Describe a model of SHRM and identify the key elements of good practice

CHAPTER OVERVIEW

The main elements of HRM were described in Chapter 1 using the Harvard model which emphasizes the importance of integration between different elements of HRM practice, the overall fit of the organization's HR system with the external environment and the importance of conceptualizing staff as a critical resource. Strategic HRM approaches elaborate on these principles and suggest that organizations that have an explicit strategy to use their human resources gain competitive advantage through better use of human capital. Thus, SHRM approaches emphasize that HRM can shape and contribute to strategy in addition to implementing it.

Contemporary SHRM, as the name suggests, also incorporates key ideas from the broader strategy literature as well as reflecting some of the different perspectives within the field. Therefore, in order to properly understand SHRM we need first to appreciate some of the main theories and techniques of strategic management which SHRM draws upon. The first section of this chapter therefore outlines the key approaches to organizational strategy focusing on industry positioning and the resource-based view (RBV) of the organization – both of which provide a strong rationale for regarding the management of HRM as strategic. Fundamental tools for conducting a strategic analysis are also described.

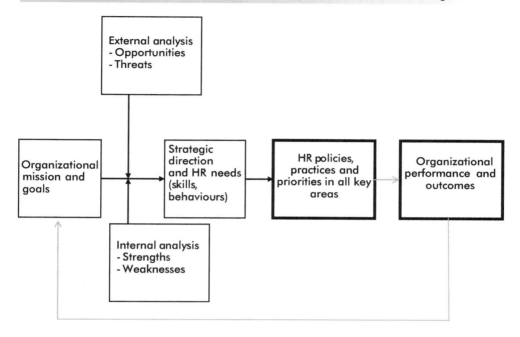

FIGURE 2.1 The strategic human resource management process and SWOT analysis

THEORIES OF STRATEGY

Strategic management involves the use of analytical methods to consciously position the organization within its competitive external environment. It typically takes account of opportunities and threats in the external environment as well as an assessment of internal strengths and weaknesses. The formulation and enactment of strategy is aimed at developing a plan that incorporates the organization's overall purpose into coherent and consistent goals, policies and actions, and the allocation of resources to support these. Since strategy enactment involves the deployment, direction and redirection of staff activities, HR has a central role in shaping and implementing strategy. The classic view of strategic management presents the 'process' as involving six steps.

1   Clarification of corporate mission, goals and values.
2   Analysis of the organization's external competitive environment to identify strengths, weaknesses, opportunities and threats (a SWOT analysis – described in detail below).
3   Analysis of the organization's internal operating environment to identify strengths and weaknesses (again using a SWOT analysis).
4   Selection of strategies that build on the organization's strengths and correct weaknesses, to take advantage of external opportunities and counter-external threats.
5   Strategy implementation.
6   Strategy evaluation with corrective feedback to the implementation phase.

A SWOT analysis as depicted in Figure 2.1 is a simple tool for analysing the strategic position of an organization, or part of an organization, by identifying strengths, weaknesses,

TABLE 2.1 Example of a SWOT analysis

Internal factors	Strengths	Weaknesses
Company culture Organization structure Key staff Resource access Experience Operational capacity Operational efficiency Financial resources Patents Customer knowledge and contacts	• Strong financial base • Growth area for your product • Group of skilled volunteers • Support from local businesses • Support from local politicians • Support from local service organizations • Well-equipped club house • Well-structured committee • Enthusiastic and capable committee	• Weak financial base • Diminishing need or desire for your product • Few volunteers • No support from local businesses • No support from local politicians • No support from local service organizations • Out of date ill-equipped club house • Poor committee structure • Overworked and tired committee • Fewer new members • Lack of interest in your sport

External factors	Opportunities	Threats
Customers Competitors Intensity of competition in market Suppliers Partnerships and alliances Change Political issues Economic environment	• Promotion of sport by government authorities (e.g., renewed 'Life in it' campaign) • New population of potential users moving into the area, housing estates with children • Grants by local authorities to encourage sport • Grants by state authorities to encourage sport • Grants by federal authorities to encourage sport • Organizations looking to sponsor local activities • Seasonal interest in particular sports, cricket in summer, football in winter	• Organizations giving up sports to sponsor to concentrate on other areas • Seasonal interest in particular sports which is in direct competition with your own sport (e.g., different types of football) • Promotion of sport to different gender which competes with your sports interest (e.g., netball and soccer for girls)

TABLE 2.1 continued

• New technology • International or national interests in sports (e.g., Commonwealth or Olympic Games) • Promotion of sport to different age group (e.g., lawn bowls to teenagers) • Promotion of sport to different gender (e.g., all types of football – to girls)	• Other interests including hobby groups, television video games, school activities, part-time work for teenagers and so on • Time-related issues, for example, competition for volunteers time, longer working hours, both parents working – children unable to attend, limited available free time for both children and parents • Other organizations with better facilities • Lack of knowledge and interest in your product

(Source: adapted from NSW Department of Sport and Recreation, 2007)

opportunities and threats. HR related factors, such as skills gaps, often occupy a central position in the conduct of a SWOT analysis. A SWOT analysis considers any and all internal and external factors that impact on the organization and its operations. Internal factors are typically identified as strengths or weaknesses while external factors are identified as threats or opportunities. For example, the strengths and weaknesses identified in the workforce analysis could form the basis for changing recruitment and training strategies and practices and build a workforce with stronger client relationship skills. Table 2.1 is adapted from New South Wales (NSW) Sport and Recreation and is in reference to the operation of Sporting Clubs (NSW Department of Sport and Recreation, n.d.).

Conducting a SWOT analysis as part of a strategic planning process such as that referred to above is consistent with the two most influential theoretical frameworks on strategy: The Porter industry positioning model and the resource-based view (RBV). Both the Porter model and the RBV present complete and alternative ways of looking at strategy but they emphasize different aspects of the SWOT model and can therefore be used together to consider different aspects of strategy. While the Porter model mainly deals with the opportunities and threats impacting the organization's external competitive positioning, the RBV focuses primarily on the internal strengths and weaknesses of the organization and how they can be leveraged as resources to improve organizational responsiveness to evolving competition. In other words the Porter model has, primarily, an external focus whereas the RBV has, primarily, an internal focus. In practice it is important to obtain a good level of alignment between the external strategic position of the organization and the internal environment. The degree of alignment is referred to as 'strategic fit'. The Porter and RBV approaches are outlined in the following section along with examples of how they link to SHRM.

Michael Porter (Porter, 1979) developed a tool for analyzing an organization's competitive position within an industry which is generally referred to as the five forces model. This analysis is performed as a preparatory exercise to assist an organization with the identification of its correct strategic direction. The five forces are as follows.

1 *Overall industry rivalry*: this identifies the intensity and patterns of competition. This is not only influenced by the other four factors but also by separate factors such as industry growth, the level of product differentiation and barriers to exiting the industry – for example, competition for members between golf clubs in the same geographical catchment area.
2 *Barriers to entry*: the obstacles to entering the industry presented by the need for economies of scale, access to scarce resources or the need for large amount of capital – for example, limits on numbers of franchise teams in a league.
3 *Buyer power*: the level of choice available to customers – for example, there may be several fitness centers to choose from in a particular geographical area.
4 *Supplier power*: this is dependent on factors such as the number of suppliers in the industry – for example, being the only tennis center in town.
5 *Threat of substitutes*: the number of alternatives available to consumers and the switching costs associated with consuming an alternative product – for example, fans switching from baseball to soccer.

Porter suggests that when positioning itself relative to competitors in an industry, an organization can only outperform its rivals in two fundamental ways: by operational effectiveness and by strategic positioning.

The first concept, operational effectiveness, means performing similar activities better than rivals perform them. While this can be a source of competitive advantage, few organizations have competed successfully on operational effectiveness alone for an extended period of time. Easily imitable areas such as technologies and input improvements do not typically provide organizations with long-term advantage because they are quickly copied by competitors. Therefore, a fitness center's purchase of the latest fitness equipment might provide a short-term advantage, but this position could quickly erode as competitors buy similar or even newer machines.

The second concept, strategic positioning, on the other hand refers to performing different activities from rivals or performing similar activities in different ways. According to Porter the two generic sources of sustainable competitive advantage lie in either cost leadership or product/service differentiation relative to competitors. If a fitness center was competing on a cost leadership basis, it might employ staff at close to minimum wages and have a 'churn and burn' approach to staffing based on plentiful supply of available labor. Alternatively, if the fitness center was following a differentiation strategy, it might not only have the latest in equipment but might also offer a range of exercise programs that were unique to that center and have more highly qualified and trained staff to give better advice to customers. The SHRM implications of the latter model would likely be that the fitness center would seek to retain more highly skilled staff, pay higher wages and probably provide more job security.

A third possibility is for an organization to focus on a particular segment or niche rather than compete across the board in a given market. In this case the fitness center could be exclusively for women which would differentiate it clearly from rivals. Such a strategic choice has implications for HR. A female only fitness center would likely seek to have a different customer interaction model than more generic centers and accordingly seek to employ staff with different skill sets and demographic characteristics.

When an organization works out its competitive position in an industry, it is important to analyze ongoing opportunities and threats as depicted in Figure 2.1 and Table 2.1. A complementary but more detailed review of the external environment (and somewhat overlapping) can be conducted using the PESTLE framework. PESTLE refers to political, economic, social, technological, legal and environmental, and is a more wide-ranging analysis of the macro-external variables that may be impacting upon an organization. In sport organizations some typical examples of factors that might be considered in a PESTLE are as follows.

Political:
* Government commitment to increasing participation in sport – for example, current concerns about obesity have resulted in government increases in funding for children and youth sport programs in many countries.
* Government targeting of certain ethnic/age or gender groups for increased participation.
* Government funding for sport infrastructure – for example, the Olympic Games in Sydney generated many improvements in local sports facilities which greatly assisted many sports federations in their development.

Economic:
* The potential of sport to create employment.
* The potential to use sport as an adjunct to promoting tourism – for example, Golf in Ireland, Surfing in Hawaii.

Social:
* Aging populations, health issues, diversity agendas, population growth, etc.
* Urban/rural growth and decline and the need to rebalance sporting infrastructure in changing communities – for example, the decline of small rural towns in many countries which leads to the loss of players for town sporting clubs.

Technological:
* Competition from the Internet computer games vis-à-vis children's sport.
* Use of the Internet to better promote sport – for example, to advertise and sell tickets online.
* Alternative technologies – for example, online sports betting or virtual football.

Legal:
* Changing laws relating to working with children.
* Legal precedents on malicious injury requiring the introduction of strong codes aimed at curbing violence in contact sports.

Environmental:
* Restrictions on the use of water and chemicals for golf courses.
* Noise and traffic issues around sporting venues in urban areas.

Although positioning within an industry is an important element of strategy it is not sufficient to give a complete explanation of the success of some sport organizations in relation to their competitors. In fact some studies suggest that industry structure accounts for as little as 8–15 per cent of the variance in an organization's performance (Black & Boal, 1994). This is because industry structural factors impact upon the entire industry and do not adequately explain the sustained competitive performance of some firms but not others. Critics of the industry structure model therefore argue that a significant component of strategic success must be explained by factors within the organization which bring us to the second perspective on strategy.

A contrasting view of strategy is provided by the RBV (Barney, 1991). This theory argues that the source of an organization's competitive advantage lies in its internal resources such as patents, copyrights, proprietary technologies as well as human and intellectual capital and its ability to manage these resources strategically. From this perspective, a sport organization's resources are viewed more widely than can be understood in the formal accounting sense. Instead, resources include any aspect of the sport organization with value-creating capabilities including those that are intangible such as the 'culture' of the organization and its ability to convey a certain image or embody a set of ideals. The RBV has important implications for SHRM because many of the most important resources held by an organization are embodied in or represented by the people who work for it.

An example of how the RBV applies in the HRM area is given by Lado and Wilson (1994) who argue that HRM systems can facilitate the development of competencies that are specific to the organization in the sense that they are contained in social relations that are embedded in an organization's history and culture. These competencies generate tacit organizational knowledge which allows for efficient execution of tasks in the same way that tacit knowledge in a mature sporting team allows players to 'know' what other players are about to do and coordinate their own movements accordingly. From this perspective an HRM system can be unique in two senses. First, because the outputs of the system – that is, the employee actions resulting from it – are unique. Second, because the system itself is a source of competence as it, for example, attracts employees to work for the organization. For example, Nike is rated 29th in the *Forbes* magazine's Best Companies to Work For in 2013 and is acknowledged for its team-based values, learning culture and opportunity to work with a talented workforce (Forbes, 2012). It is therefore useful to define HRM competence as tangible (HR performance, planning, training, selection systems, etc.) and intangible (shared mindsets, team synergies, accumulated operational experience in creativity and problem solving, etc.).

At the heart of the RBV approach is the argument that the intangibility of such resources gives the organization holding them a competitive edge because it means that they cannot be easily replicated by competitors. Implicit in this view is the idea that such resources can sustain an organization's competitive advantage over a long period so long as such resources are valuable, rare, imperfectly imitable and non-substitutable. An example of such a set of resources in professional sport might be found in a successful team's scouting network, which brings talented young players into a junior academy. Such networks are often established in longstanding relationships with key scouts or feeder clubs who are generally loyal to one senior club. The scouting network is reinforced by other intangibles such as a club's playing history, traditions and its glamour, its reputation for looking after young players, and its ability to provide opportunities for player development not offered by other clubs.

Valuable and rare resources can only be sources of competitive advantage if the organizations that do not currently possess these resources cannot obtain or imitate them. Organization resources can potentially be imperfectly imitable for three reasons. First, because obtaining the resource is dependent upon unique historical conditions. Second, because the relationship between the resource possessed and the organization's sustained competitive advantage is causally ambiguous. Third, because it is socially complex in nature (Barney, 1991). A study using the RBV theory of strategy to assess sustainable competitive advantage of intercollegiate athletics programs found that competitive advantage was often located in the 'history, relationships, trust, and culture' that had developed within coaching groups over many years. Further, 'Such complex and interdependent organizational resources tend not to be subject to imitation' (Smart & Wolfe, 2000: 144).

Employing an RBV analysis of professional football (soccer) teams, Gerrard (2005) explained how sustainable competitive advantage and sporting and financial success can be related to ownership status and the way in which professional sports teams use their resources (athletes) and allegiance (their fans). The increased financial efficiency of stock market listed teams provided the basis for improved financial performance and did not have any significant negative impact on the teams playing talent and sporting performance. As implied in the discussion of the conditions of inimitability, proponents of the RBV argue that, in most cases, competitive advantage cannot be traced to a single or isolated component, but instead is derived from an effectively executed combination of human capital elements such as the development of skill stocks, the encouragement via effective performance management systems of strategically relevant behaviors and generally supportive people management systems. Such intangible assets, it is argued, confer upon the holder the ability to implement strategy more effectively than competitors and thereby provide a strong basis for a potential source of competitive advantage.

The growth in popularity of the RBV of the organization has focused the attention of both practicing managers and academics to the internal configuration of resources in the organization and led to many initiatives in areas such as learning systems, knowledge management, intellectual capital, organizational culture and above all strategic human resource management.

THE SHRM PROCESS

Strategic human resource management (SHRM) builds on the insights provided by both the Porter view and the RBV because it emphasizes the need for alignment between the external and internal environment (strategic fit) and the importance of an organization's internal resources and capabilities in helping it achieve its strategic objectives. Sport organizations need to consider formulating and implementing strategies that differentiate them from their competitors and develop superior human resources so as to outperform competitors. Superior human resources are particularly powerful in service industries, such as sports, where employee-customer interactions are central in determining the 'value' of the transaction for the customer (as opposed to just the price of a particular service).

Wright and McMahon (1992: 298) define SHRM as 'the pattern of planned human resource deployments and activities intended to enable an organization to achieve its goals'. For example, a sport consultancy organization will generally seek to employ only the most intelligent candidates with sophisticated interpersonal skills because they recognize that the caliber of their consultants confers a competitive advantage. Similarly, a sport organization that recognizes its dependence on volunteers may seek ways to 'retain' volunteers through matching them to the task via appropriate managerial action (Kim, Chelladurai & Trail, 2007).

The essential idea of SHRM is to treat employees and volunteers as investment assets, who through a series of organizational practices develop a strong psychological commitment to the organization and unique ways of working together that delivers superior performance levels. From this perspective, sport organizations can attain a strategic advantage over their rivals because, unlike other assets such as technology, human assets are inimitable in the short term.

Key features of organizational practice associated with SHRM are not only 'pure' HR techniques such as rigorous selection systems, but also a range of associated management practices related to high-commitment work systems, employment models, leadership philosophy and style.

The implication of this perspective is that the choice of strategy is not only limited by the existing capabilities possessed by an organization, such as how intelligent its staff are, but also by deficiencies in organizational capability to implement strategy effectively, such as the ability of staff and volunteers to work together effectively at the necessary pace. Almost inevitably strategic decision making involves people-related issues; therefore, a logical corollary to this is that HR implications should be considered when strategic decisions are made.

Another argument for SHRM is that in the last two decades there has been a growing recognition among theorists and practitioners alike that traditional sources of competitive advantage such as technology, product innovation and location are being eroded more quickly due to fiercer globalized competition and a more rapid pace of diffusion, and that a committed, skilled and flexible workforce can confer a long-term advantage for an organization that is inimitable by competitors. From this perspective the essence of competitiveness lies in better business processes or higher levels of 'core competence' and 'core capabilities' (Prahalad & Hamel, 1990) rather than just specific technologies or products. The key to better processes often lies in the HR domain, for example hiring the right kind of employees, retaining volunteers or stimulating more effective teamwork to allow different sections of an organization to work together more efficiently.

Referring again to Figure 2.1 and Table 2.1 we can see that use of a SWOT analysis in an organization will typically consider three critical strategic questions:

1 Where will we compete? (In what areas and/or using what products?)
2 How will we compete? (On the basis of cost, differentiation, focus? What is our customer value proposition?)
3 With what will we compete? (How do we acquire/develop and deploy our resources in order to compete?)

HR implications can emerge from each of these strategic questions, but it is in relation to the 'with what will we compete' question that HR has the most obvious involvement in formulating strategy. Take for instance a community-based sport association that is dependent on a large volume of volunteers to run the organization, coach the children, manage squads and act as officials. In order to attract and retain an adequate pool of quality volunteers, Little Athletics organizations around the world highlight their vision of developing children of all abilities by promoting positive attitudes and a healthy lifestyle through family and community involvement in athletics activities. The emphasis of positive family and community involvement provides fundamental strength for the organizations as participants' parents and community members can be targeted as volunteers. In terms of 'With what will we compete?' Little Athletics can refer to schemes which provide training for volunteer judges, time keepers, umpires and recorders. Typically this training offers four levels of official gradings commencing at the local level with D Grade, progressing through to C Grade for Zone level, and B and A Grades for State and National level officials. Rewards and recognition are usually given via badges to qualified officials, and there are strong support networks with newsletters and other publications that acknowledge volunteer contributions. Intangible benefits such as being out on the field where it is all happening, having fun and gaining an increased appreciation of their child's activities are also critical. This example illustrates the importance of ensuring that the sport organization's HR planning, policies and activities for volunteers build on its strengths to strategically build its resource base.

Another example is a commercially orientated sport organization expanding operations beyond its domestic borders for the first time. They may face critical questions relating to staffing. How will we get properly trained staff in our new market? Should we send domestic staff as expatriates or hire locally? Are the staffing problems in relation to the overseas branch so great that we should reconsider our original decision to enter this new market? This problem was exactly what confronted many overseas organizations when they first entered the Japanese market because typically the best Japanese employees preferred to work for Japanese and not for foreign organizations. In fact many Western organizations were eventually forced to withdraw from the Japanese market because the staffing problems were too great. This is a vivid example of unforeseen HR problems derailing a strategy. The ESPN case in Box 2.1 provides an evaluation of an application of the 'industry positioning' and 'RBV' of the firm perspective.

BOX 2.1

ESPN: global expansion, recruitment and talent management

• ESPN places high importance on organizational culture and talent management.

ESPN is the world leading multinational, multimedia sports entertainment company, with the broadest portfolio of multimedia sports assets with over 50 entities (ESPN, 2014a). Based in Bristol, Connecticut (USA), ESPN is a global enterprise, with 7,000 employees worldwide (ESPN, 2014a).

The ESPN culture

'Here is a culture that breeds talent. An assembly of premier performances, out-of-this-world technology and challenges that push the boundaries of your skills. It generates confidence, pride, and the will to do better and better. That's why we're pioneers in the sports entertainment world – and why you'll enjoy the thrill of your accomplishments.

'BusinessWeek ranked the Walt Disney Company (parent company of ESPN/ABC) as one of the top companies to start your career, it also ranked Disney #11 on internship opportunities for undergraduates. Disney was ranked No. 7 in *Fortune* magazine's Top 100 Most Desirable MBA Employers, and *Fortune* also named Disney the World's Most Admired Entertainment Company. Boston College's Carroll School of Management has Disney topping the list of 50 companies recognized as leaders in corporate social responsibility' (ESPN, 2014b).

'It's all about triumph.'

'It's what our company is built on. From the day our signal was first televised to the countless milestones along the way, we live to defy the odds and continuously outdo ourselves. Our culture is designed to bring out the best in our professionals. It's in the way we listen to ideas, encourage development and seek out the best and brightest. You don't have to be an avid sports fan to have an ESPN job. You do, however, need to be passionate about your skills, your goals and having a bit of fun' (ESPN, 2014c).

Talent management

ESPN recognizes talent management as a critical business priority. The performance management processes and rewards programs are closely linked. To improve workforce performance, ESPN has focused on leadership development and inclusion. This involved the launch of various development programs, including:

- 'Leadership Premier', a program based on executive leadership development.
- 'Perspectives', a learning and development based program which focuses on development of middle management.
- 'ESPN Dimensions', a specific development program targeting development of managers.

Additionally, in 2010 ESPN launched a companywide program to establish personalized career development plans for all individual employees (Talent Management, 2014).

Succession planning

ESPN has a two-tiered process of succession planning that is carried out across all divisions and all departments. An annual talent review is conducted, where employee profiles are updated and reviewed in light of strategic business objectives. This creates an individualized development strategy for the employee and highlights potential opportunities. During the second stage, talent planning and succession discussions are conducted with the senior management of ESPN's parent company, Walt Disney Co. (Talent Management, 2014).

Inclusion and diversity

ESPN prioritizes diversity, education and development among its workforce and has established eight employee resource groups (ERGs) to support inclusion and diversity strategies. These ERGs were established to address: Young Professionals, Women, Asians, People with Disabilities, Latinos, Families, African-Americans, and Gay, Lesbian,

Bisexual and Transgender employees. These groups are formed on similar interests or areas of diversity and are managed on a volunteer basis by ESPN employees. Their areas of focus include (ESPN, 2014d):

- education and promoting cultural diversity
- networking and learning from others
- developing professional skill sets
- adding value to the business
- expanding the recruitment base
- enhancing retention initiatives
- tapping underutilized resources.

ESPN's diversity mission statement

'ESPN will embrace diversity to better serve our fans and customers. We strive to attract and retain talented and diverse people, and to create an inclusive environment where all employees can contribute to their fullest potential. In a changing world in which we endeavor to grow our business, it is imperative that ESPN's workforce reflects the diversity of cultures, thinking and perspectives of its current and prospective fans and customers. Tapping the skills, ideas and perspectives of a diverse workforce will make us a better and more profitable company, and is key to sustaining our continued growth' (ESPN, 2014e).

A few of the diversity awards that ESPN has won (ESPN, 2014e)

- Asian-American Journalists Association 2010 Leadership in Diversity Award
- DiversityInc's Top 50 Companies for Diversity
- DiversityInc's Top 10 Companies for Latinos
- Women in Cable Telecommunications (WICT) – Best Companies for Women in Pay Equity
- Gay & Lesbian Alliance Against Defamation (GLAAD) – Outstanding Digital Journalism Article
- Gay & Lesbian Alliance Against Defamation (GLAAD) – Outstanding TV Journalism

ESPN is also actively involved in employee education and understanding of the overall business strategies and goals. It created the ESPN Expo, an internal job fair, where employees are provided with an opportunity to interact and share information among their colleagues from different organizational departments (Talent Management, 2014).

Discussion questions

1 Discuss the application of the 'industry positioning' and 'RBV' of the firm perspective to the ESPN case.
2 Is there any evidence that ESPN is following a SHRM approach?

Clearly, HR needs to be involved in strategic decisions, although the actual degree of integration of HR with strategy formulation may vary between organizations depending on the philosophy of the company. At the most basic level HR has to implement the people-related aspects of any strategy. Therefore, the most primitive type of involvement is for HR to be engaged in strategy in the role of an administrative adjunct or in other words a receiver of strategy. A second and more sophisticated level of involvement is where HR issues are considered at the same time as strategy through a process of consultation, whereby HR is informed of and asked to comment on HR aspects of a strategic plan drawn up by a strategy team such as an Executive Committee. Finally, at the highest level of integration, HR may be fully involved in all aspects of strategic decision making. This is often facilitated by appointing the most senior HR person on to the sport organization's Executive Committee so as to be involved in all aspects of strategic decision making and to comment specifically on the organization's internal capabilities. The latter position is consistent with the logic of the RBV of the organization since HR is a key source of internal resources.

After a sport organization has completed its strategic analysis and formulated a strategy, it must then effectively execute the agreed strategy. As noted earlier, implementation has come to be seen as the most important component of all the steps in overall strategic management. General organizational issues to be considered when implementing strategy typically concern:

- the allocation of sufficient resources (financial, time, technology and support)
- setting up an organizational hierarchy and chain of command or some alternative structure (such as cross-functional teams)
- delegating responsibility of tasks or processes to individuals or groups.
- managing the process. This includes monitoring results, comparing against benchmarks or good practices, evaluating the effectiveness and efficiency of the process, and making adjustments to the process as necessary.

When implementing more specific programs, implementation may also involve acquiring the requisite resources, developing the process, training, process testing, documentation and integration with (and/or conversion from) existing processes.

Effective implementation of strategy requires not only decisions in relation to all of the above but also the coordination of a number of HR practices especially the core HR areas of Recruitment and Selection, Training and Development, Compensation and Performance Management. The correct choice of practices will result in the sport organization developing the required HR capability in terms of skills, ability and knowledge as well as the right attitudes and behaviours from the staff.

The final component of the strategic management process is that of evaluation. Evaluation involves measuring progress against agreed objectives and taking corrective action as necessary. Sometimes this corrective action can be so fundamental as to lead to a new strategic direction being taken. This is referred to as an emergent, as opposed to fully pre-planned, strategy and is an increasingly important component of the overall strategy process given the turbulent environment within which most sport organizations operate today. Historically, evaluation was done using mainly financial measures and ratios but more recently there have been attempts to measure progress using wider organizational measures. For example, the Balanced Scorecard (Kaplan & Norton, 1996) measures organization progress against four criteria: financial, customer focus, learning and growth, and internal business process improvement.

In the academic literature on SHRM there are two main schools of thought concerning the link between HRM practices and organizational performance. First, there is the so-called 'best practice' approach that is associated with the work of researchers such as Pfeffer (1998). This approach can be seen as directly in the tradition of the Harvard approach, discussed in Chapter 1, as it advocates what is essentially a normative approach to HRM. Based on extensive research of successful organizations, Pfeffer identified seven HRM practices that closely correlated with exceptionally high performing and profitable organizations. In combination these practices led to high-performance work systems that added value to the organizations' overall performance, including financial, in ways consistent with the RBV of the organization. Notably, the top performing organizations in Pfeffer's study were in industries characterized by intense competitive rivalry. These high-performance work systems involve sophisticated HRM practices aimed at the following.

1 Selective recruitment.
2 Developing a decentralized organization which supports self-managed teams.
3 Providing employment security.
4 Providing high rewards relative to other organizations, but based on performance.
5 Extensive training.
6 Sharing information.
7 Reducing status differentials in the workplace.

Essentially, the 'best practice' approach argues that a well-executed investment strategy in people will always pay dividends irrespective of industry. This view has been criticized primarily for underestimating the importance of external factors which may limit the opportunity to invest in people. Thus, a national sporting organization might devise an HR policy which emphasizes competitive recruitment for all positions, accompanied by an attractive reward package, access to regular training and development and a collegiate team-based work environment. However, a change in government funding, a change in personnel and power structures on the board of directors, or the loss of a major sponsorship or media deal might compromise the delivery of these practices. Cuts to funding and revenue streams may require that training and remuneration is cut back and changes to the Board may result in the senior management team being replaced by personnel that have close connections to the new board members.

The second approach is best described as a 'contingency' approach and addresses the key limitation of the best practice approach. This approach argues that HR practices should be closely integrated with organizational strategy and structure, and recognizes that different behaviors may be required from individuals in order to enact different competitive strategies. For example, a sport organization following a cost minimization strategy will have a different HR imperative than a sport organization seeking to innovate. Thus, a sport and recreation center following cost minimization may seek to retain its current staffing profile, provide basic training and development, and have a traditional performance management and reward system. On the other hand a sport center intent on pursuing an innovation strategy may seek to hire individuals with higher qualifications, establish training and development initiatives that promote creativity and innovation, and use reward incentives that recognize employee innovation and risk taking.

Research on SHRM, irrespective of the approach, provides a body of evidence which establishes a link between good HRM practices in the areas of selection, training, performance management and reward, and higher levels of organizational performance (Lepak & Shaw, 2008). Overall, this research suggests that while there is no universal normative list of HR practices that will lead to good organizational performance outcomes in all circumstances, there are certain key practices that, if used in the right combination for a particular sport organization, will stimulate good performance outcomes. However, variations in the demands posed by the business environment may result in a different pattern of HRM across different organizations.

SUMMARY

This chapter identified the origins of the SHRM approach within the broader strategy literature and linked it specifically with the RBV of strategy. A model of SHRM was presented which makes an explicit link between the goals of the organization and the need for congruence in the HR system. The model serves as a useful guide for both strategy planning and strategy implementation in relation to various HRM activities. Finally, this chapter outlined two competing theories – best practice, and contingency models – explaining the links between SHRM and organizational performance.

DISCUSSION QUESTIONS

1   Exercise: Conduct a SWOT or PESTLE analysis for a sport organization that you know well. Take the perspective of a CEO planning the organization's strategy for the next three years.

2   Use the four attributes of the RBV to analyze a sport organization that you think has a competitive edge in the marketplace. How does HR fit into this analysis?

3   Using the same sport organization discussed in Question 2, review the organization's HR practices and discuss the level of fit with Pfeffer's seven best practices.

CHAPTER 3

Human resource planning

LEARNING OBJECTIVES

After reading this chapter you will be able to:

- Understand and work with the key steps in the HR planning process
- Identify how to conduct a job analysis and associated techniques
- Comprehend the key components of job descriptions
- Explain different approaches to job design
- Discuss key aspects of succession planning
- Outline the purpose of HR outsourcing

CHAPTER OVERVIEW

As discussed in previous chapters, the dynamic external environments that sport organizations operate in creates an imperative to develop a strategy which encompasses current and future workforce requirements. HRM planning translates these broad strategic objectives into detailed operational plans. Effective planning requires that the organization has a clear picture of its current workforce including strengths, weaknesses and potential. The assessment of the current state of play is conducted within the context of the organization's ability to achieve its goals and objectives – that is, to deliver on its strategy. The next step in planning is to examine future directions, requirements and capabilities to ascertain how the workforce can meet future needs and then determine what plans need to be put in place to address any gaps or concerns. Workforce planning can assist organizations to clarify their future human capital needs (Goodman, French & Battaglio, 2013). For example, HR planning provides the means for organizations to avoid the 'short-termism' that Moore and Levermore (2012) found to be characteristic of small and medium-sized English professional football clubs. They noted that longer-term strategic activities such as HR planning are rarely in evidence and 'HR practices do not extend much beyond what is required for the day-to-day running of the organization' (2012: 203). Much of the short term planning is related to these clubs' driving imperative to achieve on-field success as the revenue flow and future of the enterprise is dependent on winning.

This chapter presents a model of HR planning and discusses dimensions of development and implementation within the context of delivering organizational goals through HR. The reasons for outsourcing HR functions are also considered.

A STRATEGIC APPROACH TO HUMAN RESOURCE PLANNING

The planning of HR is an integral part of how an organization is going to achieve its mission, by ensuring that it has the right people, with the right skills and knowledge in the right positions. The HR plan generally takes one of two forms, depending on the size/resources of the organization: as a component of a general strategic plan; or as a separate HR strategic plan. In both forms the plan developed is the basis for implementation of actions to achieve goals, strategies and measures pertaining to recruitment, retention, employee development and succession. The approach to HR planning will vary. Typically, large multifaceted organizations with complex HR issues to manage will have formal strategic planning processes in place, while smaller organizations may be less formal and more flexible in their HR planning. For example, a sport center that identifies expansion into new locations as part of its overall strategic plan would require a formal and detailed HR plan for staffing its new centers. On the less formal side, a regional basketball association may take the opportunity, when presented, to bring in an internship student to develop a membership benefits package, even though the association had not previously identified this position or job task as a priority area.

Effective HR planning serves many purposes. It allows an organization to deploy its people to meet its strategies and goals, assists with cost reduction by anticipating and dealing with labour shortages or surpluses in a timely manner and ensures optimum use of each individual's skills and knowledge while capitalizing on the talents of a diverse workforce. One component of this is the use of existing attrition and retirement data of current employees in conjunction with the strategic plans of the organization (Schuler, Jackson & Tarique, 2011). The rapidly changing internal and external environments of sport organizations present several challenges for HR planning. These challenges include changes to the way in which the sport is organized and delivered; increased competition for staff, volunteers, participants and clients; changing demographics; the need for a workforce skilled in new technologies and specialized areas; and workforce diversity. Such challenges increase the importance of effective HR planning in the strategic planning process of sport organizations.

THE HR PLANNING PROCESS

HR planning aims to achieve a desirable workforce balance and mix through integrated HR practices such as job analysis and design, staffing, learning and development and evaluation. The planning process is a complex combination of assessment of the organization's internal and external environment and mapping of the HR requirements to meet current needs and future projections. If the assessment determines that there is a gap between demand and supply the development of an HR plan to narrow the disparity would result. The assessment takes into account the current knowledge, skills, attitudes, attributes and capabilities of the workforce, and establishes whether or not these are sufficient to meet the organization's strategic goals and priorities. A SWOT analysis, as described in Chapter 2, is also a useful framework for this assessment. Figure 3.1 is a graphic overview of the human resource planning process, with more detail on the various key elements presented below.

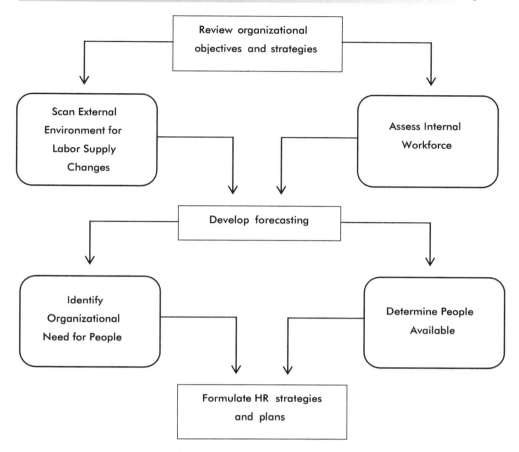

FIGURE 3.1 Human resource planning process

The internal analysis phase can be conducted at the broad macro-level and the more precise micro-level. A macro-level examination takes into account the organization's structure and the shared values, norms and expectations that guide the organization's members in terms of how to approach their work and deal with each other and customers/clients. Information about aspects such as culture or climate can be obtained via a cyclical survey process (i.e., every two to three years) or external review (often outsourced to a specialist management consultancy firm). There are many instruments that may be used to assess culture, and these range from generic off-the-shelf questionnaires to diagnostic tools which are custom designed for the organization. A micro-level analysis assesses the number of employees or volunteers, their skills, abilities and knowledge, qualifications, demographics (e.g., age, gender), level of payment, leave entitlements and records of performance appraisals. An increasing number of organizations use a human resources management system (HRMS) or enterprise resource planning (ERP) software for data management.

An example of how HR planning works in practice illustrates this process. A sport facility company with a strategy of growing its market share through the use of cutting-edge technologies identifies a trend towards greater flexibility and functionality in online customer services and social media marketing. An internal skills audit of current staff finds that a limited number of employees possess the relevant technological skills to deliver the changes needed. It is also identified that the existing selection, performance management and training policies exclusively emphasize face-to-face customer interaction skills, and rewards for success are built on this dimension of the job alone. In response, the company develops an HR plan to emphasize greater technology-orientated customer focus and uses this for recruitment, selection, training and development, rewards and career management. For all of these areas new criteria for employee skills and characteristics will be developed as part of the planning process.

HR planning is about translating strategic objectives into action plans that will deliver on key performance indicators. Although dynamic in nature, formal planning is typically undertaken on an annual basis. Managers should be able to use systematic analyses to determine if current knowledge, skills and abilities found within an organization are adequate to achieve its strategic goals. Accurate, reliable data and information on which assessments are made can be sourced in a variety of ways.

Assessing workforce supply

An assessment of the internal and external sources of supply (refer to Figure 3.1) is critical in planning. Internal analysis takes into account the likelihood of retirements, turnover, potential training needs of current employees, succession planning and future staffing requirements. Skills inventories are a common method used to collect data on current employees and volunteers. An individual or supervisor can complete the inventory form on an annual basis, updating information such as age, work/volunteer experience, job classification, qualifications, training, areas of expertise and professional association memberships.

Organizations are increasingly incorporating workforce profiles and inventory data as part of online HR systems, which allow managers access to the data for planning and performance management tasks. These systems track the numbers of new recruitments, transfers and promotions, along with retirements, voluntary departures and redundancies. Standardized processes allow an organization to capture accurate data about its current employees and performance and can provide information to use in evidence based decision making for determining any gap in an organization's supply and demand (Brown, 2010). An important component of developing and leveraging the internal workforce supply to meet demand is through succession planning.

Succession planning

Succession planning is a part of the overall process of workforce planning and involves: (1) identification of positions/roles that are suited to a succession process; (2) identification of prospective candidates for 'promotion' positions; and (3) training and development to facilitate that succession. Roles that are critical for the organization's performance success are identified as part of this process. For example, a sport event business might decide that ticketing technology specialists, social media marketers and big data analysts are increasingly relevant for their operations. For these roles, the business may focus on the use of training and development to multi-skill existing staff members – ensuring that there are capability contingencies in place in the case of a staff departure. Succession planning can additionally be person focused rather than role focused. This means targeting 'high potential' staff that have been identified as having talents that warrant promotion progression or that the organization would like to retain long term (e.g. a manager targeted to be the next CEO) or staff that have specific expertise not readily available outside the organization, especially if it is unlikely that this capability would be easily sourced externally (e.g., High Performance Logistics Manager). For these high potential and specialist staff, succession planning is likely to involve an ongoing and rigorous development of their professional expertise as well as a broader development of their management and leadership capabilities. Transferring highly specialized professional expertise to others within the organization through activities such as 'shadowing' is also critical when there is no option to 'buy in' the expertise.

Succession planning can pertain to employees and volunteers from the top of the organization, the CEO or Director of the Board, down through the ranks. Depending on the size of the organization or the position under consideration different approaches to succession and to the types of opportunities provided for employees and volunteers to gain particular skills, knowledge and capabilities, may be taken.

Most organizations focus succession efforts on senior leadership roles in the first instance, with a view to extending the process into other critical roles at lower classification levels in the future (Bernthal & Wellins, 2006). The development for these senior leadership roles may focus on ensuring that candidates experience a wide range of challenging assignments to widely develop their capabilities and include work placements tailored to individual learning needs, along with training programs and executive coaching. However, as Conlon (2011) noted, succession planning really needs to be applied to all management positions, not just to the top jobs.

Developing entire cohorts of staff or volunteers through leadership and management development and other training initiatives, rather than focusing specifically on those with current leadership positions is another approach used. These broader succession and talent management programs aim to identify and develop replacements for key groups of people over time (Rothwell, 2011). A strategy of using general training may also be more appropriate for smaller sport organizations or those organizations with a minimal training budget. For example, an Athletics Federation could use internal re-assignment to develop skills for critical roles (at minimal cost to the organization), or a Triathlon Club's volunteer director could work with a business coach and access accelerated leadership development through an externally run training program. Strategic planning will inform the processes chosen, as will future organizational needs, shifts in markets, individual potential and development, plus demographic and social changes (Schoonover, 2011).

In complement with the HR planning process succession planning should be integrated with training and development plans and the performance management system. The support of senior leaders in creating a culture where employees provide collegiate support, advice and constructive feedback is vital for effective succession management. Succession planning will vary depending on context – for example, a recent study in Asia found several unique succession challenges related to local culture fit, leadership development and the development of both global awareness and cultural intelligence necessary to lead a diverse workforce (Zhao, Smith & Campbell, 2012). See also the scenario in Box 3.1.

BOX 3.1

Succession planning in professional baseball

You are the vice president of human resources for a professional baseball team that competes in a league with 30 franchises across 25 cities in the USA, Canada and Mexico. Each team operates as an independent business but is governed by a central league office. The league is highly competitive and teams battle over many of the same resources including personnel, media attention, some marketing revenues and, at times, a shared customer base. While franchises compete against one another, there is a centralized mechanism to ensure competitive balance within the league. The average annual revenue per franchise has risen consistently for each over the past 15 years and now averages US$150 million per franchise per year.

The competitive season runs from April through to September, culminating in a championship in October for those teams reaching the playoffs. While the franchises are extremely busy during the competitive season, there is also plenty of work to be done between November and March. Thus, the industry operates on a 12-month cycle.

The organizational structure for on-field personnel is consistent across franchises, but it varies by team in the staff functions. Only 10 franchises have HR strategist positions, and only recently has that position featured vice president-level work. Generally, franchises employ between 125 and 300 staff, excluding on-field personnel.

The request

On 2 August, your team's board chair calls you to a confidential meeting and informs you that the president will be retiring at the end of the season. This is the first time you have heard about a change at the presidential level. Approximately six franchises (20 per cent) replace their president each year, so while this is not an uncommon occurrence it is a critical change within the organization. The chair asks you to develop a plan to replace the president.

To respond to the request, create appropriate recommendations for the chair about searching for and selecting a new president.

1   What are the main issues in the case?
2   Describe the information that would be most useful in forming your recommendations.
3   Describe possible courses of action for resolving the issues, and the pros and cons of each.
4   What creative approaches could be used to help understand the franchise president job?

Information from Weingarden (2008)
For the full case see http://www.shrm.org/Education/hreducation/Documents/
Top%20Choice%20Instructor%20Manual.pdf

EXTERNAL ANALYSIS FOR HR PLANNING

An external analysis looks at the demographic, occupational qualifications, eligibility and skill availability composition of the workforce in the relevant labor market. Environmental factors that affect the available labor market include the aging of labor force, immigration patterns, occupation-related supply and economic conditions. In most countries local and national level data is readily available on social/cultural changes, economic forecasts, demographic and legislative trends. The question is whether these changes will impact locally, nationally or internationally, on the organization's capacity to have a skilled workforce. The external analysis also looks at what your competitors are doing and if they are offering different employment packages/conditions to their staff. Sources of information for the external analysis include government bodies such as bureaus of statistics, employer associations, trade journals, research papers, news media, competitor/competitors' annual reports, private market research companies and community groups. The supply analysis can then be matched with a demand forecast.

FORECASTING DEMAND

Forecasting demand involves estimating the size and composition of the workforce required to meet the organization's objectives. Forecasting techniques may be quantitative or qualitative and include the predictions of experts within and outside the organization, benchmarking estimates based on similar organizations and scenario planning several potential outcomes. Each of these techniques can assist the HR planning process by identifying how many and what kind of employees may be needed. Recent research suggests that the past is not always a good predictor of the future, and that 'scenario planning' might be more effective than more traditional forecasting techniques, and that system dynamics type of modelling is particularly suited for two to five year scenarios (Hafeez & Aburawi, 2013).

Demand forecasting techniques fall into five major categories: direct managerial input; best guess; historical ratios; other statistical methods; and scenario analysis (Ward, 1996). Overviews of each are provided here.

Direct managerial input typically involves a directive that the number of people in the organization or the workforce budget will adhere to a specific number. For example, the budget of a state sport organization is set at US$1.5 million per annum for staff and consequently the organization either appoints new staff or reduces current staffing levels to meet this ceiling. This technique, while easy to calculate, is not linked to actual workload requirements and does not distinguish between critical and non-critical skills. From a strategic planning point of view the weakness of this approach is that analysis of the human resources required to best meet organizational objectives is often not undertaken.

Best guess involves a managerial judgment process. Data on the demand for employees and/or skill and knowledge requirements are collected from the manager of each section (e.g., marketing, accounts, community development, etc.) and collated for an overall projection. Each manager estimates the impact of anticipated productivity, technology and business changes. Assessment of the current staffing profile alongside the anticipated positive and negative changes guides the future estimate. While this approach provides a great deal of flexibility, it assumes that all managers have the time and ability to produce an accurate forecast.

Historical ratios capture trends in the organization's demand for human resources. Overall requirements for staff can usually be strongly correlated with other factors such as the number of programs delivered, size of membership or number of competitions held. Consider an example using simple ratio analysis. In this case, a sport company has identified that it takes 10 employees to produce 100 tennis racquets a day. A recent sponsorship signing of a top 10 men's tennis player, a crowd favorite, has led the company to forecast an increase in demand to 150 tennis racquets a day; thus, five more employees will need to be hired to meet production demand.

The major strength of this approach is that it can be easily developed with simple methodologies such as Excel spreadsheets and keeping track of changes (increases and decreases) over time and according to certain conditions (e.g., program or product demands, fluctuations in revenue, weather). Its weakness is that it requires adjustments for a potentially rapidly changing sport environment, and the ability to make adaptations may be beyond the skills of the individuals developing the projections. For instance, quick adjustments may be needed for unexpected weather conditions that result in lower than anticipated snowfall for a ski resort, as the resulting poor ski conditions correlate with lower customer demand and consequently impact staffing requirements.

Other statistical methods include regression, linear programming, simulations and demand flow models. These more sophisticated approaches consider multiple variables that are believed to be key to forecasting demand. The major drawback associated with these models is that they typically require a large sample size and its complexity is difficult to master. Software packages such as SAP® and Peoplesoft® incorporate forecasting tools to assist with this process, but these are generally only used in larger organizations and require specialized HR planning skills.

Scenario analysis involves the development of alternative workforce scenarios through brainstorming sessions that rely on workforce environmental scanning data. Environmental scanning involves a systematic approach to collecting and analyzing information from the external environment. It provides the basis for understanding the nature of trends and drivers of change that are likely to impact the sport organization. This approach encourages blue sky, outside the box thinking, and can be done within the organization or developed with the use of experts. One method, the Delphi technique, involves getting a group of experts to provide individual forecasts, which are in turn collated and then sent back to each individual, usually presented anonymously, for another round of forecasting, the process continuing until a consensus is reached by the experts. For example, the Confederação Brasileira de Futebol (CBF) could use this method to forecast the growth of local football in the wake of hosting the 2014 FIFA World Cup. Experts in the impact of hosting mega-events and modelling post-competition changes, football experts and individuals with detailed knowledge of the Brazilian environment and economy, and other relevant experts could form the basis of the Delphi group. Each expert would be asked to map out their predictions and rationale, all the individual responses are then anonymously distributed, each expert would take these into consideration and develop replies, with the distribution of responses continuing until a general consensus is reached.

The Delphi method is a convenient way to incorporate the opinions of several experts, independently and then in an integrated fashion. A weakness is its ability to deal with complex forecasts involving multiple factors, and, as forecasting contains a large amount of uncertainty, a high degree of error is possible.

Scenario analysis is a forward-looking forecasting process of creating possible future stories and considers the unthinkable. The steps are, first, develop credible scenarios; second, list key success factors and HR requirements for the organization to deal with each scenario; and third, focus resources on initiatives that promote these requirements. The benefits are building into HR strategy an awareness of impending changes and forward planning for these changing conditions. However, there is scant evidence that sport organizations are employing scenario analysis for HRM.

The supply analysis is matched with the demand forecasting work and any apparent gaps indicate either a projected unmet need or a surplus, either of which presents a challenge. The next step is then to develop action plans to close the supply–demand gap, outlining objectives, specific activities, recruitment and selection, including succession, training and development, outsourcing and contingency staffing, performance indicators, rewards and evaluation methods.

JOB ANALYSIS AND DESIGN

Job analysis is a basic HR activity and a critical aspect of HR planning as these activities aim to provide relevant data and a framework for taking decisions about the organization's workforce composition. Job analysis also forms a foundation for other HR functions, such as, recruitment, employee selection, performance appraisal, training, compensation and so on. There are various methods by which job analysis information can be collected and used to construct job descriptions and specifications. Job analysis and design provide the basis for understanding work and how it is organized to 'ensure that the organization's strategic business objectives are being supported and employee needs are being met' (Stone, 2010: 150).

Job analysis is a systematic analysis of the tasks and responsibilities of a given job, along with the skills, knowledge and experience needed to perform the job. Systematic identification of the duties to be performed in any given role provides the basis for effective HR planning. What a 'sports development officer', a 'competition coordinator' or a 'membership liaison manager' does in their job may vary from organization to organization. Therefore, a shared understanding of the expectations of the position within the specific sport organization is essential. Analysis is an ongoing process within the organization as the tasks comprising most jobs will change over time owing to technological innovations or other reasons. Up-to-date job analysis may provide an indication of when jobs need redesigning because of task content changes.

For example, a competition coordinator for a state sport organization may have been hired when the organization was relatively small and mainly used manual systems for record keeping and communication. Subsequent changes may have included the introduction of online customer relationship management programs and databases, and much greater use of social media for communication with members. Ongoing job analysis would identify and document the new duties, providing a better understanding of the current responsibilities of the competition coordinator. If the incumbent competition coordinator left the organization then the position description for the replacement competition coordinator should consequently reflect the job at that time rather than when the position was originally filled. Thus, the new competition coordinator would need to have relevant customer and social media skills.

Accurate job analysis is required for an effective recruitment and selection process. Job analysis produces a job description and a job specification. Job analysis provides data for performance appraisal that can be used to compare an individual's actual performance with the specified job expectations. It is also the basis for wage and salary determination and can be used to evaluate and compare jobs for wage and salary purposes. In addition, job analysis data should feed into the organization's training and development strategy.

Job analysis has become increasingly important as it forms a component of legal requirements for hiring, promotion wage and salary, and other personnel practices. Legal regulations vary from country to country and it is important that all sport organizations are aware of any relevant government requirements in this regard. In the USA, federal regulations provide that each employment practice of the federal government, and of individual organizations, use a job analysis to identify:

- basic duties and responsibilities
- knowledge, skills and abilities required to perform the duties and responsibilities
- factors that are important in evaluating candidates.

Additionally, the US Federal Guidelines for job analysis and *Equal Employment Opportunity Commission's Uniform Guidelines for Employee Selection Procedures, 29 C.F.R. Part 1607[1]* provides a framework to help assure that hiring, evaluation or promotion processes are employed in a non-discriminatory manner. Furthermore, it states that a thorough job analysis is needed for supporting a selection procedure. This may have implications for proving or disproving that discrimination has taken place. For example, a job description may be tendered in laying charges of discrimination against an organization charged with paying a female less than a male in the organization, even though the woman is performing what is essentially the same job as her male counterpart.

Job analysis information

The most frequently used technique for collecting information for a job analysis is the *interview*. It is used to collect data from the employee who is performing the job or the job incumbent's manager. Critical incident interviews, where the individual or manager describes incidents where underperformance or success has eventuated, are used to identify vital skills and abilities required to perform the job. A weakness of this approach is its subjectivity. Employees may overstate the duties they perform or they may neglect to mention certain responsibilities which are infrequent but critical. On the other hand, the manager may speculate about what they think the employee is doing rather than the tasks that are actually being performed.

Structured questionnaires, completed by the employee or manager and others who have some relationship to the job, are also commonly used. To avoid problems of respondent bias many organizations use some form of 360 degree feedback where the job holder, peers, direct reports and managers all answer questions about the one job. The data is then collated to provide a 'rounded' perspective on the job.

Direct observation of the individual performing a job, with a record taken of the observations, is used where work behaviors are observable. The subjectivity of other methods such as interviews or self-complete questionnaires is removed, but there is a danger that the employee may change his or her behaviors if they know they are being observed. *Diaries or logs* in which employees record their daily activities and tasks can also be used to record what the job entails.

Combinations of the four methods outlined above will usually provide better results than just using one method alone. Regardless of the method used, the information collected should be comprehensive and align with an organization's vision and strategic goals.

Job descriptions and specifications

Two primary outcomes of job analysis are the provision of information for job descriptions and specifications. Where the job description outlines the duties and responsibilities attached to a position, the specification delineates the qualifications and skills required. While in practice aspects of the specification are likely to be embedded in the job description, it is a useful exercise to conceptually differentiate between the two as each has a different purpose. The job specification and description act as a guide for recruiting the right person into a job that the sport organization needs performed. The description also provides the basis for determination of the level of remuneration and is used in performance management.

A *job description* should be concise, accurate and contain achievable tasks. The job is identified with a title (e.g., Athlete Investment Officer), location of the job within the organization (e.g., Finance and Investment division) and the reporting relationship of the job (e.g., to the Senior Investment Officer). The job's definition is contained in a summary statement that includes the purpose of the job, its function and its relationship to the organization's strategy. The job delineation includes the duties, responsibilities, reporting relationships and other tasks or functions and is the lengthiest part of the description. In general, job descriptions tend to be less specific at higher levels within the organization such as for senior managers or executives than for lower level positions and to focus more on objectives to be achieved rather than tasks to be undertaken.

The *job specification* outlines the minimum qualifications required to perform the job. This would typically include education, experience or skills. Determining the base-level qualifications for a job requires a thorough job analysis and a good understanding of the skills needed to perform the work effectively. For example, in the case of the competition coordinator, knowledge of appropriate competition software packages and the ability to operate website software systems would be included in the job specification. This job specification would enable the organization to engage in targeted recruitment and selection procedures. An Athlete Investment Officer Position example is presented in Box 3.2

As jobs change over time, and the incumbents in an existing job may modify their approach to performing the jobs to deal with such changes, the job analysis process is vulnerable to potential inaccuracies. While it is not realistic to expect that the job descriptions are continuously updated with every change, there is a need for a systematic review process. Responsiveness to change in this regard needs to be balanced with the legal requirements for documentation. Flexibility can also be maintained through an active job-design approach.

JOB DESIGN

Job design is the process of outlining the way work is performed and the required tasks, using job analysis and contextualizing this information by locating the job within the workgroup. Job design takes into account the needs of both the workgroup and the organization in the design of the job. De Cieri, Kramar, Noe, Hollenbeck, Gerhart and Wright (2005) note there are four basic approaches to job design: (1) motivational; (2) mechanic; (3) biological; and (4) perceptual-motor. Each approach has implications associated with its use.

BOX 3.2

Position description UK Sport

Job title: Athlete Investment Officer
Team: Finance & Investment
Reports to: Senior Athlete Investment Officer
Grade: 3

Job purpose

- To plan, deliver and monitor UK Sports' Athlete Personal Award (APA) investment across a portfolio of defined sports, working with Performance Team, National Governing Bodies (NGBs) and Athletes.
- To manage, and undertake where appropriate, project work/developmental work/ analysis of information relating to Athlete's on the World Class Performance Programme.
- To be the main point of contact for Athlete Investment related queries, and proactively promote the work of the Athlete Investment Officer Team through a customer service approach both internally and externally.

Key result areas

Administration of Athlete Personal Awards
- Manage the Athlete Personal Award (APA) grant programme for Podium and Development level athletes for a portfolio of sports, ensuring the operation of an efficient and effective system, including:
  - Planning the timetable with Performance Advisers and sports, and proactively co-ordinating the process ensuring this is met so athletes receive their APA payments on time.
  - Review athlete nominations put forward by sports, to ensure the right athletes have been identified in the right performance categories, raising with NGB/ Performance Advisors any nominations that require further discussion.
  - Assess athlete applications requesting additional information/clarification from athletes if required and calculate APA amounts in line with agreed UK Sport policy and any agreed sport specific criteria.
  - Issue Award Letters for APAs, including Terms & Conditions of Awards and any other relevant documentation.
  - Maintain athlete records, including relevant data on the Grant Management System.
  - Set up APAs and payment schedules on the Grant Management System (GMS), including checking payments and bank details before the pay-run.
  - Highlighting any issues to the Senior Athlete Investment Officer requiring further discussion.

Investment Monitoring & Information Reporting
- Generate and provide accurate APA budget information to input into the forecasting of UK Sport funding budgets and APA reimbursements to NGBs.
- Monitor individual athlete performance in major championships against targets, using results data to verify appropriateness of athletes' existing performance category and feed results into the Mission 2012 process in order to measure performance against sport KPIs.
- Research, source and compile athlete data in order to respond to internal and external requests (e.g. Annual Review, Parliamentary Questions, Freedom of Information requests, Team 2012).
- Highlight issues and themes arising and pro-actively contribute to the formulation and continuous improvement of athlete services, policies and processes, including relevant guidance notes.

Investment Relationship Management
- Be the front-line key contact for athletes, providing information and support on APA and related issues, resolving queries and making referrals where necessary, acting at all times with a high level of customer service.
- Liaise with staff at all levels within sport governing bodies and other system partners (e.g. BOA, Home Country Sport Councils, EIS, Performance Lifestyle Advisors, BAC) as necessary. Building relationships in order to generate trust and a successful working partnership, along with developing their knowledge and understanding of the APA system and the regulatory status attached to the APA.
- Provide support to Performance Advisers, the Senior Athlete Investment Officer, other Investment Team colleagues, and other UK Sport teams by advising on athlete policies and processes, providing results data and other information.

Projects
- Manage specific Projects as identified by the Senior Athlete Investment Officer.
- Participate in relevant investment projects, in particular implementing solutions identified through the Mission 2012 review process.
- Undertake any other activities consistent with the responsibilities of the AIO post.

Key internal/external contacts
- Senior Athlete Investment Officer
- Finance & Investment Team
- Performance Team
- Performance Lifestyle Advisers
- Other UK Sport colleagues, in particular the Governance Team
- Officers from Home Country Sports Councils and Institutes
- Staff at executive levels in sport governing bodies and system partners, in particular the British Athletes Commission
- WCP funded athletes
- Suppliers/consultants
- Internal and external auditors.

This job specification is not to be regarded as exclusive or exhaustive. It is intended as an outline of the areas of activity and will be amended in light of the changing needs of the organization.

Competencies: Athlete Investment Officer

Technical competencies
- Educated to degree level or equivalent.
- Good analytical skills and ability to analysis data.
- Proven experience in an administration and/or a project related role.
- IT literate, with a high level of competency in the use of Microsoft packages and databases.
- Understanding of high performance sport in the UK and particularly challenges facing athletes.
- Experience in the development of policy and processes desirable.
- Previous experience of data analysis desirable.

Job-related competencies
- Building partnerships
  - Identifying opportunities and taking action to build strategic relationships between one's area and other areas, teams, departments, units or organisations to help achieve business goals.
- Contributing to team success
  - Actively participating as a member of a team to move the team toward the completion of goals.
- Gaining commitment
  - Using appropriate interpersonal styles and techniques to gain acceptance of ideas or plans; modifying one's own behaviour to accommodate tasks, situations and individuals involved.
- Planning and organizing
  - Establishing courses of action for self and others to ensure that work is completed efficiently.
- Follow up
  - Monitoring the results of delegations, assignments, or projects, considering the skills, knowledge and experience of the assigned individual and the characteristics of the assignment or project.
- Quality orientation
  - Accomplishing tasks by considering all areas involved, no matter how small; showing concern for all aspects of the job; accurately checking processes and tasks; being watchful over a period of time.
- Continuous improvement
  - Originating action to improve existing conditions and processes; using appropriate methods to identify opportunities, implement solutions and measure impact.

- Decision making
  - Identifying and understanding issues, problems and opportunities; analysing data to draw conclusions; using effective approaches for choosing the course of action; and developing appropriate solutions.
- Living the mission and values
  - Knows and understands the mission and values.
  - Operates within the values on a daily basis.
  - Understands and can explain how their role contributes to the mission.
  - Gives input to discussion and feedback within the values.

Information from UK Sport (2014)

The *motivational* approach acknowledges the psychological needs of employees and how the fulfilment of these, when built into job design, can lead to increased job satisfaction, motivation, performance and involvement. Motivational components may include:

- autonomy – level of independence in carrying out job duties
- intrinsic job feedback – the work in itself is motivating
- extrinsic job feedback – external sources of feedback are provided
- social interaction – avenues for team and collegiate work
- task/goal clarity – job requirements are clearly delineated
- task variety – the job involves engaging in different activities
- task identity – a complete, indefinable piece of work is produced
- ability/skill level requirements – the knowledge level required is high
- ability/skill variety – use of different skills and knowledge
- task significance – the job is interconnected and important to other jobs
- growth/learning – opportunities for learning are provided
- recognition – scope for reward and acknowledgement of good work.

The use of motivational approaches to job design such as job enrichment (providing more decision-making responsibility), job enlargement (widening the scope of tasks), job rotation (moving employees around a range of jobs), flexible work practices and self-managing teams, all focus on increasing the potential of the job to motivate. A well-designed job based on this approach will typically result in an increase in number and level of skills required. Research shows that motivational techniques, while increasing satisfaction, do not necessarily lead to better performance quality. The relationship of job design to motivation is discussed in more detail in Chapter 8.

The *mechanistic* approach was dominant throughout the 20th century and is underpinned by principles of scientific management, time and motion studies and work simplification. The premise of this approach is that there was one best way to do a job, and by analysing workers' movements the most effective way to perform a job could be designed. The key components considered in this approach are:

- job specialization – the degree to which specialization of tasks is possible
- specialization of tools and procedures – the degree of special purpose use of tools and procedures
- single activities – whether the job can be done one task at a time
- skill simplification – the basic skill and training required
- repetition – the repetitiveness of the tasks
- spare time (decrease) – the time between tasks is minimized
- automation – what tasks can be automated?

The mechanistic approach is orientated towards HR efficiency and flexibility outcomes such as staffing ease and low training times. As such, it suggests designing jobs with reduced mental demands. The benefits of this work design approach are decreased costs of training, lower staffing difficulties, fewer errors, decreased mental overload and fatigue. The disadvantages are that the mechanistic approach is associated with increased absenteeism and boredom, together with decreases in job satisfaction and motivation (Das, 1999). Its task focus suggests a 'dehumanization' of work.

The *biological* approach (Campion, 1988) is based on the human factors related to work design, and is also referred to as the *ergonomic* approach. It is based on the science of biomechanics, or the study of body movements, and is concerned with the design of jobs and physical environments to match the physiological capabilities and limitations of people. This approach analyses the physiological needs and physical conditions under which work is undertaken, considering elements such as:

- physical size – aspects such as the need to be of certain height or weight
- strength – requirements of lifting or muscular endurance
- agility – ability to carry out work that requires physical manipulations.

The aim of a thorough ergonomic analysis and subsequent job design is the reduction in workplace illness and injuries, and fostering of good employee health.

The *perceptual-motor* approach also has its roots in the human-factors literature. The focus is on human mental capabilities and limitations. The aim is to design jobs in a way that ensures that they do not exceed the mental capabilities of the job holder primarily by striving to reduce the attention and concentration requirements of jobs, while improving reliability, safety and user reactions. This approach emphasizes:

- facilities – adequacy of lighting, workplace layout and design
- equipment – ease of use of equipment
- materials – access to manuals; information used in performing the job
- information – considerations of the information input required and processing to do the job and information required to be produced by the job.

The benefits of this approach are related to lower error rates, fewer accidents and reduced training requirements; however, its use has not been found to increase job satisfaction or motivation.

Stone (2010) suggests that in planning work and designing jobs it is important to understand the contemporary context of the work and seek to design jobs that maximize outcomes for both the organization and the individual. There is an increasing use of 'new' forms of job design such as high performing teams, virtual locations, tele-commuting and other flexible formations. These are a reflection of the demands that contemporary sport organizations face and must be responsive to if they are to ensure organizational sustainability. Meeting the needs of employees, volunteers and customer expectations requires continuous change, improvement and responsiveness. Together with this is the changing and increasingly diverse workforce, with greater representation of women, dual working couples, cultural diversity, higher-educated employees, and an aging workforce in most Western countries. Workplace tenure changes mean that employees now expect to change organizations several times during their career or run their own businesses. The extent to which existing job design approaches can respond to these changing environments will be an increasingly paramount issue.

OUTSOURCING THE HR PLANNING FUNCTION

Some sport organizations that do not have the staff, expertise or volume of work to justify the operation of a separate HR function within the organization may outsource some aspects of HR such as HR planning, assessment or recruitment. Outsourcing involves entering into a contractual arrangement with an external service provider to deliver a product or service for the organization, such as HR tasks that would have otherwise been performed in-house. Considerations in decisions to outsource usually revolve around either more effective provision of the service in terms of cost and quality or the need for expertise, knowledge or skills that are not present in the organization. Typically, outsource providers are specialists able to provide a central product or extensive service across a range of organizations and thus gain economies of scale, such as recruitment, benefit plan design, retirement services and HR information management systems. The outsourcing arrangement should be assessed in terms of organizational effectiveness and its impact on the internal workforce. For example, a relatively small sport organization might outsource an activity such as the development of an HR strategy and action plan based on workforce assessment. Stone (2010) suggests that reasons for outsourcing include: increased focus on core business; cost and quality; access to improved technology; and elimination of union problems.

Within outsourcing it is common to develop a service level agreement (SLA). SLAs are contracts between service providers and sport organizations that define the services provided, the metrics associated with these services, acceptable and unacceptable service levels, liabilities on the part of the service provider and the customer, and actions to be taken in specific circumstances. An example of an SLA for HR services is provided below.

Service level agreements – HR outsourcing
1. Recruitment and selection
Pre-advertisement
Advise on workforce planning, strategy and recruitment policy.
Assist in job/role design.
Undertake job analysis/evaluation and compliance matters as necessary.
Campaign planning.

Advertising
Agree advertisement text with organization representative.

Liaise with advertising agency and place advertisement in agreed media.
The organization representative will respond to requests for approval.

Preparation of documentation
Prepare and agree electronic and hard copy job packs for candidates.
Collate all job applications and enter all applicants onto database.
The organization representative will carry out shortlisting exercises and decide candidates to be interviewed.

Interview
Advise on interview arrangements.
Obtain references.
The organization representative will:
- invite candidates to interview
- organize interview venue
- organize selection arrangements
- organize panel and interview pack for panel members
- make verbal conditional offer to successful candidate, including negotiation of salary.

Appointment offers
Issue conditional offer letter and contract including relevant Terms and Conditions and organize medical clearances. Notify unsuccessful applicants.

Another form of outsourcing in HR relates to contracting another body to deliver a specific service or product whereby HR is built into the arrangement. For example, the SLA may be a contract for facility management, and as part of the arrangement the contracted body is also responsible for the organization's staff development and training. An example would be when a local government authority enters into an SLA to operate a swimming facility and manage all the staffing requirements associated with the facility's operation. The SLA should provide clear performance indicators and serve as framework for evaluating the outsourced HR activity. See, for example, the case study in Box 3.3.

BOX 3.3

Case study: 2012 London Olympic Games and HR planning

Volunteers

The London Organising Committee of the Olympic and Paralympic Games' (LOCOG) volunteer program involving the recruitment, training and deployment of 70,000 individuals, has been highly praised. Prior to the recruitment process, LOCOG clearly articulated the commitment required by volunteers. This included approximately 20 hours of training and a minimum of 10 shifts. Establishing these expectations early was a key factor in the low attrition rate through the interview, selection and deployment stages. The initial invitation period was divided into two stages. The first stage was specifically targeted to disabled groups and sports specialists. Forty-six large disabled groups were targeted, which proved highly successful with a much higher proportion of disabled applicants than any previous Games. The specialist specific recruitment campaign was also highly successful, with specialists accounting for approximately one-third of all volunteers. The second stage was opened up to the general public.

The recruitment campaign commenced in July 2010; however, applicants were not informed of successful application until January 2012. During this period, LOCOG maintained communication with all applicants, including online engagement through a dedicated volunteer website.

More than 250,000 people applied for volunteer roles. Forty per cent of these applicants stated that the 2012 Olympic Games had inspired them to volunteer for the first time. LOCOG encouraged applications from outside of London, establishing nine regional recruitment centers.

Volunteer training involved three core stages: orientation, role specific and venue specific. The general orientation training integrated volunteers with paid staff and contractors, implemented to develop team spirit and cohesion. Role specific and venue specific training targeted specific functions, duties and facilities' detail.

Paid staff

The functioning of organizing committees is pivotal during preparation and delivery of Olympic Games. They are responsible for managing relationships and partnerships both internally and externally. LOCOG designed cross-functional teams to manage multiple stakeholder relationships. These 'task forces' were non-hierarchical and coordinated key individuals from various areas of LOCOG and external agencies to address issues that spanned across teams or functions.

Through the seven-year period of Games' preparations, organizing committees changed dramatically. LOCOG started in 2005/06 with less than 50 people. By 2012, approximately 200,000 people, including staff, volunteers and contractors, were being managed. In the few weeks following the Games these numbers dropped to hundreds and then tens, and in June 2013 LOCOG was closed.

LOCOG recognized the importance of the early stages of building an organization. High priority was placed on recruiting the right people for each position. Recruitment was based on strong and consistent leadership and focused on flexibility in structure and people to adapt through the phases of planning and implementation. Employment was based on short-term contracts, referred to as time-limited employment, which provided flexibility to increase or decrease staff numbers as required. It was recognized that key to the success of this staff program was continuity of personnel at senior levels.

LOCOG employed a mix of people who had previous Games experience and expertise, with those without major event experience. Recruiting inexperienced staff gave LOCOG a different perspective and challenged the traditional way Olympic Games had been delivered. This balance of experience and fresh enthusiasm created a dynamic environment while maintaining trust and credibility with partners and stakeholders.

A critical factor in establishing LOCOG was the recruitment of high-caliber people, who importantly exemplified the Games' vision. Senior management's roles and responsibilities seamlessly evolved through the different phases of the Games' organization. Embodying the Games' vision allowed leaders to portray their commitment to the Games, promote innovation and enthuse other employees.

LOCOG prioritized internal communication and engagement among their paid workforce. Regular staff brief sessions, workshops and engagement days were conducted and as the team grew in size and geographical scope an intranet and cascade briefing system were introduced. Through implementation of a solid governance structure, which directly reflected the operational structure, decision-making power was directed to groups of directors and managers, who ensured the Games' budget aligned to key activities.

Another key factor in LOCOG's successful delivery of the Games was their ability to adapt and evolve. Immediately prior to the Games, OCOGs' workloads significantly increase and the organization must be as adaptable as possible, refining structures and decision-making procedures. The strong leadership through LOCOG and effective organizational design was critical for the movement of people and flexibility of structures during transition from planning, testing to event delivery.

Information from International Olympic Committee (2013a)
and National Audit Office (2012)

Case discussion points

1   What were some of the key considerations in LOCOG's HR planning strategy?
2   Outline some of the operational outcomes of the above considerations.

SUMMARY

HR planning processes such as those discussed in this Chapter provide a framework and alternative techniques for sport organizations to assess where they are, where they want to go, and how they plan to get there. Strategic implementation of HRM means performing planning activities that support the organization's mission accomplishment and measuring how well those activities contribute to achieving strategic goals. The critical aspect of HR planning is that the organization engages in efforts to anticipate and take actions to ensure that the organization will have the requisite human resources in place to meet its goals.

The HR planning process examines the organization's internal and external environment and uses this information to determine HR requirements required by the organization to meet its goals. An organization may include succession planning as part of their strategic workforce planning process, by identifying critical positions or targeting specific employees for targeted succession plans. Job analysis and design are key activities in the planning process. Job analysis is an examination of the tasks and sequences of tasks necessary to perform a job. Job descriptions are a product of job analysis and list the tasks, or functions, and responsibilities of a position which include reporting relationships and specifications such as the qualifications required. Job design is the process of outlining the way work is performed and the required tasks using the job analysis and contextualizing this work within the workgroup. The challenge for job design is to acknowledge the trade-offs that have to be made between using the different approaches to job design and structure jobs that will be able to meet future challenges and create a motivating and satisfying workplace.

DISCUSSION QUESTIONS

1   Develop an internal workforce profile template for a sport organization where you have worked or volunteered, or with which you are very familiar. What information would be critical to include? (Consider how this would relate to education, training, biographic attributes, competencies, work experience, and any other relevant data/information.)

2   How would you assess the internal and external workforce supply available for an organization that is planning to launch a new product line (e.g., an athletic footwear company launching an athletic apparel line; a fitness club introducing ballet barre classes)? How would you forecast the workforce demands associated with this expansion?

3   Describe who you would include (and why) in a Delphi process of scenario analysis to forecast demand in the situation(s) noted earlier.

4   Conduct a job analysis of the most recent paid or volunteer position of a classmate or workmate. Do this based on interview questions alone and fully consider what to ask so that you collect the most relevant information (e.g., What do you do on a daily basis? Describe critical incidents. How do you handle problems that arise? What would I see if I watched you do your job? What things would be most important for you to record in a daily log about your job?).

5   Find at least two currently advertised sport industry job descriptions on the internet. Compare the elements of each description: What are the key job specifications? What does this tell you about the position(s)? Are the job descriptions adequate? What else would you want to know about the position?

6   Discuss how succession planning can contribute to SHRM in a sport organization you are familiar with. What might be some of the barriers/constraints to its implementation? What are some of the benefits of filling a position through succession planning? And some of the drawbacks?

CHAPTER 4

Recruitment and selection for sport organizations

LEARNING OBJECTIVES

After reading this chapter you will be able to:

- Articulate the strategic importance of recruitment, selection and placement to an organization and arguments in support of judicious hiring
- Appreciate the links between recruitment and selection and other human resource management (HRM) activities
- Describe different sources and methods for generating a pool of job applicants
- Explain current trends in recruitment including the impact of 'new media'
- Identify a variety of selection techniques and the advantages and disadvantages of each
- Recognize the sources of bias in selection decision making

CHAPTER OVERVIEW

Recruitment and selection are terms that are often used as synonyms. In fact they are separate but linked processes. Recruitment refers to the activities and processes undertaken by an organization in order to generate a suitably qualified pool of candidates for employee and volunteer positions. Selection refers to the techniques and methods used to choose the best candidate from the pool that has been generated by recruitment.

This chapter begins by noting the reasons why recruitment and selection are such important human resource (HR) activities. It then describes a sequential process of managing both activities from the beginning to the end. Various alternatives are outlined in relation to each activity and the advantages and disadvantages associated with each are outlined.

AN OVERVIEW OF RECRUITMENT AND SELECTION

Chapters 2 and 3 introduced the concept of strategic human resource planning and associated techniques. This chapter should be read in conjunction with Chapter 3 as the HR activities of attracting and selecting employees and volunteers are closely connected with workforce planning and defining the tasks, roles and responsibilities of jobs. HR planning identifies the human resources required to provide the organization with the ability to implement its strategy. The 'work' of the organization may be undertaken by employees, volunteers or it may be outsourced (or a combination thereof). In most large organizations the recruitment and selection process is managed by the HR department in conjunction with line managers. In a small- to medium-sized organization, such as many sport organizations, recruitment and hiring decisions tend to devolve to line managers and in some case to the Board of Directors.

Attracting and selecting the right individuals for the organization is a critical strategic human resources management (SHRM) decision. In the words of the former Chief Executive Officer (CEO) of General Electric, Jack Welch, 'Strategy begins with the people that you hire.' A key premise of SHRM is hiring the right people to ensure that the organization meets its goals. There are a number of reasons for this emphasis on selecting the right persons for your organization.

First, people are at the center of all organizational processes and the amount of discretionary effort that they put in can vary enormously. Getting the right people can literally mean the difference between success and failure in an organization as indicated in research on the topic. Studies on the productivity of workers in self-paced jobs have found that the gap between the best and the worst performers varies on average by a factor of two or more (Goleman, 1998; Schmidt & Hunter, 1983). In another study, high-performing employees were found to outperform a control group by 129 per cent on average (Boyatzis, 1999). Such findings indicate that attracting and selecting the right people is perhaps the single most important part of the entire HRM process. This is reflected in the often cited aphorism among employers that it is better to hire for attitude and train for skills rather than hire for skills and try to train the attitude. For example, when hiring staff for a summer sport camp, a critical attribute is genuine enjoyment of working with children, an outgoing, adaptable, flexible and diligent nature, and the ability to live in a cabin or a platform tent with children or co-workers for 9 to 11 weeks. In a job like this where fun and sociability are more critical for the participants than high-performance sport outcomes, the aforementioned attributes are often more important for staff than technical sport competence as having the right attitude is critical to success.

Second, recruiting people that have a positive contribution to make to the culture of an organization can help the organization achieve its goals. Using a sport analogy, the introduction of a new player into a team or the appointment of a new coach can galvanize performance and provide the impetus for a team to improve their performance and increase success. When power forward Alana Beard joined the Washington Mystics of the Women's National Basketball Association in 2006, the coach Ritchie Adubato noted that her contribution made a massive difference to the team's success. A teammate, Mystics forward DeLisha Milton-Jones added: 'Having her on this team is invaluable ... she's a great luxury because she can do so many things' (Gallo, 2006: 6). The Mystics went on to make the 2006 playoffs after having missed out in the previous season.

The culture of an organization is both influenced by, and influences, selection decisions. It impacts whether new people will fit in, based on their values and expectations. And it impacts the attractiveness of the organization to potential new employees – that is, whether good people will want to join. A study by Zhang and Gowan (2012) affirmed that socially responsible companies are more attractive to potential employees than less socially responsible companies. Uggerslev, Fassina and Kraichy (2012) examined applicant attraction to certain companies and concluded that perceived fit between the applicant and the organization was the largest predictor of applicant attraction across all recruitment stages. And in a 2013 study into employee engagement, commissioned by Randstad, the second largest HR services and staffing company in the world, it was found that company reputation and culture are significant factors in attracting new employees. From a sample of over 3,200 individuals, 96 per cent reported that it is important for their new company to have a good reputation among current employees, and 86 per cent recognized the importance of good reputation in the community. Moreover, 68 per cent of respondents reported that their new company should be engaged in corporate social responsibility (CSR) activities (Randstad USA, 2013). As an organization's culture can potentially encourage or exclude good candidates from joining it is a notable force in recruitment.

Third, consistent with the resource-based view (RBV) of the organization that was outlined in Chapter 2, organizations today are more reliant on internal transformation processes that build, for example, speed and efficiency, than on traditional sources of competitive advantages such as location and technology. Therefore, attracting the right talent (i.e., people) becomes a key strategic process in ensuring the organization's future.

Fourth, looking at the direct and indirect costs associated with sub-optimal hiring decisions also provides compelling reasons to recruit and select carefully. Selecting the wrong candidate can result in disruption to an organization because of reduced productivity, poor interpersonal relationships and team morale, reduced customer service levels and high associated costs. In direct monetary terms alone, an incorrect hiring decision has been estimated to cost between 40 and 60 per cent of the total annual compensation for a given position (Byham, 2001). An extreme example of the cost of a wrong hire is illustrated by events that happened at Nike. In 2004, Bill Perez was handpicked to be Nike's new CEO by Nike co-founder Phil Knight. However, Knight forced him out of Nike after just 13 months, noting that Perez just didn't understand what Nike was about and that there was too much for an outsider to learn. It is estimated that Perez received a severance package, coupled with salary and bonus that totaled US$19.4 million. This was a very costly mistake in hiring.

Figure 4.1 represents an overview of the recruitment and selection process showing the various stages and options. The remainder of this chapter discusses each of the major components and the options which are available to managers in working through the recruitment and selection process from the beginning to the end.

RECRUITMENT

As noted at the start of this chapter, the overall purpose of recruitment is to generate a pool of qualified candidates that will assist the sport organization to meet its strategic goals. An effective recruitment process will:

- be well-informed about upcoming internal supply and demand for new personnel
- scope out the external labor market conditions for different groups of staff and volunteers
- identify the best channels and materials for attracting employee and/or volunteers to the organization
- determine appropriate techniques for assessing the effectiveness of different recruitment methods and relevant legal obligations.

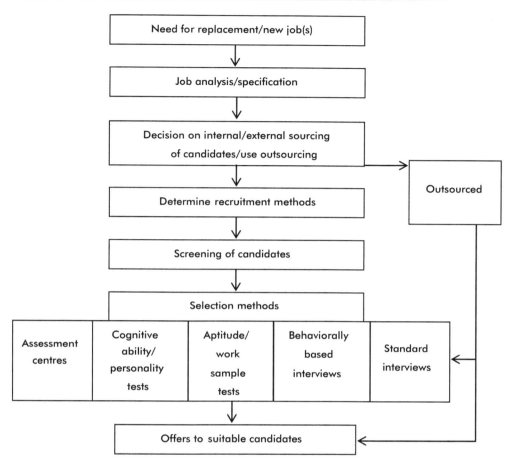

FIGURE 4.1 An overview of the recruitment and selection process

The actual process of obtaining job applicants is about both reaching qualified applicants and stimulating enough interest so that candidates apply for the job. Candidates may be sourced internally or externally depending on organizational policy and the nature of the positions. Internal recruitment sources include current employees, friends and families of employees and internal transfers. The main advantages of recruiting internally are that it is less costly and reduces risks for both the candidate and the organization because each has more accurate information about the role and the required skills. Internal recruitment also provides greater scope for career development within the organization. The major disadvantage with internal recruitment is that the organization is choosing from a small pool of candidates and may become insular or miss out on better options as a result. External recruitment is when the new employee or volunteer is sought from outside the organization. External recruitment involves additional costs, risks and longer training and adjustment periods than internal recruitment, but recruiting externally means that you can access a wider pool of potential talent. Most organizations will employ a mix of external and internal recruitment approaches.

RECRUITMENT METHODS

With reference to Figure 4.1, once an organization has determined a job specification it must then make a decision about whether to recruit internally, externally or through an external contractor. Internal recruitment methods tend to be simple and often revolve around the efficient dissemination of job information. Thus, in a national sport association office the recruitment of an internal person into a newly created Volunteer Manager role might involve the executive director and senior managers notifying or speaking with the current staff members who they have identified have the right qualities and competencies for the position. Personnel identified through the organization's succession planning process (see Chapter 3) as suitable for this position would most likely either be directly appointed or progress through an informal selection process. Intranet bulletin boards which advertise positions may also be used. Larger organizations may employ more sophisticated approaches by searching the HR information system databases for qualified candidates or using data analytics in conjunction with succession management techniques, such as those discussed in Chapter 3, for senior jobs. There are many instances where internal recruitment is judged as the most appropriate way to fill a vacancy. For example, after a major corporate restructure, Octagon Worldwide appointed Rick Dudley as its new President and CEO. Dudley had formerly been President of Octagon North America and had a long and successful track record in sports marketing.

With regard to external recruitment, the need to be more attractive to employees has led many organizations to try to build an employment 'brand' by becoming an 'employer of choice'. To become viewed as an 'employer of choice' sport organizations will commit themselves to offering reward packages, fringe benefits or job opportunities that make them stand out. The Adidas group, for example, has an 'Employer of Choice Approach' that focuses on 'creating a work environment that stimulates innovation, team spirit, engagement and achievement' (Adidas Group, n.d.: para 2). The company monitors employee engagement scores and reports industry employee of choice recognition awards. It is not uncommon for organizations to promote such employee benefits in their direct advertising and/or seek to become recognized as a 'best employer' by an independent external body. There are competitions that seek to identify the best organizations to work for, including *Fortune* magazine's 100 Best Companies To Work For (Time Inc., 2014) and Aon Hewitt's Best Employers in Asia 2013 Awards (Aon Hewitt & Associates, 2013). However, organizations that promote themselves as employers of choice should be mindful that they need to live up to the designation on an ongoing basis and some employee surveys indicate a growing level of cynicism relating to this practice.

External recruitment methods include traditional methods such as hard copy and online advertisements in newspapers or trade journals, the use of public employment agencies, internships and recruitment of graduates direct from universities. The use of *e-recruitment* has become a major component of the recruitment strategy for a wide range of sport organizations and is now a common method for job seekers in searching and applying for jobs. Dedicated websites include Sports Recruitment International (with regional offices in the UK, Switzerland, Singapore and Australia), Globalsportsjobs, Sportspeople.com, SportJobs in South Africa, Cosmos Sports Jobs in Canada and JobsInSports.com. The latter not only lists current positions that are vacant but also provides a database of professional sports team contacts, a sports internship database for entry-level candidates and a resume writing service.

The Internet is used to facilitate any or all of the main processes of attraction (advertising/ recruiting), selection and assessment (screening and testing). In addition, e-recruitment systems can be used, in parallel, to support applicant tracking and workflow systems. Advantages of e-recruitment relates to ease of use; amount of coverage, both geographical (worldwide) and in terms of target audience (all candidates looking for jobs in certain fields can be automatically notified of vacancies); reduced costs per hire when compared with traditional methods; shorter hiring cycles; improved quality and frequency of candidate responses; and recruitment can be tailored more precisely to the required job/candidate profiles.

Let us look at how this might work in practice. The national peak body for golf has just approved funding for an exciting and innovative project with the objective of increasing female participation in the game. A women's golf development officer job description is then written and posted on an Internet recruitment site. This is complemented by advertisements placed in professional golf magazines and in regional and national newspapers as well as the organization's own website. All applicants are requested to access an online application form, complete this form and submit their applications online. Job seekers that have signed up with the Internet site and that fit the profile of the candidates being sought will be notified of this vacancy. The Internet recruitment agency will also provide the golf association with data relating to remuneration practices to assist with setting an appropriate reward package for the position. When the applications are received the agency will assess each applicant and determine those who meet the key selection criteria. The list of potential interviewees will then be forwarded to the golf association for approval and the agency will notify unsuccessful candidates. The agency may then exit from the process at this stage or they may undertake the full selection process and recommend the appointment of the best applicant to the golf association.

However, Internet-based recruitment does come with disadvantages, as front-end efficiencies can often be counteracted by inefficiencies at the back end related to having to filter good applications from the hundreds or thousands of inappropriate or irrelevant ones. This highlights the need to use effective filtering software or services which can be sensitive to well-defined criteria relating to candidates who may fit the job profile. Other challenges encountered by organizations in implementing e-recruitment include problems with technology and difficulties in tailoring e-recruitment systems to meet specific needs in a recruitment process. When simultaneously operating both online and paper-based systems, it is critical to integrate e-recruitment systems with existing HR systems. Some of the earlier concerns about excluding potential applicants have diminished with the huge growth in the use of the Internet and it is now the preferred application method for a large majority of candidates in developed economies.

A common practice if the organization is handling large numbers of candidates or is recruiting for a highly specialized or senior role, is to outsource the recruitment and screening to a professional employment organization as represented in Figure 4.1. Professional employment organizations come in two main forms. First, there are full service recruitment consultants who will help the client organization to define position requirements, advertise, interview and provide a shortlist of candidates, some of whom will be on the consultant's placement books. In this sense, some consultants act as brokers or agents for prospective staff as well as for organizations seeking staff.

The second type of professional employment organizations are executive search firms that specialize in finding staff for very senior jobs. These firms may use a combination of advertisements (which often do not indicate the client organization's identity) and their own research, networks and databases to find candidates. Typically, these 'head hunters' (as executive search firms are colloquially known) are expensive and can charge in excess of 50 per cent of the first year's salary for a successful placement.

Another more recent approach to recruitment is the increased use of referrals and networking sites. In this approach people working in the organization use their personal and professional networks to spread the word about jobs. This is a more or less constant search for top quality candidates and relies on organizational staff spreading information about available positions.

Organizations may also target trade shows, customer contacts, academic connections, alumni networks and professional associations. Specific initiatives include sending current staff members to industry professional associations and conferences where they are likely to meet potential candidates and the use of professional association websites, listservs, social media sites and magazines to advertise for professional staff.

The choice of recruitment method will vary depending on the type of sport organization, the state of the labor market and the type of position being filled. For example, a small community sport organization might recruit using local networks and partnerships whereas a global company such as IMG might use recruitment consultants for senior positions.

Recruiting volunteers

In many Western countries the provision of community sport revolves around the resourcing and use of voluntary labor and volunteers have been found to be critical to their survival and success (Cuskelly, Taylor, Hoye & Darcy, 2006; Østerlund, 2013). Volunteers are also central to some governments' policies to grow sport participation (Nichols, Padmore, Taylor & Barrett, 2012). However, there appears to be an increasingly prevalent view that many sport organizations are struggling to recruit sufficient volunteers and studies report that volunteer numbers in many countries are declining (Breuer, Wicker & von Hanau, 2012; Koskia, 2012).

It is worth noting here that while sport volunteering is deeply rooted in many countries around the world, it is by no means a universal practice. In many countries there is no volunteer culture or tradition, and indeed in some cases volunteering is devalued as it is judged as giving away your capital for no return. As the *Final Report on Volunteering in the European Union* (GHK, 2010) highlighted in presenting census data on volunteering across Europe, it is still extremely difficult to recruit and retain volunteers in many former communist countries within the EU. Typically, the higher the GDP of a country, the more its citizens volunteer – underpinning the relationship of volunteering to income, education and general socio-economic status. However, there are exceptions to this, such as the Arab Gulf States where the relatively small indigenous population has high disposable income levels and low participation rates in non-paid sport volunteer activity. In countries such as these, the recruitment of sport volunteers needs to take into consideration what is appropriate to the specific cultural context and develop the most relevant approach.

The first step in maintaining a cohort of committed volunteers is their effective recruitment (Park & Kim, 2013). In this first stage, it should be emphasized that volunteers are valued by the sport organization and are not just being recruited to fill a position that no one else wanted or just to save the organization money. In non-profit sport organizations voluntary positions such as board members may be elected or appointed on an ex-officio basis. In the latter situation recruitment is by nomination and selection is via election.

The recruitment process for most volunteers is typically informal, and attracting a sufficient number of qualified applicants can be difficult. The most common pathway for involvement in voluntary work in a sport organization is through friends, family or the social networks of individuals already involved in the organization. A personal approach to asking people to volunteer is the best way to recruit volunteers into sport organizations. In the early stages of the recruitment process the potential volunteer should be given a realistic overview of what the role entails before they are asked to commit their time and energy to a position. This should include a job description with meeting times, major tasks and average weekly or monthly time commitment. Gaining an understanding of the characteristics and competencies of sport volunteers provides the organization with the basis to target appropriate individuals for volunteer roles (Kim, Zhang & Connaughton, 2010).

Volunteer recruitment for large-scale mega-sport events such as the Olympic Games, Football World Cup, World Championships and high profile events such as the Super Bowl in the United States, are quite different to sourcing volunteers for community sport. Most mega events will recruit via advertisements, announcements, partnerships and target volunteering associations, sporting organizations, professional groups, multicultural groups, educational institutions and sponsors. Various volunteer positions are needed and range from specialists (e.g., sport technical roles) that require specific knowledge of a particular sport to general roles (e.g., spectator services, transport, community liaison) that have very basic competency requirements. The scope of recruitment for such events is extensive. For example, in the 2010 Winter Olympic Games in Vancouver, 18,500 volunteers worked during the events (International Olympic Committee, 2013b). For the 2012 UEFA European Championship in Poland/Ukraine, 23,965 volunteer applications were received and more than 5,000 volunteers were selected and worked during the tournament (Union of European Football Associations, 2014). In the 2013 World University Summer Games in Kazan, Russia, 19,970 volunteers from 37 regions across Russia and 38 countries around the world were deployed (Summer Universiade in Kazan Executive Directorate, 2014). For the 2014 Winter Olympic Games in Sochi, Russia, from more than 180,000 registered applications, approximately 25,000 volunteers were involved in the Games. Controversially, for the 2010 Commonwealth Games Delhi 20,000 people registered as volunteers; however, approximately half failed to turn up for their duties or failed to return after a couple of days of volunteer work (Magnay, 2010). It is thought that the key factor in the high attrition rate was the attraction of the uniform as many volunteers collected the uniform and then subsequently failed to carry out their volunteer duties (Magnay, 2010).

In a study of volunteers at the 2010 Vancouver Olympic and Paralympic Winter Games, Dickson, Benson, Blackman and Terwiel (2013) recommend that sport event organizers could be more strategic in their volunteer recruitment. This is possible by targeting people who may have the interest and time to volunteer after the event, and by using recruitment and training prior to the event to get the volunteers thinking about post-event volunteering.

Selection of employees or volunteers can be made through a range of different methods and techniques, and the next section outlines the most common of these approaches.

SELECTION METHODS

Once the organization has screened out unsuitable candidates, a number of selection options are available. Some of the more commonly used methods are presented in Table 4.1, together with indicators of the cost and validity associated with each technique. When choosing selection techniques, account should be taken of the reliability and validity of each method.

In relation to selection, reliability refers to the extent to which a selection technique is free from random error or, to put it another way, the technique produces a consistent result with repeated use. Research on selection methods reveals that easily observable competencies, such as verbal fluency, can be more reliably measured using an interview than, for example, leadership ability, which is far more complex and deeply embedded in the individual's personality and therefore not easily assessable during a selection interview.

Validity refers to how well a measure on a selection technique relates to the individual's actual performance in a job. That is, the extent to which a selection measure is a predictor of effective job performance. Using our verbal fluency example from above, while the ability to effectively communicate may be measured reasonably reliably in an interview, it does not necessarily mean that verbal fluency is a good predictor of performance for a given job. On the other hand, a website design task used as a selection technique for a social media position is likely to have a high validity since it directly measures a significant job component.

The selection process may require different techniques to be used for reasons of validity, even if the actual technique has a lower reliability score. Perhaps the best example of this is the traditional interview, which has often been found to have a low reliability score, but is still considered essential in most selection procedures because of the need to judge a candidate's sociability and other attributes that can be reliably observed in an interview situation and which have a high validity in relation to the ability of a candidate to 'fit in' with an organization's culture and values.

As can be seen in Table 4.1, some techniques have greater validity than others, and choosing the right technique or combination of techniques will vary according to each selection scenario. The advantages and disadvantages associated with each of these techniques, and the situations in which each one is most appropriate, are discussed in the following section.

TABLE 4.1 Common selection methods, cost and validities			
Selection technique	*Cost*	*Validity*	*Reliability*
Behaviorally based interview	Low	Very good	High
Assessment centre	High	Very good	High
Cognitive ability test	Medium–low	Very good	Medium
Work sample test	Low	Good	High
Aptitude test	Medium–low	Good	High
Standard interview	Low	Poor	Low
Personality inventories	High	Poor–medium	Variable but average overall

Cognitive ability tests

Cognitive ability tests differentiate people on their mental capacity and can involve tests of verbal comprehension, numerical ability, abstract reasoning, inductive reasoning, pattern recognition and memory. These tests are often used to evaluate candidates for more complex jobs and have been used since the early 1900s. Cognitive ability tests are generally reliable and have good validity and an Internet search will reveal volumes of these that can be taken as samplers. Such tests are typically used for middle to senior-level positions; however, they are being increasingly deployed as an online screening step by multinational and large national organizations as part of the 'multiple hurdles' approach. That is to say, passing such a test does not qualify a candidate for the job, but failing it may legitimately be used as a basis for eliminating a candidate from further selection procedures. For example, a professional sport organization is recruiting a business administration trainee in the corporate partnerships section. The position requires research, communication and investigation skills. Therefore, a standard cognitive ability test that measures verbal reasoning and numerical tests would be appropriate as such tests have shown high validity for jobs requiring these abilities. Try your hand at: https://pg.sitebase.net/pg_images/taleo/practicetest.htm

Work sample tests

Work sample or job performance tests attempt to simulate a job in the controlled conditions of a selection process or require candidates to provide samples of their actual work, such as a portfolio. Candidates tested via a simulation are asked to complete verbal or physical activities that closely mirror real work tasks. For example, a potential manager of an aquatic and recreation complex might be asked to do an 'in basket' exercise in which the candidate is given a hypothetical situation and a range of tasks to undertake that require managerial level decisions to be made in a short time frame. Such tests usually require the candidate to evaluate and prioritize the multiple requests outlined and devise a plan of action to address the issues in the most logical way. Thus, the exercises given to the candidate for the aquatic and recreation complex position might include being asked to respond to a customer service complaint; a notice of non-compliance of safety equipment operation; a sudden resignation of the head lifeguard and a last-minute request for additional lifeguards for a school swimming event to be held later in the day. As a result of the close association with real jobs, work sample tests have a high reliability and validity. The major problem associated with these tests is the possibility of less than optimum performance due to anxiety in the testing environment.

Aptitude tests

Aptitude tests attempt to simulate work sampling tests in situations where the candidate has not previously worked in the job for which she/he is being recruited. The key issue with these tests is the validation of the test as a good predictor of success in relation to the actual job. Tests can be used to cover a range of areas, with the most common relating to clerical and numerical aptitude and mechanical or physical dexterity tests. For example, applicants for a technology position in a sport information company that provides sports statistics and information services online could be assessed using a programming aptitude test. Some of these will use 'pseudocode', flowcharting or assembly language.

Cognitive ability, work sample and aptitude tests can sometimes be purchased from HR consultancy firms or can be obtained directly from professional associations. Various versions of these tests are also found on the Internet and are relatively inexpensive. Research suggests that generic tests are equally good predictors of job success as specifically tailored tests. See www.shldirect.com/numerical.html for some examples.

Personality tests

Personality refers to a combination or profile of relatively stable traits that describe, and in turn predict, how an individual reacts in certain situations, including interacting with others. A sport organization may be particularly interested in uncovering candidates' personalities in order to gauge the likelihood of those individuals fitting into a particular job, a workgroup setting and the organization as a whole, and the likelihood that they will perform well there. Personality inventories may be used to gain insight into individuals' traits as part of the selection process. These inventories are usually comprised of statements or questions relating to attitudes and behaviors with which the subjects are asked to agree or disagree by choosing from a number of alternatives. Personality inventories attempt to measure the major psychological characteristics of a person using standard personality constructs such as the so-called 'Big Five' dimensions of personality. These characteristics are listed below along with a list of adjectives that describe their sub-scales.

- Extraversion (social, gregarious, assertive, talkative, expressive).
- Adjustment (emotionally stable, non-depressed, secure, content).
- Agreeableness (courteous, trusting, good-natured, tolerant, cooperative, forgiving).
- Conscientiousness (dependable, organized, persevering, thorough, achievement orientated).
- Inquisitiveness (curious, imaginative, artistically sensitive, broad minded, playful).

There are numerous commercially available psychological inventories but they can be expensive and there is considerable debate about their usefulness in assessment with many questions about their reliability and validity. The basic factors of the Big Five have been found to explain and predict individual differences and work performance (van der Linden, te Nijenhuis & Bakker, 2010).

Assessment centers

Assessment centers employ a comprehensive approach to selection and are mainly used for management candidates, often at entry to mid-manager level where the organization is trying to assess potential beyond the immediate position. Assessment centers incorporate a range of techniques typically based on behavior assessment. Some very large organizations run their own assessment centers, but it is more common for smaller organizations to use the assessment center services of HR consulting firms. Candidates in an assessment center will undertake a range of observed group-based and individual problem-solving exercises that simulate actual managerial tasks. Assessment candidates may also be required to complete psychological and cognitive ability tests, work sample tests and interviews. The components of assessment center activities are usually evaluated by multiple, professionally trained raters. Performance of candidates is typically measured using competencies profiles. Assessment of values can also be covered by assessment centers, which can provide good opportunities for determining whether or not a candidate will fit in with the prevailing culture of an organization (motivational fit).

As an example, a state governing body of rowing is looking to appoint a development coordinator. The position is generally responsible for the overall management, promotion and development of the sport and its affiliated rowing clubs and competitive and recreational members throughout the state. Specifically, the development coordinator is responsible for rowing campaigns focusing on junior athlete and coach pathways and the development of junior activities for beginner levels to high performance. An assessment center approach could be used to assess potential candidates, whereby each person would be required to complete a series of activities and tests to assess their interpersonal skills, and their demonstrated ability to inspire and elicit cooperation of people across a wide range of organizations – including teenagers, volunteers, rowing clubs and secondary high schools. Organizational skills and ability to set priorities, plan work programs and meet deadlines could also be assessed. The assessment center program might include aptitude and cognitive ability tests, 'in basket' exercises, scenario simulations, a presentation to the 'board of directors', and a group exercise involving teenagers and volunteers. Personal data could be collected via a CV and credential checks to determine if candidates had relevant experience and sufficient rowing knowledge including national rowing coach accreditation.

Overall, assessment centers provide a well-rounded measure of a candidate's abilities and potential and have a high level of reliability and a high validity for managerial jobs and executive appointments, particularly those with complex competency profiles. The major drawback of assessment centers is the cost and time involved in putting candidates through the center and completing the assessments.

Standard interviews

While the standard or traditional interview is the most commonly used selection technique it is also the method that is most susceptible to error in its use because of its inherent subjectivity. Low reliability and validity with the use of interviews can relate to faulty processing of interview data and poor judgments about appropriate questions and responses which are often the result of poorly developed interview skills. Some of the common subjectivity problems that can occur with interviews are 'halo' and 'horn' effects, where interviewers either like or dislike one characteristic of a candidate and this biases all other judgments. For example, an interviewer might dislike the dress sense, hair style or jewelry worn by the applicant. At a more subtle level, the effect might manifest itself in stereotypical labels being applied such as 'typical accountant/IT person/jock'. Other subjectivity problems might arise through 'contrast effects', where very good or bad candidates can affect the judgments made about others or 'leniency/strictness' effects, where different interviewers employ varying standards to judge candidates.

Despite the well-known potential problems, recent research on standard interviews (Gatewood, Field & Barrick, 2011) has indicated that they are more reliable and valid than previously thought when designed and used correctly and in the right circumstances.

Of particular importance here is the need to clearly identify the attributes that need to be measured in the interview. Initial impressions can heavily influence interviewer evaluations (Barrick et al., 2012); therefore, it is important to have a formal structure for the interview process. However, as Dipboye, Macan and Shahani-Denning (2012) caution, the interview should not be an interrogation and while rigor is important, the interviewer should also aim to develop rapport and use the interview as an opportunity for both parties to assess if there is a good fit with the organization. In recent years there has been massive growth of the competency-based, or behavioral, selection programs and interviews within organizations. The behaviorally based approach uses the interview to ascertain how a candidate deals with certain situations based on actual experience of real events (as detailed in next section).

Behaviorally based interviewing

Weinstein (2012) argues that employers should know how to effectively use behaviorally focused techniques in order to minimize potential selection mistakes. Behaviorally based interviewing is predicated on the idea that past behavior and performance are the best predictors of future performance, and that past behavior can be closely examined via structured interviews based on:

- questions built around job-related information
- questions aimed at revealing in some detail how candidates have handled situations and tasks involving similar competencies to those of the job in question and the results of those actions
- questions that unearth the true nature of the candidate's knowledge, behaviors, motivation and values.

Interviews based on behavioral rather than situational criteria – that is to say interview questions should gather data on what candidates really did in past situations rather than what they 'might do' in hypothetical future situations – elicit higher levels of predictive validity (Pulakos & Schmitt, 1995).

The process of conducting behavioral interviews begins with the construction of a list of competencies which are specific to the job in question – for example, certain technical knowledge and expertise, social skills, leadership ability, physical skills or ability to work in a group setting. Within the competency framework for the job, the interviewers will question the candidates about their qualifications and skills, about specific experiences where they have used the skills and the results of this usage, and about the underlying motivations behind their actions and behaviors. For example, if a sport travel company is looking to select a new sales person and one of the key dimensions is persuasiveness, the behaviorally based interview should be built around getting the candidates to talk about situations where they were required to be persuasive in previous jobs. Questions might follow a sequence similar to that set out below, where each question probes further into the detailed actions, consequences and underlying motivations of the candidate.

- Describe a situation where you had to overcome extreme buyer resistance to get a sale.
- What was different about this situation?
- What objections did the client raise?

- How did you answer them?
- How did you respond to the client's negativity?
- What did you say next?
- How did you close the sale?
- What was the result of your action?
- How did you feel at the close and why?

By probing for such detail about real events, the behavioral interview almost becomes a re-enactment of the candidate dealing with a previous work situation. In this way, 'real' behaviors can be observed and any pretense on the part of the candidate can be brought to the surface.

The selection process for volunteers may involve a number of steps which mirror those taken when hiring a paid employee. However, few community-based sport organizations are in a position to conduct a formal volunteer selection process, and often the number of vacant positions is greater than the number of people prepared to volunteer. On the other hand, many major events have quite sophisticated and robust selection procedures for volunteers.

As noted earlier, the Sochi Organizing Committee for the Olympic Games received more than 180,000 applications and selected 25,000. Volunteers were assessed for their Olympic values and ideals, ability to work in a large team and leadership qualities. There was a screening stage, where applicants were required to demonstrate communication skills, friendliness, and a willingness to help to solve the most unexpected and challenging tasks. Others undertook a test and were interviewed in the Volunteer Centers. The 26 Volunteer Centers across Russia provided volunteers' training (Sochi 2014 Organizing Committee, 2013).

Considerations in volunteer selection can include appropriate accreditation or preparedness to undertake a relevant course (e.g., coaching certification), experience in working with teams, good communication skills, specialist skills (e.g., accounting expertise, website design), and reliability and trustworthiness. Reference checks are advisable when appointing individuals to a position that involves close contact with children and in many countries criminal history checks are a legal requirement if the volunteer is working with under 18-year-old children. A positive outcome of such policies is that people have confidence in the good faith of coaches and officials.

At the conclusion of the selection process an organization must make decisions about who to hire. It is at this point that organizations will often check candidate references if this has not been done earlier. Written references generally have a low validity so it is advisable to exercise caution at this point. In fact many large organizations now refuse to provide written references because of the potential for legal action from disaffected former employees and will instead provide only a letter confirming the dates between which a person was employed. 'Off the record' telephone interviews are more likely to generate a candid and truthful response from former employers but these too should be used with caution. A final check that the organization should make relates to the qualifications the candidates claim to hold. Surveys by recruiting companies have revealed a high level of false claims about qualifications from job applicants. After making the necessary checks, the organization is then in a position to make offers. A common practice in many organizations is to rank candidates by order of preference and make offers accordingly. In this way organizations have alternative candidates should offers to candidates be declined.

SOCIAL MEDIA IN THE RECRUITMENT AND SELECTION PROCESS

Social media has changed the landscape for both job-seekers and organizational recruiters. Traditionally, external candidates have been solicited through various media channels and professional networks and then subject to a number of different selection processes, as outlined above. However, in many countries the rate of social media adoption has accelerated and now employers have access to vast amounts information about candidates, and this has raised a number of ethical questions regarding the extent to which this information influences appointment decisions. Social networks that allow personal interaction such as MySpace, LinkedIn, Twitter and Facebook are now part of the recruitment process. There are also companies that specialize in recruitment (search firms) that solely use social networking sites as a business model.

Social media is mainly used first to find candidates and second to screen applicants. It is also used for employee engagement, increasing retention, management, evaluation and monitoring. There is currently little empirical evidence on whether social networking sites are a valid and reliable source of effective/successful employees. However, anecdotally it appears that social media is becoming a key part of recruitment strategy, with LinkedIn the most favored tool for this process. Social media offers potential time and cost savings over traditional methods, but it does limit the marketplace to social media users. The use of social media should be ethically transparent and candidates should be informed if they are to be screened using social media.

There has been much debate about the ethical issues associated with using social media to screen potential candidates. A 2012 study by Reppler of 300 US recruiters reported that 91 per cent used social networking sites to screen prospective candidates, 47 per cent used this information to decide whether or not to interview the candidate and 69 per cent admitted to rejecting a candidate based on what they discovered from their social media profiles (Sutherland, 2013). As social media provides employers with information that they might not obtain otherwise such as race, ethnicity, religion, marital status, disabilities, political affiliations and other personal interests, there may be possible discrimination elements. As a result of some high profile cases, many states in the USA have now passed legislation to make illegal the practice of forcing job applicants to disclose their social media login details. Companies such as Reppler provide a service that manages a person's online

---

BOX 4.1

A contemporary dilemma

Based on the discussion above, discuss/debate the following in class:
- Employers have the right to use information gleaned from social networking sites to make hiring decisions.

Versus
- What an employee or prospective employee posts on social media sites are his/her own business and should not affect employment decisions.

image across different social networks, continuously monitors the content, shows how the person is perceived across social networks, identifies any potential issues and risks, produces an image score and tracks changes that could affect the individual's online image.

BOX 4.2

Work for decathlon campaign

Social media spotlight: recruitment through Facebook?
This sports brand proves it can be done

As LinkedIn takes steps to push its social elements further and make the world of work more engaging, Facebook's shortcomings in the job sector have become increasingly apparent; it's a sector left relatively untouched and is surrounded by general confusion as to how it could be used effectively in the sport industry.

However, Indian sports brand Decathlon Sports has just set an interesting precedent. Based on Facebook (with conversations mirrored on Twitter and, of course, LinkedIn), the 'Work for sport' campaign aims to recruit over 100 sports enthusiasts into a variety of the company's departments, including retail, finance, IT, logistics and legal.

After five days of online teasers hinting at job prospects for sports lovers, the campaign was revealed in full with five short video clips illustrating how sporty types would be better off working at Decathlon, where they can work alongside like-minded people with shared passions. The video clips portray a clear message in a humorous way, telling the viewer, 'If sport is your life, make a living off it.'

Users are then encouraged to 'like' the page in order to submit an application with Decathlon – which they can do directly within Facebook.

Since the inception of the campaign at the start of September, the page has received over 26,000 likes. These aren't idle 'Why not?' likes, or likes in an attempt to win a prize or because it's a cool thing to like; these are likes from genuinely interested, relevant users who already know the brand (how else would they find the otherwise vaguely titled 'Work for sport' page?) and are authentically engaging with the page in order to apply for work (there's really no other reason to like the page).

The result? Decathlon gets 26,000+ job applications from switched-on, appropriate individuals, and the brand gets a reputation boost thanks to its clever viral videos and progressive HR thinking.

Facebook recruitment naysayers take heed – this is a strong precedent for future campaigns.

Information from Social Media Influence (2013)

SUMMARY

Recruitment and selection and judicious hiring are critical to a sport organization's success. There is a critical link between recruitment and selection and other HRM activities. There is a variety of sources and methods for generating a pool of job applicants, as well as a variety of selection techniques, each with their own advantages and disadvantages as well as issues relating to reliability and validity. No one method will be right for all situations and, thus, the choice of technique should be considered in relation to the circumstances of each selection decision. Sources of bias and subjectivity in selection decision making are important considerations. There is a recent trend towards using social media for recruitment and selection; however, it is not without its own issues. At the end of the day, uncertainty in selection can best be reduced by the use of multiple techniques, provided the time and resources are available.

DISCUSSION QUESTIONS

1   What are the key reasons for claiming that recruitment and selection are *the* most important of *all* HR processes?
2   Identify the sources of bias in relation to interviews. How can bias be minimized?
3   Using the job advertisement in Appendix 1, outline three different recruitment methods you could use for the position. What would be the advantages and disadvantages of each?
4   Using the job advertisement in Appendix 1, construct an interview schedule using the behaviorally based interviewing method described at the end of this chapter. Focus on:
   • proven ability to be a visionary
   • proven ability to lead
   • excellent interpersonal and communication skills.

(Optional role play: in pairs practice interviewing each other using the behavioral method to probe the experience of the other person for each of these competencies.)

APPENDIX 1: SAMPLE JOB ADVERTISEMENT

High Performance Manager – Archery Canada
Nature of position: Part-time professional employee (0.5 position with the possibility of a 0.75 to full-time position in the next 1 to 2 years)
Immediate supervisor: Executive Director
Work location: National Office (Ottawa) preferred but not a requirement. Telecommuting is an option.

The High Performance Manager's (HPM) work plan will be guided by Archery Canada's High Performance (HP) plan. The HPM is responsible for leading/assisting with the implementation, monitoring and evaluation of specific elements of Archery Canada's high performance strategic plan and the 3D archery program. As well, the HPM is responsible for the day-to-day management and the ongoing monitoring of Archery Canada's HP program. The HPM regularly communicates and works with and provides support and leadership to the High Performance Committee (HPC) and appointed volunteer National Team staff. The HPM may be called on from time-to-time to work with and provide expertise to the Coaching Certification Committee and the Long Term Athlete Development (LTAD) Committee.

Areas of responsibility/ primary focus
- To lead and/or assist with the implementation, monitoring and evaluation of specific elements of the High Performance (HP) strategic plan. Specific elements to be determined by the HPC and the Executive Director.
- To annually revise the HP strategic plan, as deemed necessary by the HPC and the Executive Director.
- To work in collaboration with the volunteer Coordinators of the Senior, Para-Archery and Youth Programs (comprising the HPC) and the V-P of 3D Archery Program, on high performance matters such as: national team criteria and selection; ranking criteria and updating; Archery Canada funding criteria; event and program budgets; carding criteria and nominations; national team staff selection; staff manual; athlete and staff agreements; criminal/vulnerable sector background checks; training camp opportunities; competition opportunities; communications with athletes.
- To work in collaboration with the above volunteer Program Coordinators and/or the appointed volunteer National Team Leaders to coordinate arrangements for all Teams that fall within specific portfolios including: travel, accommodation, team staff and registration.
- To work in collaboration with the Executive Director and other appropriate volunteers, on high performance matters pertaining to the lodging of complaints, appeals, doping infractions, as deemed required by the Executive Director.
- To communicate with the above volunteer Program Coordinators and/or the appointed volunteer National Team Leaders (including 3D Archery) about needs and requirements for each National Team.
- To coordinate Senior, Para-Archery, Youth developmental opportunities as set out by the HPC.

- To prepare reports for HPC and Executive Committee meetings and for the Archery Canada Annual Report.
- To attend and participate in meetings of the following organizations: HPC (face-to-face meetings and teleconferences); Board (Executive Committee); Canadian Olympic Committee, Canadian Paralympic Committee; Summer Sport Caucus, Sport Canada; Own the Podium, other partners, as deemed required.
- To record and distribute HPC meeting minutes (face-to-face meetings and teleconferences).

Education and experience
- University degree or college diploma in sport management/sport administration or a related degree/diploma or combination of experience.
- Experience in high performance sport programming and/or sport management; program and project management; budget design and management; logistics coordination.
- Experience with a national or provincial sport organization.
- Background and knowledge in competitive archery is preferred but not essential.
- Knowledge of the Canadian amateur sport system and of the programs of Archery Canada's key sports partners, including Sport Canada, Own the Podium, the Canadian Olympic Committee, the Canadian Paralympic Committee and the Coaching Association of Canada.
- Bilingualism (English and French) is preferred. English is essential.

Essential skills and abilities
- Proven ability to be a visionary.
- Proven ability to lead.
- Excellent interpersonal and communication skills.
- Proven ability to work with volunteers.
- Well organized with the ability to:
  - manage multiple tasks and projects concurrently
  - establish priorities and meet deadlines
  - develop and execute work plans
  - work under pressure
  - follow up on correspondence for projects requiring responses/future actions, in a timely manner.
- Strong computer skills. Ability to use Microsoft Office, Outlook, Excel, PowerPoint and to use the Internet as a search and research tool.
- Proven ability to develop, manage and evaluate programs.
- Proven ability to develop and manage project and program financial budgets
- Sound judgment and decision making .
- Ability to work independently.
- Ability to work within a team environment.
- Working knowledge and application of social media such as Twitter, Facebook, Joomla/WordPress.
- Flexibility in working hours. Available to travel and to work some evenings/weekends.

CHAPTER 5

Orientation and organizational culture

LEARNING OBJECTIVES

After reading this chapter you will be able to:

- Explain the importance of orientation in sport organizations
- Describe the stages of organizational socialization
- Describe a variety of orientation strategies and practices
- Understand the importance and process of orienting sport volunteers
- Describe organizational culture and its role in newcomer orientation

CHAPTER OVERVIEW

Orientation may be viewed as the final step in the recruitment and selection process, or as the first phase in an employee or volunteer's involvement in an organization. Either way, it is a critical part of effective strategic human resource management (SHRM). This chapter examines how orientation can facilitate a successful transition experience for individuals moving into a new job, role and workgroup, and to the organization as a whole. All newcomers (whether they are new to a position, to the organization or to the workforce itself) experience the three basic stages of socialization, which coincide with pre-entry, entry and adaptation to the new work environment. Role clarity, self-efficacy and social acceptance/integration may be enhanced through organizational socialization from the outset and are ultimately factors in individuals' job satisfaction, commitment and retention.

Orientation also gives newcomers a chance to align, or realign, their preconceived expectations about the organization. The notion of an individual's psychological contract is introduced here as the orientation process can play an important role in ensuring that one's understanding of the mutual expectations between him or herself and the organization are consistent. Orientation also provides a chance for an individual to judge the degree of personal fit with the organization.

A framework outlining the three stages of organizational socialization is presented, along with strategies and further orientation practices that can be deployed for effective socialization at each stage. One of the key aspects to which newcomers must be socialized is the culture of the organization. Organizational culture is the values, beliefs and assumptions that underlie how things are done within an organization. It is critical for newcomers to get a handle on this as quickly as possible as culture is an important guiding force for members. The last part of the chapter focuses on the meaning and role of organizational culture in the workplace, including its place in newcomer orientation.

THE IMPORTANCE OF ORIENTATION IN SPORT ORGANIZATIONS

Orientation or 'induction' may be seen as the final stage of the recruitment and selection process (Booth, Fosters, Robson & Welham, 2004) and a critical aspect of successful human resource management (HRM). Substantial time and resources may have been put into looking for, screening and ultimately hiring new staff and volunteers who are expected to make a meaningful contribution to the sport organization. To ensure that newcomers to the organization hit the ground running, do the work that is expected of them and stay with the organization, it is essential that they have an appropriate introduction to their new work environment. It is contended that the 'period of early entry is one of the most critical phases of organizational life' (Kammeyer-Mueller & Wanberg, 2003: 779). Newcomers' initial work attitudes are strong indicators of attitudes and behavior several months down the road, including the likelihood that they will stay or leave (Bauer, Bodner, Erdogan, Truxillo & Tucker, 2007). Effective orientation can help new staff and volunteers adjust to their job, workgroup and workplace. This, in turn, will contribute to their job performance, satisfaction and commitment to the organization (Bauer et al., 2007), and reduce the stress and anxiety that is commonly associated with facing an unfamiliar situation (Saks & Ashforth, 1997).

Figure 5.1 depicts the organizational adjustment process for newcomers, highlighting the outcomes that are the ultimate objective of systematic orientation. Specifically, newcomer adjustment to the organization is indicated by role clarity (understanding one's job tasks and task priorities), self-efficacy (sense of task mastery and confidence in one's role) and social acceptance and integration (perceived approval and inclusion by peers and the workgroup). In combination, these factors have been shown to have a direct impact on job performance, job satisfaction, organizational commitment and intentions to remain with the organization (Bauer et al., 2007; Kammeyer-Mueller & Wanberg, 2003). Figure 5.1 also outlines the factors that contribute to newcomers' adjustment – namely, individuals' pre-entry knowledge about the organization and further information-seeking initiatives, and

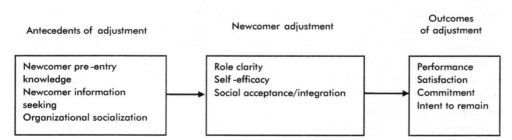

FIGURE 5.1 A model of newcomers' organizational adjustment (Source: Adapted from Kammeyer-Mueller & Wanberg, 2003; Bauer et al., 2007)

organizational socialization efforts. These factors in the newcomer adjustment process are examined below.

New staff and volunteers may have acquired some degree of familiarity or pre-entry knowledge about the organization and their particular role there as part of the recruitment and selection process. Well-prepared candidates for a job can be expected to have familiarized themselves with the mission, mandate, products, services, programs and structure of the organization, at least before applying for the job and certainly before being interviewed for a position. Candidates may have gained further insight by walking around and talking with current staff during the interview process. This is, of course, important for them to get a sense of whether the organization is, in fact, a place they would like to work. For example, a potential board member for a community sport club would likely ask questions before agreeing to stand for a position; 'What would I do?' and 'How often are meetings?' would be typical questions of someone considering volunteering their time to help out. A prospective collegiate basketball coach would be likely to ask questions about the team's budget and would want to check out the facilities as part of the recruitment and selection process. She might want to know upfront about other expectations with regard to contributing to the work of the athletic department. As these examples illustrate, some preliminary orientation to an organization may have taken place during the recruitment and selection process; however, it is critical that newcomers have a formal orientation to their new work environment upon entry. Pre-entry knowledge, as we shall see below, can sometimes be inaccurate and insufficient, and research indicates that formal organizational practices can have a substantially stronger impact on newcomer adjustment than leaving newcomers to seek information on their own (Bauer et al., 2007). The often challenging process of recruitment and selection would not be complete without further orientation of new staff and volunteers.

ORGANIZATIONAL SOCIALIZATION

Orientation is essentially familiarizing oneself with something new. This corresponds with the process of socialization, whereby 'a person learns and acquires the values, attitudes and beliefs, and accepted behaviors of a culture, society, organization, or group' (Tosi, Mero & Rizzo, 2000: 35). We are socialized whenever we become involved in a new situation – when we're born, when we first go to school, when we go to (new) work and when we move to a different country or culture. Socialization is the process of orienting oneself to the customs, language, expectations and so on of the new environment. One may be socialized into several different environments at the same stage of life – for example, a new job and a new city. It is important to become familiar with the new setting, to learn what is expected and accepted there, so that one can fit in more quickly and effectively.

While an individual inherently wants to be comfortable in a new situation as quickly as possible, a sport organization also wants its new hires or volunteers to fit in right away so that they can begin contributing to the organization. *Organizational* socialization is defined as 'the process by which a person learns the values, norms and required behaviors which permit him to participate as a member of the organization' (Van Maanen, 1976: 67). This is still a broad definition; to what, exactly, is the newcomer being orientated? Aspects of the organization with which a newcomer needs to become familiar in order to develop role clarity, task self-efficacy and peer and workgroup acceptance and integration include the following.

- Formal work-related aspects of the organization (e.g., mission and goals, organizational structure and chain of command, reporting relationships, the evaluation and reward system).
- Formal personnel-related policies and procedures (e.g., employee benefits, health and safety standards, disciplinary and grievance procedures).
- Role and assigned tasks, including the skills required, and specific reporting requirements.
- Workgroup, including supervisor(s) (e.g., individual personalities, group norms and expectations).
- Physical layout of the workplace or where work is done (in the case of virtual workplaces; see Chapter 11).

One additional aspect with which the newcomer should become familiar is the culture of the organization.

Organizational culture is the core values, beliefs and assumptions about how things are done within the organization. It is represented by visual artefacts, such as logos, displayed pictures and awards, as well as stories, myths, rituals and styles of dress. These things reflect what the organization is all about and what is valued there. Values, beliefs and assumptions about the organization are also manifested in organizational processes, such as communication (formal and informal lines), decision making (who gets to be involved) and rewards (as an indicator of what is valued). To the extent that organizational culture reflects a shared understanding, it serves as a control mechanism such that members understand 'how things are done around here.' For example, there may be an unspoken rule that you 'arrive before, and leave after, the boss', or it is understood that the best, or most important, work is really done over coffee, or on the golf course, or when skiing, surfing or cycling. Organizational culture is important to maintaining strategic direction, because of the coordinating effect it has on members. Thus, it is important that an organization's culture – what is valued and understood to be the 'way of life' (Johns & Saks, 2011: 268) – is aligned with the organization's corporate strategy (McKenna & Beech, 2002). Newcomers' orientation to organizational processes and artefacts can provide a lot of insight into the organization's culture. Organizational culture is reviewed in more detail below.

Newcomers

There are several types of newcomers in an organization: (1) those who are new to the organization and the workforce in general; (2) those who have previous workforce experience but are new to the organization; and (3) those who are veterans of the organization but new to a different role or part of the organization. Individuals require at least some orientation to new situations. Not all newcomers have the same background experience, which may be an important consideration in the orientation they require.

'Neophytes' or novices (i.e., student interns, graduate management trainees, recent graduates and those with little or no work experience) are new to the organization and to the type of job, and may be new to the industry and the full-time working world as well (e.g., Carr, Pearson, Vest & Boyar, 2006). These recruits may fill entry-level jobs, where relatively basic skills are required and the organization has an opportunity to groom them for further roles – for example, sales associates with a sporting goods retailer or a sport event facility. Organizations also recruit and select veteran staff and volunteers with prior experience in the organization, in the industry or in a particular type of job (e.g., Carr et al.,

2006). For example, a sport development co-ordinator is moved into a management position within the organization, or a collegiate sport media relations officer moves to a position in a professional sports franchise. These individuals are promoted or hired because of their previous experience and the knowledge and skill sets they can offer to the organization. The focus of their orientation is really resocialization to a new work environment. Resocialization may also be required when existing staff or volunteers are faced with major changes to the organization. It may be strange to think of employees being 'newcomers' in their own organization; however, an individual who moves from a staff to a managerial position may be expected to face at least some uncertainty with his or her new role and the expectations that accompany it. Orientation is critical to the effective SHRM of any type of 'newcomer'.

Stages of socialization

It is helpful to think of orientation to a new job or organization as occurring in stages, as an individual transition from 'newcomer' to 'insider' (Wanous & Colella, 1989). There are three basic stages in the work socialization process (Feldman, 1976): (1) anticipatory socialization; (2) encounter socialization; and (3) role management. Instead of focusing exclusively on orientation that begins when an individual first enters the organization as a member, and ends once they have met everyone and become familiar with the organizational/unit policies and procedures, this framework acknowledges that a newcomer's understanding about an organization begins before they even enter the workplace and continues as they adapt to their role. The three stages are depicted in Figure 5.2.

The first stage of the organizational socialization process occurs before entry to the organization (Feldman, 1976). As a result of anticipatory socialization, most newcomers have some preconceived ideas or expectations about what it means to work in a particular segment of the sport industry, in a particular role or in the new organization itself. These pre-entry ideas, expectations and knowledge may be formed as part of the individual's formal education, previous work or volunteer experiences, and through other sources of information (e.g., friends, family, fans, media). Sport management students often declare that they want

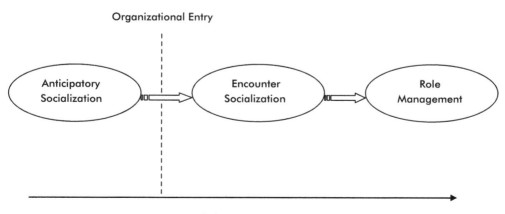

FIGURE 5.2 The stages of organizational socialization (Feldman, 1976)

to work for a particular (perhaps their favorite?) professional sports team. While this may be a worthy career goal, there may be gaps between what an individual thinks it will be like to work for a given team or organization, and what it is really like. According to Hofacre and Branvold (1995: 174), 'the potential for a discrepancy between expectation and reality seems especially high in careers … in professional sports'. A job in pro sport may be perceived to be glamorous, where employees get to rub shoulders with sports stars. Yet, the reality is more likely long hours, low pay and little glamour (Hofacre & Branvold, 1995). In a study of the expectations and realities of a front office career in minor league baseball, Hofacre and Branvold found that 'job seekers' believed having knowledge of baseball and sports in general was significantly more important to a successful career in minor league baseball than did current front office staff. Job seekers also had unrealistically high expectations about advancement opportunities, decision-making power, job stability and receiving a good salary in a career in professional baseball. The authors concluded that the job seekers may have been in for a 'reality shock' (Hall, 1976) and disappointment in a baseball front office career, because of the seeming discrepancy between their pre-entry expectations and the reality of the job. Zeng (2011: 12) also found that university physical education graduates' expectations surpassed what they experienced in reality in their careers. The author concluded that the graduates are 'unaware of [the] practical target' of their job search.

These pre-entry expectations about what individuals will experience in an organization form the basis of their psychological contract with the organization – that is, an individual's understanding about what they owe the organization, and what they can expect from the organization in return (Lewis, Thornhill & Saunders, 2003). (The concept of psychological contract is discussed in more detail later.) Many of these pre-entry experiences and understandings may have been what made the organization attractive to the individual and the individual attractive to the organization. However, that anticipatory or pre-entry socialization contributes to newcomers' ideas and expectations which may be at odds with what the organization or job is really like, and what values, norms and behaviors are considered important and required for effective contribution to the organization. According to Kammeyer-Mueller and Wanberg (2003: 782), 'those who have accurate information about all aspects of the job will be better able to assess the extent to which they will "fit" in their new positions and will be in situations that better match their abilities and preferences'. Research supports this contention such that newcomers with more accurate pre-entry knowledge about their job report better adjustment (Bauer et al., 2007). At the least, it is critical to recognize that newcomers will have varying degrees of pre-entry knowledge about the job and the organization, which will have implications for their further socialization there. Any disparities will become evident during the second stage of encounter socialization.

The second stage of encounter or accommodation socialization takes place at or immediately following entry to the organization or new job. At this point the individual experiences the organization 'for the first time as one of its members' rather than as someone who is just trying to get in (Tosi et al., 2000: 102). This is when the individual begins to gain deeper insight into the reality of the organization, and his or her identity in the organization begins to form (Beyer & Hannah, 2002). The newcomer is formally introduced to his or her task and is initiated into the group. According to Johns and Saks (2011: 256), if accommodation is reached, 'the recruit will have complied with critical organizational norms and should begin to identify with experienced organizational members'.

A formal opportunity to learn what newcomers want and need to know about their new work environment may be particularly important with veteran newcomers, who have more extensive anticipatory socialization and thus pre-entry knowledge. Research suggests that veterans are more likely to be effectively resocialized when they are oriented as if they were novices (Rousseau, 2001) – that is, they are given opportunities and encouragement to gather information, discuss and negotiate its meaning, and make sense of their new environment, rather than assuming that they 'know the ropes'. In fact, organizational socialization tactics have been shown to have a greater impact on the adjustment of veteran newcomers than neophytes (Bauer et al., 2007), perhaps underscoring the importance of resocialization to a new work environment. Through a strategically designed orientation process, the organization can take advantage of the formal opportunity to communicate what it wants neophyte and veteran newcomers to know.

The third stage – role management – is a process of adaptation socialization that involves fine tuning one's expectations about the organization and understanding reciprocal obligations after some time in the organization. This stage may not be as clearly defined in terms of start and end points as the first two stages. It is more likely defined by the new member than by the organization, as the individual comes to terms with the final stage of adjustment to task mastery, role clarity, workgroup integration and political knowledge. Nonetheless, it is important to recognize that orientation to the organization does not necessarily end for newcomers after the, perhaps more formal, entry stage of encounter socialization.

(RE)ALIGNING EXPECTATIONS

Anticipatory socialization suggests that individuals are likely to enter the workplace with preconceived ideas about their new job, the organization, the sport and the industry. These pre-entry expectations form the initial basis of a psychological contract that new staff and volunteers develop with a particular organization. The psychological contract is an unwritten agreement that represents shared expectations between an individual and the organization. It is a pattern of rights, privileges and obligations that is established during orientation, yet it is continuously negotiated throughout one's career or time with an organization (Tosi et al., 2000). As noted earlier, during orientation an individual may find inconsistencies in what he or she understands about and expects from an organization – for example, the working conditions, co-workers, opportunities for advancement and so on. Thus, it is an important stage during which one's psychological contract will undergo some meaningful development.

During the orientation process, newcomer staff or volunteers may also experience for the first time an awareness of the alignment between their own values and beliefs and those of the organization. This will give them a further sense of what is known as person-organization fit, or 'congruence between organizational values and [one's] own individual values' (Tosi et al., 2000: 102), than what they may have felt during the recruitment and selection process. Research indicates that accuracy of expectations and perceived person-organization (P–O) fit has direct implications for newcomers' short-term job satisfaction and retention (Tosi et al., 2000).

The psychological contract

The employment relationship is a social exchange or transaction where member effort and loyalty is given in return for fair rewards. Beyond the formal agreement which forms the basis of that relationship is an individual's psychological contract with his or her organization. The psychological contract comprises an employee's or volunteer's beliefs about what they can expect to receive from the organization in return for their work, effort, performance and commitment. Perhaps most importantly, the psychological contract is based on the individual's belief that it is a mutual agreement between themselves and the organization – that is, both parties understand their respective obligations. What employees expect to receive in return for their effort, loyalty and commitment may vary from one person to another, and from one organization to another. However, expectations generally include fair compensation, guaranteed work of a minimum specified duration, a safe work environment, socio-emotional security, training and development as required, and a sense of community (Taylor, Darcy, Hoye & Cuskelly, 2006).

Volunteers, by definition, will not have any expectations for financial compensation; however, their psychological contract may comprise expectations that their needs and motives for volunteering will be met – for example, that there will be an opportunity to make a difference and to connect with others through sport volunteering (Cuskelly, Hoye & Auld, 2006). In a study of the psychological contracts of community rugby volunteers in Australia, Taylor et al. (2006) found that the participants were, in fact, most focused on the intrinsic characteristics of their volunteer role – specifically their expectation for rewarding work, social environment and networking opportunities, and recognition and appreciation for their contributions. Their next greatest focus was working conditions – specifically, expectations about the number of volunteers to do the work and support from the club.

The psychological contract is essentially a member's way of compartmentalizing his or her expectations of the organization, and the organization's expectations in return. The contract is violated when an individual's expectations are not met by the organization, or that person does not meet the expectations of the organization. For example, a manager of merchandise for a professional sports franchise finds out that she does not actually have as much decision-making discretion as she thought she was going to have with regard to selecting new products. The fallout may be frustration, dissatisfaction or disillusionment on the part of the member, with further implications for the individual's work behavior (Johns & Saks, 2011). The likelihood of a perceived violation or breach of the psychological contract is increased when an individual has an inaccurate understanding of the mutual obligations between himself and the organization. In their study of community rugby volunteers, Taylor et al. (2006) further found that club administrators had different expectations than the volunteers, focusing particularly on volunteers performing their role professionally and reliably in line with the club's policies and standards (recall that the volunteers, in contrast, were focused on being given rewarding work, social opportunities and recognition). The authors concluded that there is a distinct possibility of psychological breach in the community rugby club setting because of the discrepant expectations and obligations.

Unrealistic expectations about the job or organization likely develop during anticipatory socialization. It may be the fault of the organization itself if it portrays an inaccurate image of the reality of the workplace and the organization's expectations during the recruitment and selection process. The discrepancy may become apparent over time as an employee or volunteer comes to realize that what was expected from the organization is not being offered. It can also happen in the short term as newcomers learn, as part of their orientation, that what may have been expected will not be realized. This 'reality shock' can have important implications for reduced obligations on the part of the newcomer, as well as lowered satisfaction and increased stress from realizing expectations will not be fulfilled.

The psychological contract is of concern to systematic orientation because it is important for the newcomers and the organization to develop a mutual understanding that is based on realistic expectations about the reciprocal relationship. 'It is important that newcomers develop accurate perceptions in the formation of a psychological contract' (Johns & Saks, 2011: 257), many of the terms of which are established during the anticipatory socialization phase of orientation.

Person–organization fit

According to Cable and Parsons (2001: 1), 'person-organization (P–O) fit, or the compatibility between people and the organizations in which they work, is a key to maintaining a flexible and committed workforce that is necessary in a competitive business environment and a tight labor market'. Research suggests that 'operating in an environment consistent with one's values is a more positive experience on many levels' (Meglino & Ravlin, 1998: 380). Indeed, in a study of the American Youth Soccer Association volunteers, Kim, Chelladurai and Trail (2007) found that person-organization fit, in terms of perceived alignment between the volunteers' and Association's values, was a significant predictor of volunteers' sense of empowerment (self-efficacy and perceived control over one's work) there.

Right from the start, newcomers will likely ask themselves whether and how they fit in with the organization. In fact, this is likely a key consideration during the employee selection process where both the organization and the candidate assess whether he or she seems to 'fit' that workplace. Once in the organization, if individuals perceive that their values do not match those of the organization, they will deal with this dissonance by either changing their perceptions (i.e., their personal values) or leaving the organization (Cable & Parsons, 2001; Kristof-Brown, Zimmerman & Johnson, 2005).

Organizational values are highlighted and clarified through the orientation and socialization process and thus newcomers can quickly begin to determine whether they fit in. For example, a new coach may become more comfortable and feel a greater sense of fit in his new work environment after meeting with other coaches and gaining an understanding of formal and informal practices in the organization. Cable and Parsons (2001) found that certain orientation or socialization strategies were significantly associated with P–O fit – namely, sequential, fixed, serial and investiture approaches, which are discussed below. We can expect veteran newcomers to have a more positive perception of P–O fit from the outset as they are likely to seek out and join a new organization where they perceive they fit (Cable & Parsons, 2001).

ORIENTATION STRATEGIES

Individuals tend to be active participants in their own socialization, in terms of seeking out information they need to help understand their new environment (Allen, 2006). This can involve probing about aspects on which one is unsure and in a manner with which one is comfortable (Ashforth et al., 2007). It may also include acquiring information and insight from a review of organizational documents, informal conversations with colleagues, general socializing and simply observation. However, proactive socialization by newcomers can be expected to vary according to, for example, the degree to which they are comfortable reaching out and feel the need for personal control in a new situation (Ashford & Black, 1996). Proactive socialization may also be more likely with veteran newcomers, who may be more comfortable in the work environment in general, and in the organization itself if they are moving within, as they will have more confidence and awareness regarding what they need to know. Finally, the degree of proactive socialization can also be expected to vary depending on the extent to which the organization engages in systematic orientation of its newcomers. Given the importance of orientating newcomers to the organization and likely variations in the extent to which newcomers will be proactive in their own socialization to the new setting, organizations should not leave it to newcomers to find their own way. Rather, various strategies and practices may be used as part of a systematic orientation process and are presented here.

Van Maanen and Schein (1979) proposed a framework that describes different types of orientation strategies that may be utilized in an organization. The six strategies are arranged as dimensions representing contrasting approaches:

1   collective vs. individual
2   formal vs. informal
3   sequential vs. random
4   fixed vs. variable
5   serial vs. disjunctive
6   investiture vs. divestiture.

With the collective approach, a sport organization may provide orientation to several newcomers as a group. One advantage with this approach is that the organization can orient several members at once rather than individually. Another advantage is that the group of newcomers has an opportunity to learn about the organization together, helping each other to understand and sharing individual perspectives. The group is given standardized or common information about the organization, which can help to reduce uncertainty and contribute to a sense of shared values as individuals know they are learning what others are learning (Allen, 2006). The collective approach is favored when there are several newcomers commencing at the same time and all require orientation to the same information. This might be the case with venue staff at a stadium or special event volunteers where hundreds or even thousands may have formal orientation at the same time. It would also be favored for more routine and more technical jobs where newcomers need to know the rules and procedures in order to do their job effectively – for example, staff at the front/reception desk of an aquatics facility, or sales staff. It is possible that a collective approach would be used on an individual basis, when standardized information is the focus yet only one newcomer is coming on board. In contrast, an individual approach focuses on orientation that is tailored to each new member. This approach is most appropriate when standard information about the organization and job is seen as less valuable than on-the-job training as a means of organizational socialization. This might be the case with less routine jobs – for example, a head coach or a marketing director position.

Formal strategies involve a planned approach to orientation where the information to be shared is strategically selected and the means to impart the information is carefully designed. Informal strategies are the opposite, where orientation is essentially unplanned and impromptu. It is more likely to be on an ad hoc or 'as need' basis and involves on-the-job learning rather than formal sessions. As such, formal strategies tend to present a more consistent message, whereas information imparted through informal strategies may be more varied, from one individual or group to another, or from one job to another.

Sequential orientation strategies rely on a step-by-step formula that has been determined to provide appropriate stages in learning about the organization. For example, a newly hired swimming instructor who has the required qualifications may be expected to be orientated through a sequence of formal learning about the facility, programs and specific safety and risk management measures (either through an interactive orientation session or reading a manual), followed by observing or shadowing a current instructor, and finally teaching a class himself while being observed by a supervisor. In contrast, a random approach is less of a staged process. Orientation to the job and workplace tends to be arbitrary or 'figuring it out as you go'. A sequential approach may be expected to reduce a newcomer's uncertainty or anxiety about whether there will be a thorough orientation when it is seen as an organized process (Allen, 2006).

Another dimension of orientation strategies is whether the approach is fixed or variable. A fixed approach refers to orientation that occurs within a set timeframe (e.g., three days, one week, or three months). A variable timeframe means that there is no specific end to the orientation; rather, it may be assumed to continue until the newcomer has adjusted (i.e., achieved task mastery, role clarity, workgroup integration and political knowledge). Fixed orientation can be suited to newcomers' needs and learning curves (e.g., novices may require more time than veterans). This approach can also ensure that there is an opportunity to develop and test competence on the job (Allen, 2006). Variable orientation is more open-ended and flexible, allowing for individual differences along the way.

Another orientation strategy dimension – serial vs. disjunctive – refers to whether regular members are directly involved in the orientation of newcomers. The serial approach involves current members directly in newcomers' socialization – for example, through formal mentoring or the use of role models and hosting orientation sessions. This may be the case when new lifeguards are hired and oriented to the facility by a more senior guard. The orientation may involve formal information sessions, on-the-job shadowing by the new guard and, finally, monitoring and evaluation by the senior guard. Disjunctive orientation, on the other hand, does not formally involve regular members in newcomers' socialization. Rather, they tend to be left to their own devices, to figure it out on their own. The major benefit of the former approach is integrating newcomers with regular members for social learning. Another benefit is the opportunity for informal socialization that can take place in this shared environment – that is, learning about the organization and its people beyond the planned or required information sharing. Organizational culture can be transmitted through stories and myths that are passed along to new members and from informally observing member behavior.

The final dimension of orientation strategies is the investiture vs. divestiture approach. The former involves inducting the newcomer into the organization by focusing on what positive and unique attributes they have to contribute to the organization. This can help the individuals to understand how they fit in, and begin to build a positive personal identity in the workplace. Investiture provides 'positive social support from experienced organizational members' (Allen, 2006: 240). In contrast, divestiture involves inducting the newcomer to the ways of the organization through breaking down any misconceptions they may have about the organization upon entry. Divestiture often involves debasement or humiliation through one or more 'tests' that are intended to show the newcomer that they do not, in fact, really know what goes on in the organization. Divestiture is essentially 'negative social feedback [about preconceptions] until newcomers adapt' (Allen, 2006: 240). This approach is most common in the military and on sports teams, and is consistent with the notion of hazing – tearing new members down in order to build them back up. Once the newcomer's preconceptions have been rescinded, orientation focuses on socializing the individual to the desired ways of the organization. This approach is more likely to occur in entry-level jobs where the organization wants to start with a clean slate. Consider Box 5.1, which gives an example of staff orientation at GoodLife Fitness Clubs Inc.

BOX 5.1

New staff orientation at GoodLife Fitness Clubs Inc.

GoodLife Fitness Clubs Inc. is a recognized leader in the fitness industry with clubs located across Canada. At GoodLife, understanding the company's culture is of paramount importance to the organization's leaders. For this reason, the company promotes the GoodLife Promise, including its purpose and core values, during on-boarding and learning of new 'Associates' (staff). This takes place through a 'Base Camp' orientation, online training modules, and in club training, with the intent of integrating the new Associates in to the organization and their role.

All new Club Associates attend a Base Camp within their first two months. Base Camp is a one to three day experience (depending on the club position) for classroom learning that focuses on learning and mastery of skills through role play, feedback, peer evaluation and more role play. Activities are designed to help new Associates learn about their role within the organization and the specific details required of their job. New Associates also complete online training activities. The online 'Learning Path' includes complete modules for knowledge acquisition and role playing for skill perfection. As part of this early training all new Associates also receive a copy of the book *Living the GoodLife* written by CEO and founder David Patchell-Evans. The book explores the company's history and journey since inception. New Associates are tested on their knowledge acquisition through online and written tests and their skill performance through role playing as part of the Learning Path and Base Camp. Most new Associates complete their Learning Path requirements during their first three to four months of employment.

Within the club, new Associates participate in job shadowing, which pairs them with a more experienced person in their role and allows them to learn more about the job through observation, practice and feedback on their performance. The role play takes place during their 10 minute 'caring meeting' with their direct supervisor each shift. Feedback on their performance is given to keep the new Associates sharp and performing at a high level. The daily meeting ensures the relationship between each Associate and their Manager is strong and focused on the individual's growth and development.

Each new Associate receives a performance evaluation at the 3-month mark. This review is facilitated by their direct supervisor, whether that is the General Manager, Assistant General Manager or Fitness Manager. GoodLife provides each Manager with a series of interactive tools designed specifically for on-boarding and engaging new Associates. These tools help the Manager to learn more about the new Associate and coach/guide them to achieving their growth and development goals, as well as their financial and personal goals.

The company holds a separate orientation for the General Manager and Fitness Manager positions, which is the 'GoodLife Boot Camp'. These sessions are also centralized, and new General/Fitness Managers travel from across the country to participate as a group. At Boot Camp, Managers learn about such things as Member retention, Associate engagement, employment law and company operations. Senior executives attend these sessions and present information on their respective departments and how they function (e.g., Associate Relations, Corporate Wellness, Sales, and Finance). At the club, typically incoming Managers will not have anyone to shadow for their particular job as they have either replaced the former leader or assumed that role in a new club. Instead, the Divisional Manager and Management Development Instructor (for General Managers) and the Personal Training Regional Manager (for Fitness Managers) teach these new leaders how to perform at a high level in their role. Part of the new General Manager learning program is to experience and complete the learning for each Associate position in their club. This ensures the General Manager is familiar with all areas of club operations.

At GoodLife Fitness Clubs Inc., introducing new Associates to the organization's culture through various documents, formal and on-the-job training, and constant feedback helps integrate the core values for new Associates. These procedures have contributed to the organization being repeatedly recognized as one of Canada's 50 Best Managed Companies.

> Prepared by Eric MacIntosh with information
> from GoodLife Fitness Clubs Inc.

Discussion questions

1   With reference to Van Maanen and Schein's (1979) framework, what type of orientation strategies does GoodLife Fitness Clubs use for its new Associates? What strategies does it use for its new General Managers?
2   Do you think these are the best strategies for the different positions? If not, what could be done differently?

The six socialization approaches outlined by Van Maanen and Schein (1979) can be grouped into two patterns of socialization (cf. Johns & Saks, 2011). *Institutionalized socialization* comprises collective, formal, sequential, fixed, serial and investiture strategies. It reflects a more structured process of socialization which has been shown to promote newcomer loyalty, commitment and consequently reduced turnover (Ashforth & Saks, 1996; Bauer et al., 2007; Cable & Parsons, 2001; Griffeth & Hom, 2001). Allen (2006) found that collective, fixed and investiture tactics in particular had the greatest effect on newcomer commitment or embeddedness in the organization. That is, orientation in the group setting, for a set period of time, that focuses on what the newcomers bring to the organization and where they will fit in, will be most effective. Other research reinforces the importance of investiture tactics in particular (Bauer et al., 2007).

In contrast, *individualized socialization* comprises individual, informal, random, variable, disjunctive and divestiture strategies. It reflects a relatively less-structured approach to newcomer socialization and parts of it are consistent with leaving newcomers somewhat to their own devices, to engage in proactive socialization. These strategies tend to particularly impact newcomer adjustment (role clarity, self-efficacy, social integration), in the shorter term, as individuals gather the additional information they feel is necessary (Bauer et al., 2007). Still other research indicates that individualized socialization enhances the impact of institutionalized tactics on person-organization fit (Kim, Cable & Kim, 2005). Together, the research suggests that a combination of tactics will be most effective for newcomer orientation. Reconsider the orientation process at GoodLife Fitness Clubs Inc. in terms of whether that organization uses more of an institutionalized or individualized socialization process.

ORIENTING SPORT VOLUNTEERS

References throughout this chapter to the orientation of both employees and volunteers have been intentional. In general, the same stages of socialization (Figure 5.2) and adjustment (Figure 5.1), and the same orientation strategies and practices, apply to both groups of personnel. As with paid employees, 'a well-designed and thorough orientation and training process is important for new volunteers. The orientation process is critical to ensure volunteers are welcomed, that they feel a valued part of the club and most importantly, that they are comfortable in their role and can work productively' (Australian Sports Commission [ASC], 2014a: para 1). New volunteers should be: (1) provided with general club information (history, mission, goals); (2) introduced to and provided with the names and contact information of key volunteers and any staff; (3) familiarized with the responsibilities and accountabilities of their new role and how their role relates to others in the organization; and (4) familiarized with any facilities, equipment or resources that are used by the organization on a regular basis, and its risk-management procedures (ASC, 2014a). It should not be assumed that new volunteers know what they are supposed to be doing, how, when and with whom, just because they have offered their free time to help a sport organization. Rather, it is important to effectively orient volunteers, so that they develop a strong, realistic psychological contract with the organization (Taylor et al., 2006).

Turning to sport event volunteers, training is deemed to be a critical component of event volunteer management (Chelladurai & Madella, 2006; Van der Wagen, 2007). Event volunteer training is analogous to orientation as it typically coincides with volunteers' organizational entry or the first time they experience the organization as one of its members. As with staff and volunteers who are new to an organization, we may expect that volunteers who are new to an event have experienced some anticipatory socialization. For example, citizens of Sherbrooke, Quebec would have been very familiar, through media and word-of-mouth communication, with the fact that the city bid in 2009 to host the quadrennial Canada Summer Games in 2013, and that the Games were successfully awarded to the region later that same year. Following that, local citizens would have been aware of the progress of capital enhancements to the region in the form of new and upgraded sport facilities and the need for 5,000 volunteers to stage the event. All of this information and these experiences would have given them some background on the nature of the event, its progress, political issues and so on. In fact, 'media announcements' was one of the main factors that led citizens to sign up as volunteers at previous Games in other cities (Doherty, 2003). Thus, we can presume that each volunteer became involved with the event organization with some pre-conceived ideas and expectations, although these were not necessarily accurate or complete. For the successful operation of the Games it was important for the host committee to ensure that the, ultimately, 6,000-plus volunteers had a common understanding of the vision, mission and planned legacies of the Games, the management structure and venue management plans, and available positions and responsibilities. This information was shared at a general Games information session held for registered volunteers three months before the Games began.

According to Chelladurai and Madella (2006: 61), this preliminary orientation phase of event volunteer management is critical for sharing with volunteers 'the nature and goals of the event, its functioning, key roles, persons and responsibilities, and role of volunteers and specific human resource policies and procedures applying to them'. It can also be used to 'create a good atmosphere and to develop ownership in the volunteers with respect to the event' (Chelladurai & Madella, 2006: 61). The preliminary orientation phase may be part of, or in addition to, further task-specific training. This was the case with the 2013 Canada Summer Games, where venue orientation sessions took place about a month after the general orientation session (and after volunteers had been given their assignments). During these types of task-specific training sessions, newcomers are typically still learning about the organization, its expectations and adjusting their own expectations about being involved. Volunteers may be oriented to their specific venue team of volunteers and the various roles involved, and provided detailed written and verbal information about transportation and parking issues, security, accreditation, customer service, conflict resolution, cross-cultural awareness, disabled integration and dealing with the media. Such a formal information session may be accompanied by a venue walk-through to familiarize volunteers with the physical space where they will be working.

ORGANIZATIONAL CULTURE

The concept of organizational culture has its roots in anthropology. Culture refers to the social context in which people live. Just as a group, community or society has shared meanings and values, so too does an organization. Organizational culture is an underlying system of values, beliefs and assumptions about how things are done in an organization (Schein, 1985). Just as our individual values and beliefs guide our behavior, organizational values and beliefs serve as a guide to individual behavior in the organization. Thus, organizational culture is a key component of SHRM.

Schein defined organizational culture as:

> A pattern of basic assumptions – invented, discovered, or developed by a given group as it learns to cope with its problems of external adaptation and internal integration – that has worked well enough to be considered valid and ... to be taught to new members as the correct way to perceive, think, and feel in relation to those problems.
>
> (Schein, 1985: 9)

Core values, beliefs and even further underlying assumptions about 'how things are done around here' may be difficult to know directly. Instead, they are manifested or reflected in organizational practices and member behavior. These are more visible artifacts that represent what is valued in the organization, believed to be important and assumed to be acceptable. To the extent that these values, beliefs and assumptions are known, and accepted, by members of an organization, they serve to guide or control organizational behavior. Therefore, it is to the organization's advantage to ensure newcomers understand and embrace the culture of the organization. Similarly, it is to the newcomers' advantage to understand as quickly as possible how things are done around their new workplace.

Organizational culture has consistently been shown to be associated with staff attitudes and behavior. The extent to which particular values and beliefs are perceived to be manifested in an organization has been shown to engender workplace satisfaction, organizational commitment, increased effort and reduced turnover (e.g., Choi, Martin & Park, 2008; Lok & Crawford, 1999; MacIntosh & Doherty, 2005; MacIntosh & Doherty, 2010; MacIntosh & Walker, 2012; Sheridan, 1992; Silverthorne, 2004) and further organizational performance in the long term (Carmeli & Tishler, 2004). The positive influence of organizational culture is likely due to a combination of members' understanding and acceptance of how things are done.

A 'strong culture' is one where the values, beliefs and assumptions about the organization are widely understood and strongly accepted across the organization. It can be expected that a strong culture is more of a guiding force for members (McKenna & Beech, 2002). However, a strong culture can be a liability when it is characterized by values, beliefs and ways of doing things that run counter to an organization's corporate strategy, HR plan and overall best interests – for example, restricted communication, intolerance of differences or resistance to change. In an interesting historical analysis of leadership and governance practices in FIFA, Tomlinson (2014: 7) described 'how the workings of the FIFA system have been [consistently] open to misuse, and how the pursuance of private and personal interests has long been accepted as the norm in FIFA'. This appears to be a direct contradiction to its mission and branding as 'a model of fair play, tolerance, sportsmanship and transparency' (Tomlinson, 2014: 1).

In contrast, a 'weak culture' is one where the values, beliefs and assumptions about the organization are not widely known or not strongly accepted. As a result, culture is less of a guiding force for members. Newcomer orientation is an opportunity to strengthen an organization's culture by imparting to the newcomer desired behaviors and the underlying values and beliefs. Additional mechanisms by which a desirable organizational culture can be developed, strengthened and maintained, and a less than desirable culture may be changed, are discussed below.

We can also consider that within an overarching or 'dominant' culture there may be several differentiated subcultures (Martin, 1992). Subcultures are unique sets of values, beliefs and assumptions that develop over time within an organizational group or unit. Subcultures may form among individuals who work in the same functional area (e.g., marketing, sales, coaching, administration), at the same hierarchical level (e.g., management, operations staff) or in the same geographical areas (e.g., sport retail chain stores of a larger parent organization, internationally dispersed units within a multinational corporation such as adidas or IMG). Subcultures reflect shared values and beliefs based on common or shared experiences of group members. Subcultures may also form among staff or volunteers who have similar socio-demographic characteristics (e.g., age, gender, retired athletes). These forms of subcultures are personal rather than work related and may be analogous to 'cliques'. While a clique can provide an important source of support for newcomers and veterans alike, it may be viewed as an exclusionary group. Subcultures that develop based on function can be very positive if they provide members with a more work-specific frame of reference in the workplace. However, culture or subcultures are only positive from the organization's perspective if the values and beliefs they represent, and the further behavior they engender, align with the strategic focus of the organization.

The notions of a dominant culture and subcultures are not necessarily antithetical, as some might suggest (Martin, 1992). Rather, 'a subculture could consist of the core values of the dominant culture as well as the values of the area to which they relate' (McKenna & Beech, 2002: 93). In a study of the dominant culture and subcultures in a large multi-franchise fitness organization, MacIntosh and Doherty (2005) found that the corporate values of passion, peak attitude, fitness and organizational performance were perceived to be more prevalent by club staff than head office staff. The authors concluded that the distinct subcultures were likely consistent with the respective functions of the two different groups. For example, it was not surprising that the corporate value of fitness was more pervasive in the club subculture 'given that the mandate of the clubs is to provide quality fitness services to clients. In contrast, head office is responsible for [a myriad of organizational operations] and is not as directly involved in the delivery of fitness services' (MacIntosh & Doherty, 2005: 17). In a later study of culture across the fitness industry, MacIntosh and Walker (2012) identified the presence of subcultures, with personal trainers and club managers, in particular, having different perceptions about the degree of formalization and focus on fitness programs in their clubs (both lower for the personal trainers who work more independently and on their clients' specific programs). The possible existence of subcultures within a dominant culture means that the newcomer may need to be socialized to the values and beliefs of the group as well as to the broader culture of the organization.

There are many different ways to describe the nature of a particular organization's culture. It is argued that culture is unique from one organization to another, and therefore the only way to know it is to examine the visible manifestations (i.e., organizational practices, member behavior, symbols, myths) and talk to people about how things are done and why (Sackmann, 2001). This can help to uncover the underlying values and beliefs that are shared in the organization. However, there are also several frameworks and corresponding instruments that comprise what are considered to be sets of key characteristics that organizations value. Langton, Robbins and Judge (2010: 377–378) suggest that the following values 'capture the essence of an organization's culture'.

- *Innovation and risk taking*: the degree to which employees are encouraged to be innovative and take risks.
- *Attention to detail*: the degree to which employees are expected to work with precision, analysis and attention to detail.
- *Outcome orientation*: the degree to which management focuses on results or outcomes, rather than on the techniques and processes used to achieve those outcomes.
- *People orientation*: the degree to which management decisions take into consideration the effect of outcomes on the people within the organization.
- *Team orientation*: the degree to which work activities are organized around teams rather than individuals.
- *Aggressiveness*: the degree to which people are aggressive and competitive rather than easy-going and supportive.
- *Stability*: the degree to which organizational activities emphasize maintaining the status quo in contrast to growth.

These characteristics can be used to describe an organization's culture profile, based on members' perceptions of how things are done there. It is possible to determine whether there is widespread understanding and acceptance of the profile (a strong culture), or whether it is unclear what is going on, what is expected or why things should be done in a certain way (a weak culture). It is also possible to determine whether subcultures exist within an organization, based on variations in the perception or importance of these characteristics and perhaps the existence of other important elements. Although these key characteristics are presumed to have universal relevance to organizations of all types, research suggests that organizational culture may be specific to different industries (Lee & Yu, 2004). Smith and Shilbury (2004) found that history and tradition were highly valued elements in voluntary amateur sport organizations, while MacIntosh and Doherty (2007a) uncovered member success and a sense of connectedness within the club as valued aspects in the fitness industry – elements that were not apparent in universal measures of organizational culture.

Organizations should have a thorough understanding of the nature and strength of the core values and beliefs of their dominant culture, as well as the presence of any subcultures, and particularly whether they are consistent with the strategic direction of the firm. With regard to orientation, there are several mechanisms by which newcomers can learn the culture of an organization, and these are discussed below.

Learning organizational culture

Organizational culture is learned as part of the socialization process. A newcomer may develop some sense of the organization's values and beliefs before entering the organization. This may happen as part of the recruitment and selection process or even prior to that, based on the individual's knowledge of the organization through personal experience or learning about the organization from others. For example, as a former client or member of a sporting goods retail store or local sports club, a new employee or volunteer likely developed perceptions about the organization's culture or how things are done there, which contributes to his or her image of the organization (Hatch & Schultz, 1997; MacIntosh & Doherty, 2007b). As noted earlier, however, anticipatory socialization may be a source of inaccurate information about an organization. It is important that newcomer staff and volunteers have a clear understanding of organizational reality.

The most meaningful orientation to organizational culture occurs, however, once the newcomer becomes involved in the organization, during entry socialization. At this point, the individual has direct exposure to cultural artifacts that reflect what is valued and considered most important. Newcomers learn about organizational culture through symbols, including such things as office furnishings and decor and manner of employee dress (e.g., formal or casual office attire, matching uniforms or individualistic dress). These symbols convey to staff and volunteers what is important, accepted and expected in the organization. Organizational culture is also passed along through stories that 'anchor the present in the past and provide explanations and legitimacy for current practices' (Langton et al., 2010: 381). For example, at Western University in London, Ontario, Canada, stories continue to be told about Mr John 'The Bull' Metras, who was a very successful head coach of the football team from 1939 to 1969, head coach of the basketball team from 1945 to 1964, and served as Athletic Director from 1945 to 1972. These stories highlight the importance of history, tradition and athletic excellence that continue to be core values at the institution to this day.

Company rituals and ceremonies are another mechanism by which culture is transmitted. A fitness club or sports retailer may have sales performance awards and ceremonies that convey the importance of this form of achievement. The orientation process itself may be seen as a rite of passage (e.g., Base Camp at GoodLife Fitness Clubs), to the extent that it is systematic and thus conveys the importance of learning about how things are done in the organization. Annual staff picnics or bowling tournaments, or entering a team in a charity tournament, are other examples of company rituals that communicate and reinforce certain values in the organization.

Observing the behavior of others and, perhaps most importantly, seeing what is rewarded (i.e., valued) and what is not tolerated by the organization is a fundamental way to learn about organizational culture – for example, seeing how members act and react in certain situations, observing patterns of formal and informal communication and realizing the tolerance for ambiguity or conflict in the organization. These visible artifacts and manifestations of organizational culture not only teach, but also reinforce the existing values and beliefs (Johns & Saks, 2011).

Strengthening or changing organizational culture

Given the potential impact of a strong, positive organizational culture – that is, one which is widely shared by members and aligns with the organization's objectives and corporate strategy – it is important to consider how it is possible to strengthen an existing culture (so that it is more widely and deeply embraced). Alternatively, it is important to understand how to change a culture that is either weak and not shared by many or is not aligned with the strategic direction of the organization.

There are several ways to strengthen or change an existing organizational culture. It is widely recognized that the founder of the organization typically sets the path for the organization at the outset (Langton et al., 2010). This has been the case with GoodLife Fitness Clubs (David Patchell-Evans), Nike Inc. (Phil Knight), Formula 1 Racing (Bernie Eccelstone), China's leading sport apparel company Li-Ning (founded by former gymnast

Li-Ning) and, of course, with Apple (Steve Jobs). The organization's leaders, which may or may not include the founder, continue to guide, or change, the direction of the culture. It is modeled and reinforced by what they pay attention to in the workplace, their own work behavior, as well as their reaction to crises or critical incidents. John Stanton 'found' running in 1981, then founded the Running Room in 1984, a sport and exercise retail chain and meeting place for runners, with outlets across Canada and the US. He continues to join staff and clients for Running Room club runs (Running Room, 2014a).

Organizational culture is also strengthened, or changed, through recruitment and selection. Hiring employees or bringing on board volunteers who 'fit' with the current or desired culture can help to perpetuate and reinforce that culture, or help to change culture in the desired direction. Continuing from the example of the Running Room, the sport and exercise retail chain hires only runners to staff its stores:

> The Running Room is truly a store for runners by runners. All team members are runners whose philosophy is that if you're out there running on the same roads as the customers, you can better relate to them.
>
> (Running Room, 2014b: para 3)

The socialization of newcomers is another important point at which existing culture can be strengthened or changed. Desirable culture can be reinforced during either formal or informal orientation, when newcomers learn about the organizational culture – for example, through symbols, stories, rituals and the behaviour of other staff or volunteers. As may be expected, socializing newcomers to an organization's culture is more difficult to do when the culture is weak to begin with – that is, when the underlying values and beliefs are not widely understood or accepted. Following orientation, culture can be strengthened and maintained by rewarding behavior that is consistent with desirable values and beliefs in the organization.

SUMMARY

Orientation is the socialization of newcomers to the organization. It is critical that both 'neophyte' and 'veteran' newcomers have a relevant and thorough introduction to the organization so that they are more likely to hit the ground running, do the work that is expected of them and stay with the organization.

New staff and volunteers ideally adjust to their new working environment as they move through three stages of socialization. The stages of anticipatory, encounter and role management socialization correspond with newcomers' pre-entry, entry and adaptation to the organization, respectively. The intended outcomes of orientation and socialization are task mastery, role clarity, workgroup integration and political knowledge. Successful adjustment is characterized by organizational commitment, job satisfaction and retention.

Orientation is critical for aligning, or realigning, newcomers' expectations about the organization and their role there. An employee or volunteer's psychological or unwritten contract with an organization is based on mutual expectations and obligations, some of which will be established and some of which may need to be aligned with the reality of the organization. A newcomer's perception of P–O fit is important to their successful adjustment to the organization; thus, orientation is critical to create or strengthen one's sense of whether their values are consistent with those of the organization.

Newcomers may be proactive in their socialization to the organization, seeking out information they want and feel they need. However, it is important for the organization to implement a well-designed orientation process that lets it control what information newcomers receive and how. A framework of six contrasting approaches highlights strategies an organization can use to effectively implement orientation. The job preview and mentoring are two specific methods of orientation that correspond to newcomers' pre-entry, and entry and adaptation to the organization, respectively.

The orientation of sport volunteers, including those involved in staging events, should not be taken for granted. Like employees, newcomer volunteers likely have preconceived ideas and expectations about the organization or event that are not necessarily consistent with organizational reality and are not necessarily complete. The various strategies and practices for orienting and socializing employees are applicable to volunteers as well.

Finally, organizational culture is the values, beliefs and assumptions that underlie how things are done in an organization. It is reflected in an organization's symbols, stories, rituals and practices. To the extent that organizational culture is understood and accepted by staff and volunteers, it serves to guide and control behavior, by letting members know what is expected and how things are done. Thus, it is important that organizational culture is aligned with an organization's corporate strategy, and that newcomers come to understand and embrace that culture as quickly as possible.

DISCUSSION QUESTIONS

1   Discuss your experience with entering and adjusting to a new organization or a new job. What socialization strategies and practices were used? Were your values and expectations aligned with the organization? Did you experience any 'reality shock'? What could the organization have done to make your orientation more effective?

2   Describe the psychological contract you have with an organization for which you are employed or volunteer. What are your expectations of the organization and what do you perceive the organization expects from you? Have you had to adjust your psychological contract during your time with the organization?

3 Using an institutionalized or individualized approach, design an orientation process for each of the following.
   a A new social media officer (new to the position and organization).
   b New summer sports camp counselors (new to the position and organization).
   c A neophyte volunteer coach (new to coaching).
   d A veteran newcomer volunteer coach (new to the organization).
   e A veteran newcomer director of sponsorship for a professional sports team (new to the organization).
   f A veteran newcomer facility manager (promoted to the position).

4 Consider the organizational culture of a sport organization with which you are familiar.
   a View the organization's website and describe what image it tries to portray regarding 'how things are done around here'.
   b Now, describe the organizational culture as you know it (consider visible artifacts such as symbols, stories, rituals, myths and behaviors, organizational processes such as hiring, rewards, lines of communication and the core values they represent). Is there a discrepancy? Are there organizational subcultures you are aware of? How strong is the culture (do staff and/or volunteers know it and accept it)? What difference does the culture make to the attitudes and behavior of staff and/or volunteers?
   c How could a newcomer learn the culture of that organization?

CHAPTER 6

Training and development in sport organizations

LEARNING OBJECTIVES

After reading this chapter you will be able to:

- Articulate the significance of training and development in sport organizations
- Understand the aims of employee and volunteer learning
- Explain the training and development model
- Describe how effective training and development contributes to organizational development and enables strategic achievement of organizational goals

CHAPTER OVERVIEW

Training and development are important ingredients of human resource management (HRM) and thus are critical to an organization's success. Broadly speaking, training and development are used to build the skills and capabilities of the organization to meet its strategic challenges. More specifically, training and development are used to close the gap identified, either implicitly or explicitly, in the actual vs. desired performance of the employee or volunteer at an individual, group/team or organizational level.

The contributions that training and development can make to a sport organization's effectiveness, competitiveness, and to employee and volunteer satisfaction are outlined in this chapter. Training and development processes and activities are discussed from the perspective of a systemic and integrated (i.e., strategic) approach to planning that can be applied to any employee group (senior executives, line managers, operational staff, volunteers). Underpinning this approach is the premise that sport organizations should ensure that their training and development initiatives are aligned with their strategic objectives and mission.

THE SIGNIFICANCE OF TRAINING AND DEVELOPMENT IN SPORT ORGANIZATIONS

Sport organizations that have well-managed training and development programs can more easily retain employees and volunteers, ensure that their human resources have the capability to deliver on the organization's strategy, and provide future leaders for the organization. The research on training indicates that it is a good investment, and that the way training is designed, delivered and implemented is critical for successful outcomes. It has also been found that various forms of training from manager training, to team training, to cross-cultural training, consistently yields positive results when the training is designed systematically and based on the science underpinning learning and training (Salas, Tannenbaum, Kraiger & Smith-Jentsch, 2012). Training and development can also assist organizations to address the challenges and maximize the benefits, related to: generational differences in motivations, expectations and approaches to learning; rapidly emerging learning technologies; and the need to develop an adaptive, flexible workforce that can adjust to changing workplaces and increasing cultural diversity.

The strategic rationale for training and development in sport organizations includes:

- increased job satisfaction and morale among employees and volunteers
- reduced turnover of employees and volunteers
- increased employee and volunteer motivation
- improved efficiencies in processes and procedures
- enhanced capacity to adopt new technologies and methods
- risk management in terms of better knowledge of compliance requirements.

Training and development is equally applicable to paid staff and volunteers. Effective training and development of volunteers is fundamental for the continued existence of many community sport organizations, as these organizations rely on developing and retaining such personnel to deliver their core services. The Australian Sports Commission's *Volunteer Management Program*, Sport England's *Volunteer Investment Program*, and Sport and Recreation New Zealand's *Running Sport Program*, just to name a few, all emphasize the importance of training practices in the management of volunteers. A study of community sport volunteers in Australia (Cuskelly, Taylor, Hoye & Darcy, 2006) found that the retention of volunteer committee and board members was positively related to training and support practices.

Training and development involves an alignment of the strategic objectives of an organization with the capability of those involved in the organization to achieve these objectives. For example, a community fitness center with a mission to be the first choice for fitness services of its local citizens might develop a specific training program focused on customer care and relationship management issues to ensure that its employees understand how to deliver customer satisfaction, ensure customer retention and develop customer loyalty. In a study of fitness center employees, Makover (2003: 91) found that 'specific training and mentoring programs can help elevate employees' awareness, efficacy, commitment and satisfaction, and as a result … improved quality of the service that they provide to customers'. A study of Canadian national sport organizations (NSOs) found that training improved both the learning and individual performance of sport managers and the organizational performance of NSOs (Millar & Stevens, 2012).

More specific objectives for training and development include ensuring that employees and volunteers are provided with opportunities to learn new skills, knowledge and attitudes that will allow them to deal with the demands of the sport organization in which they work and volunteer. Training and development can be initiated for a variety of reasons for either individuals or groups of employees or volunteers. Some common reasons for engaging in specific programs of training and development are as follows.

- To train about a specific topic or skill.
- As a component of an individual's overall professional development program.
- When a performance appraisal indicates that performance improvement is required.
- As part of a succession management or a strategic talent management process.
- As a way of developing a common and shared mindset and approach to decision making among managers.

Typically, 'training' refers to the development and enhancement of technical, job-related skills and abilities, either on-the-job or off-the-job. 'Development' is more concerned with changing attitudes and behaviors as well as skill building, and aims to improve the aggregate capabilities of the person. When a person is recruited it should be not only for his/her ability to perform a current work role but he/she should also demonstrate the potential to learn and change as the role evolves. Informal learning and development is part of the job and is the responsibility of all managers and supervisors. This means that job performance, appraisal and development of staff are undertaken by managers and supervisors in the course of their work and, as a result, they are continuously assessing the need for job improvement and career development. Understanding the role of learning in this process is essential.

EMPLOYEE AND VOLUNTEER LEARNING

The basic premise of learning, acquiring new skills, knowledge, attitudes and behaviors as a result of interactions with the environment underpins the concept of training and development. Learning occurs in context and can be achieved through active, social and reflective means (Driscoll, 1994). Learning is individualistic and people have different preferences. Some people learn best when the learning takes place within a certain environment (context), others prefer to be mentally active (active) to make connections between the new knowledge and existing knowledge and then construct meaning from their experiences, some like to work collaboratively in groups and gain from different perspectives (social), and others learn best when given the opportunity to critically think about their actions and outcomes (reflective).

There are three distinctive theories about how learning occurs that managers should understand and apply to maximize the success of training and development. These are behavioral, cognitive and constructive learning orientations. The *behavioral* approach focuses on changing observable behavior through either positive or negative reinforcement and the learner engages in the behavior in order to learn. For example, a fitness center manager might train a new instructor by complementing her/him on actions which are generally desirable, but then as the instructor gains these competencies the manager would gradually move to only praise those precise behaviors that are considered essential for the job. This type of learning can produce a relatively permanent change in behavior due to the learners' experience (Ormrod, 1999).

The *cognitive approach* focuses on mental processes and suggests that learning occurs when information is mentally processed and the result is a change in the structure of the learner's knowledge. The cognitive orientation to learning considers how people perceive, interpret and think about the environmental events they experience in a way that enables them to modify their behavior fairly rapidly (Gagne & Driscoll, 1988). Continuing the example above, the manager would provide cognitive feedback to the fitness instructor, that is, specific information about performance and his/her success or failure in delivering key aspects of his/her job.

The *constructive* orientation to learning contends that a person's knowledge, together with the learning process itself, is constructed by the learner's interpretation of their experience. Learning is taken to be a relatively permanent change in a person's knowledge or behavior. This premise consists of three components: (1) the duration of the change is long term; (2) the change involves the content and structure of knowledge in memory or the behavior of the learner; and (3) the cause of the change is the learner's experience in the environment (Mayer, 1982). Constructivism suggests that learning is an intentional, conscious activity on the part of the learner. In this approach our fitness instructor would actively and consciously engage with learning the practice required for the job through action and then reflect on the activities.

Constructed learning is a shared responsibility of the sport organization and of employees, volunteers, managers and supervisors at all levels. Employees should pursue learning that is aligned with organizational priorities and which prepares them to do their job into the future through the acquisition and maintenance of knowledge, skills and competencies related to their level and function. Managers and supervisors are responsible for enabling training that supports organizational objectives. Organizations can provide opportunities for continuous learning in order to optimize organizational learning. Sport organizations that explicitly encourage and support this learning process from a strategic perspective are called 'learning organizations'.

The 'learning organization' (Senge, 1990), 'knowledge creation' (Nonaka & Takeuchi, 1995) and 'knowledge management' (Drucker, 1995), all represent frameworks designed to improve organizational capacity for learning. A learning organization incorporates the development of organizational levels, collective intelligence and acknowledges the importance of knowledge and, in particular, tacit knowledge. To this end training-based development fosters learning in different ways (learning networks, communities of practice) than might be traditionally found in HR training and development.

In learning organizations managers, supervisors, employees and volunteers are active partners in supporting learning. Each person plays a role in identifying learning needs, stimulating and supporting informal learning, and ensuring the continuous learning of themselves and others. Organization employees and volunteers are encouraged to learn, acquire new knowledge and skills, and disseminate this knowledge to others within the organization to improve or renew existing work practices, products or services, or to initiate innovation. Training and development activities are structured to enhance the learning capacities of employees and volunteers and are delivered within an environment favorable for learning. This might include using job rotation, mentoring, self-directed study or task simulations in a stimulating work environment. In this organizational context, training and development are a form of learning and there is a strong link between learning and working. Strategic viability of all organizations is tied to the continuous training and development of employees and volunteers.

A TRAINING AND DEVELOPMENT PROCESS

The basic components of a training and development process will follow from the planning process outlined in Chapter 3. The training and development component is an outcome of what has been deemed to be central to the organization's current and future workforce needs. There are typically five steps in a systematic approach to training and development, as follows:

1   training *needs analysis*;
2   development of *training goals*;
3   *design* of the training or development intervention;
4   *implementation*.
5   *evaluation*.

Step 1: Training needs analysis

The objective of undertaking a thorough training needs analysis is to collect information that will assist in the development of training strategies and objectives. This involves analyzing what the organization is doing now and what it aims to achieve in the future. The process typically involves a three-level approach. First, an organizational level analysis is used to examine how a training and development program can support the strategic direction of the organization and be aligned with organizational goals. The question asked is, where is training needed and which organizational goals can be achieved via training? For example, a golf club identifies a performance gap shown by a declining number of membership renewals and low member satisfaction. Data used in the analysis might include the golf club's strategic goals, culture, quality assurance processes, and employee turnover and absenteeism rates. As a result of the analysis, the training requirements needed to address this issue would be identified, such as a customer service front-line training program.

At the next level of assessment, an operational task analysis is performed to identify the nature of job tasks and the knowledge, skills and abilities required to perform the job effectively. The question asked here is, what needs to be learned to do the job effectively? Data used in this level of analysis might include position descriptions, performance criteria and market research about the requirements of similar positions in other organizations. For example, after researching the training needs of officials, British Cycling developed a standardized program for training cycling officials, with a standardized format for all disciplines comprising training and hands-on experience gained over the course of six races and including child protection, communication, administration, technical and competition (see Box 6.1, 'From the field').

Finally, an individual level analysis is carried out to see how well a person performs a job. This is undertaken to ascertain which individual should be trained and the type of training that they require based on an assessment of their current performance against

BOX 6.1

From the field: Training officials in British Cycling

British Cycling identified the need to more systematically train officials (known as commissaires) and organizers who are or would like to become involved with the promotion and management of British Cycling events. The aim of this training is to encourage more people to organize races and become event officials. As an NGO British Cycling also wanted to be confident about consistency of officiating and offer a clear entry point for potential officials. The training is aligned with an overall strategy to increase standards.

British Cycling also identified that the government was taking more of an interest in sports volunteering as a whole and would like to ensure that people involved have undergone certain checks. As a sport that takes place on public roads and other places British Cycling are also increasingly under pressure from government sources (and the police and local authorities) and the training program aims to increase the confidence from these bodies as well.

The training is of benefit to the volunteers in terms of clarifying the standard British Cycling is aspiring to for events, and for British Cycling, as better organized events should mean it is more effectively protected (from a litigation point of view) as the volunteers would learn about correct operational procedures to follow in the training.

The organizer training is aimed at the organizers of small grassroots events (events where most of the budget comes from entry fees and the organizer is a volunteer). In these events the roles of organizer and chief official have become somewhat confused. British Cycling had limited resources available for organizers and little more than the rule book available for officials. So in order to start, the volunteer Support Officer from British Cycling had to assess and diagnose the responsibilities of the organizer, chief official and the competitor. In broad terms the responsibilities were divided into three types of task: administration, technical and competition.

The administration, technical and competition responsibility of each group were defined as follows.

- *Organizer*: takes the entries, sets up (and removes) the course, maintains the course during the event.
- *Officials*: check validity of entries, competitors' bikes and clothing, manage the race on the day, validate the result.
- *Competitors*: enter correctly, bring equipment within the regulations and fit for purpose, compete fairly.

This standard format could be applied to any type of cycle race and therefore all British Cycling training could be taught in a similar way. British Cycling has now written training using the same module titles to introduce officials to road racing, track racing, BMX and cycle speedway.

The training for officials covers five modules taught over one day plus an introduction and conclusion, and then candidates have to attend at least six competitions as an

Assistant Commissaire before they can become a Chief Commissaire. The modules are as follows.

1 *Introduction*: to introduce the tutors, candidates and to outline the aims of the day.
2 *Child protection (good practice)*: to give officials an idea of best practice when dealing with young and vulnerable persons.
3 *Communication*: working as part of a team and being an authority figure during an event.
4 *Administration*: necessary paperwork that a Commissaire will need to complete before, during and after an event.
5 *Technical*: issues related to the competitors bike and clothing.
6 *Competition*: discipline (sanctions there and who can issue them) using the road and race simulation.
7 *Conclusion*: evaluation of the course and what candidates will need to do next in order to qualify as a regional (Chief) Commissaire.

The course was well received and attracts both new and existing officials. It has also gone someway to reassuring officials what their roles and responsibilities are. The post-qualification assessment has also started a useful process of post-course formative assessment leading to the summative assessment when they have gained enough experience to go up to the next rung of the ladder. Again this should ensure that standards should rise over the next few years.

Discussion questions

1 Outline the steps that British Cycling undertook in this training program – as per the training and development process.
2 Discuss the aspects that you would include in an evaluation of this training program.
3 How might you incorporate a mentoring scheme or other development initiatives into British Cycling?

Prepared with information provided by Robert Jefferies,
Volunteer Support Officer, British Cycling Manchester

desired performance. It identifies who needs training at the individual level and to what degree. Employees and volunteers can require training for a variety of reasons, and these typically can be grouped into three categories as follows.

1 To update or enhance skills and knowledge.
2 To fill a performance gap that is identified during the performance management process.
3 To fill a growth or development gap, if the individual is to be promoted or to be able to fill another position in the organization.

Data used in this level of analysis would include performance appraisals, internal and external customer feedback, observation and other feedback. For example, a sport development officer might be performing well on strategic planning and implementation, coordinating and delivering activities and events, employing and training coaches and volunteer staff, and evaluating and monitoring activities using performance indicators, but struggling with their job requirement to manage financial resources and a budget. In response, they could be enrolled in an appropriate level accounting course to address this skill deficit.

Taken together, the three levels of analysis should provide the basis with which to identify the organization's training objectives and provide the foundation on which to design the training. Ideally, criteria for the evaluation of the training initiatives are also established during this phase to measure success of achieving the training objectives.

Not all organizations have procedures for systematically determining training and development needs. Those who do engage in this process are usually organizations with HR professionals or organizations, such as government departments, that are required to do so for funding or accreditation purposes. The needs analysis in small or non-profit sport organizations is generally done on a broader level. An example would be to operationally identify deficiencies such as the necessity for higher order financial skills to manage budget submissions, or required compliance standards such as legislated risk management documentation. An example of broadly identifying volunteer satisfaction as a key training and development need is provided in Box 6.2 in a 'Snapshot of a sport club'.

Step 2: Setting training and learning goals

The goals developed for training and development should state what will be accomplished as a result of the training and should be specified in light of the needs identified. These

---

BOX 6.2

Snapshot of a sport club

The Apex Football Club is a long established club with a strong community support base and successful volunteer management program. The Club has developed a systematic and committed approach to developing job satisfaction, commitment and facilitating a team environment which is underpinned by a performance culture. To establish the program the Club:

- appointed a Volunteer Program Manager;
- reviewed training requirements, identified a need for key volunteer personnel to have training in administration, first aid and medicine, and dealt with volunteer management issues;
- commenced a mentor program for all volunteers for their professional development;
- ensured that paid staff were trained in volunteer management.

will arise out of gaps and deficiencies identified in the preceding needs analysis. Training goals and objectives indicate the organization's expectation of the employee or volunteer in relation to their understanding of relevant concepts (e.g., privacy requirements), ability to perform a skill (e.g., public speaking) or demonstrate a change in behavior (e.g., improved decision making). Common training programs for the employees and volunteers in sport organizations include: communication, negotiation, customer service, developing codes of conduct, issues of conflict of interest and corporate social responsibility, good corporate governance, diversity issues, volunteer management and coaching and officiating. The latter training is usually located within a state or national accreditation framework.

All training should consist of observable and measurable learning objectives so that all stakeholders are involved in the process; this means that the trainee, trainer, manager and any other relevant party will have clarity on the expected outcomes. To take an example, a basic level training program on diversity objectives might include the following.

- Demonstrate an understanding of the value, importance and impact of managing diversity and inclusion for your organization.
- Recognize and encourage behaviors that value diversity in the workplace.
- Develop strategies that will enhance the organization's capability by capitalizing on differences and improving workplace harmony.

Once the training and development objectives are determined then the next step is to design relevant programs and ensure infrastructure support.

Step 3: Designing training and development

As noted previously, the training goals and objectives will influence design. The determination of the way in which the training will be delivered also relates to the content, method of instruction, material, exercises and sequencing. The content of the training course should link directly with the areas that were identified in the needs assessment and align with the training goals. The design of training is related to the learning goals, cognitive outcomes including enhanced knowledge and better mental models, behavioral outcomes related to acquiring a new skill or improving it, and affective learning outcomes relating to improved motivation and self-efficacy (Salas, Tannenbaum & Smith-Jensen, 2012). The design of training is a highly specialized area and it is not the intention of this book to provide precise guidelines on designing organizational training programs. However, there are some guiding principles that should be considered in assessing the appropriateness of the training design and methods.

A wide range of skills and tasks categorizations exist but, basically, these aspects can be grouped into three general categories: cognitive, interpersonal and psychomotor (Goldstein & Ford, 2002). Cognitive skills and development are related to problem solving, understanding and knowledge requirements. Interpersonal aspects are to do with interactions with others, including colleagues, volunteers and stakeholders. This covers a very wide array of skills such as leadership, communication, negotiation, conflict resolution and team building. Psychomotor skills are related to manual or physical activities that require specific movements.

Step 4: Conduct the training and/or development programs and activities (implementation)

Training methods

There are several methods that can be used to deliver the required outcomes of skill, knowledge, attitudinal or task development. The method is chosen to match the skill or task required. Training may include formal, structured learning experiences such as classroom, seminar or conference-based training or the use of online training packages, e-learning and blended learning. Technology delivered training has gained significant momentum and now encompasses just-in-time training on an individual's mobile device (e.g. phone, tablet and computer) through to MOOCs (massive open online courses) delivery. These types of portable and accessible approaches have meant that small groups or individuals and remote areas have greater access to training as location and volume are not at issue.

The choice of appropriate training design and delivery methods is closely associated with the benefits accrued from training. It is suggested that effective training employs the principles of involving trainees in the content selection of the training, providing activities that are experientially engaging and allowing trainees to have experiences that could lead to 'errors' from which they can learn. The method of training will depend on the composition and needs of the trainees.

Volunteers may need to receive more specific training to provide the information and skills necessary to effectively perform the volunteer role. Unlike most paid positions, many volunteer roles will be filled by individuals who do not have prerequisite skills or expertise in the job they will perform. Given that (1) skills and abilities are not the basis for a volunteer's recruitment, (2) several volunteers may share or rotate in a task and (3) volunteer work is often undertaken with little supervision, effective volunteer training has been found as a critical component for good volunteer management and sport organization effectiveness (Kim, 2004). For example, a volunteer may be recruited as a duty manager based on their knowledge of a particular sport rather than their experience as a manager. Once fully skilled, the volunteer will then be in a position to further develop their skills and knowledge or acquire further knowledge through engagement in developmental initiatives.

The advent of easy-to-access Internet-based training has spawned a range of online manuals, support materials and training courses, developed by government, national and state sporting bodies, and non-government organizations (NGO), that can be accessed free of charge and at convenient times. Such courses are relevant for both volunteers and paid staff working in community sport. Box 6.3 gives an example of one such online training initiative.

Employee and volunteer development

Development of individuals within the organization focuses on improving organizational performance through enhancement of the employees' or volunteers' abilities. Developmental interactions have the potential to enhance not only personal growth, through increased knowledge and career advancement, but also organizational goals, through enhanced performance and increased employee retention. The importance of the development approach is highlighted in a study of basketball referees by Warner, Tingle and Kellett

BOX 6.3

Online training: Play by the Rules program

Play by the Rules is a free, online training course for coaches, administrators, umpires and referees, participants and volunteers. The courses are short (up to two hours), may be done in part or all at once and make extensive use of case studies.

Play by the Rules states:

> We harness the combined strength and knowledge of the human rights and sports and recreation sectors to promote and provide information, tools and resources that will influence attitudes and change behaviors, leading to cultural change in sporting and recreational environments.

Focus for 2011–14

Over the next three years our work will focus on raising awareness of *Play by the Rules* and on working in partnership to integrate our knowledge, tools and resources into the policy and practice of those with an interest in sport and recreation at all levels across the country.

The courses provide up-to-date information on rules, legislation and examples of best practice. There is an online quiz at the end of each module. An official certificate is provided on successful completion of the course.

For more information see www.playbytherules.net.au (link active as of November 2013); Play by the Rules is supported by the Australian and State and Territory Governments

(2013). They found that referees who exited these roles indicated that training was an issue of concern. This was related to their training which only catered to knowledge of rules and enforcement, rather than on a development approach that could develop skills in communicating with coaches, players and spectators.

There are various forms of development-orientated activities, such as: trainee positions, job rotation, leadership and management development programs, mentoring and coaching; an array of topics of developmental interactions such as: career advice and work life support and balance; and numerous factors that may contribute to development (Higgins & Kram, 2001).

Trainee and internship positions provide an individual with specific responsibilities beyond their normal duties and/or a senior person to work with and learn from. Job rotation involves providing the individual with the opportunity to perform a number of jobs, each chosen to build their skills, knowledge and expertise across a range of the organization's activities. Orientation processes and programs are also fundamental for achieving employee and volunteer development. The place of orientation and its use in development is discussed in further detail in Chapter 5.

While training needs are organization specific, Cunningham (2012) has argued for the inclusion of diversity training in sport organizations. Based on NCAA research findings, he suggests that to be impactful, the way in which training relates the organization's mission, strategic aims, hiring and personnel evaluation, should be explicitly articulated. When this is done the trainee is 'more likely to transfer the training to their work environment, and consequently, and create a more diverse and inclusive workplace' (Cunningham 2012: 400).

Development-focused initiatives such as *mentoring* programs and *coaching* assignments have substantively gained in popularity (Eddy, D'Abate, Tannenbaum, Givens-Skeaton & Robinson, 2006). One of the reasons for the surge in the use of mentoring and coaching is the mounting evidence of the positive contributions that mentors can make to career success, and the use of these methods to achieve competitive advantage through people and as important mechanisms of professional development (Rhodes & Fletcher, 2013). Coaching and mentoring programs may reside either on or off the job, depending if the coach or mentor is located within the organization or is external. While the terms coach and mentor are sometimes used interchangeably there are differences in the role each plays.

Mentors, whether it is in a formal mentoring program or in an informal relationship, focus on the person, their career and support for individual's growth, while the coach is more job focused and performance orientated. The coach aims to assist the individual by increasing their capabilities through clear goals, techniques, practice and feedback, not unlike a sport coach. Coaches may be peers or hold a more senior role than the person being coached.

Mentoring

Mentoring is about relationship building. The mentor is usually a person who holds a more senior role than the 'mentee' and is able to impart his/her knowledge about career development. Mentoring is a formal relationship structured around developmental needs. A mentor can share wisdom and experience and provide support, advice and counsel to enable a mentee to grow and develop. Mentors can make important contributions to understanding how to get things done, ethical decision making, understanding of other people and their viewpoints, and accessing networks and identifying beneficial individuals. The relationship is mutually beneficial with mentors often profiting from communication and feedback from their mentees. Good quality mentoring (and coaching) can lead to improved awareness of self-efficacy and provide the basis to deal with situations that involve others in the goal attainment (Rhodes & Fletcher, 2013).

Most facilitated mentoring programs have a formal process which defines each step and monitors the ongoing success of the program. Although programs will differ, generally, mentoring can be classified into an eight-step process as follows.

1 *Choosing the mentee*: this may be done via a specific job or general area that needs attention and may be through a self or manager nomination process.
2 *Identifying developmental needs*: areas for improvement or further development are determined via self or managerial assessment.
3 *Choosing potential mentors*: a mentor's capability and willingness to undertake the role is assessed.

4 *Pairing the mentor and mentee*: the skills and knowledge needed by the mentee and the ability of the mentor to provide practice or guidance in those areas are assessed for fit.
5 *Orientation for mentors and mentees*: outlines expectations about time commitments, interactions, reporting requirements development-related responsibilities.
6 *Drawing up the contract*: includes the development plan, confidentiality arrangements, the length of the relationship, frequency of meetings and the role of both the mentor and mentee.
7 *Implementation and reporting*: carrying out the contract with regular reporting on the relationship and progress towards the development goals.
8 *Evaluation and follow-up*: an assessment is undertaken.

Mentoring requires commitment from both parties, a common issue arising in mentoring programs relates to finding an appropriate mentor who can provide both the professional (career) and personal (psychosocial) dimensions for the mentee. Weaver and Chelladurai (2002: 98) note that successful mentoring can result in 'positive outcomes for the protégé (advancement, growth and satisfaction), for the mentor (intrinsic satisfaction, status, respect and power) and for the organization (reduced turnover and development of management potential)'. Their study of intercollegiate athletic administrators found that mentored staff were more satisfied with the organizational supervision and respect they received, the people they work with, and their extrinsic rewards, than their non-mentored colleagues. Griffiths and Armour's (2012) study of volunteer youth sports coaches concluded that mentoring with volunteers should consider how to profitably maximize professional learning in a shared and sustained social network to address the nature of the isolated and voluntary nature of the vast majority of coach practice.

Additionally, mentoring has been identified as a way to support and encourage more women to become leaders in sport organizations. In her study of women involved in athletic leadership, Kelly (2004) concluded that the task of searching out an appropriate mentor and being an appropriate mentor, was paramount to the experience of successful leaders. Kelly also noted that professional training for women in athletic leadership was limited, and recommended more research into the establishment of a developmental process to introduce women to the demands of interscholastic and intercollegiate coaching environments. Bower's (2009) meta-analysis of qualitative studies of mentoring women within the sport industry led to a set of proposed actions for female and male mentors and protégés, practitioners and professional organizations in improving the underrepresentation of women in leadership positions in sport. These included consideration of: informal mentoring; selecting a mentor wisely; including low performer protégés as well as high performer protégés; introduce the protégé to key players; use of performance evaluations as a mentoring tool; more than one mentor; and be open to both male and female mentors.

In considering mentoring, both generally and specifically within sports coaching, Jones, Harris and Miles (2009) proposed guidelines of good practice, which included many of the same consideration as Bower (2009), along with the following.

- Focus and identify the needs of the person being mentored at the beginning of the relationship.
- Provide a challenge for both the mentor and coach.
- Training provision for mentors.

- Appreciate that mentoring is a fluid and dynamic process, requiring patience as to evolve through several stages.
- Develop mutual trust between mentor and mentee.

The bottom line is that the mentoring process should be a facilitative and nurturing relationship between the mentor and the mentee.

Coaching

There are numerous models of performance coaching but essentially coaching involves one person supporting and directing another person (the client) through encouragement, questioning and support. The client agrees to a plan of action, and the coach will help to motivate and guide them to complete their plan. The coach–client relationship is designed and defined in a relationship agreement based on the client's expressed interests, goals and desired outcomes. Interestingly, Greenberg and Baron (2008) suggest that athletic coaches and organizational coaches share many commonalities of practice, such as: analyzing performance, creating a supportive climate for development and offering encouragement.

Coaching is different from mentoring, as a coach will seldom offer advice. Coaches typically use questioning, reflection and discussion to get the client to identify their career or development goals, develop options, strategies and action plans to achieve the desired outcomes. Clients are responsible for their own achievements and success, and a coach does not expect that a client will take any specific action or attain specific goals. A coach monitors the client's progress towards the achievement of his or her action plan. A coach does not provide counseling or therapy.

As the use of coaching as a development option grows, so do the range and complexity of models, frameworks and theories on coaching. The GROW model (Whitmore, 2004) is a commonly used coaching framework. The basis of this model is that you need to know where you are going (the Goal), where you are (Current Reality) and the possible ways of achieving your goal (Options) before you can choose the best path. The final ingredient is the motivation or 'Will' to undergo change and commit to action. The four key components of the model GROW can be used to structure a total coaching program or a single session.

Transformational coaching (Hargrove, 2002) takes coaching beyond a single-loop learning model such as GROW by seeking to identify the source of an individual's behavior and frames of reference (double-loop learning) and facilitate the client to look at different ways of being (triple-loop learning). This transformational model involves coaching the client to continuously improve their current practices or do what they are already doing better, enabling them to fundamentally reshape their patterns of thinking with the intent of helping them break through impasses and learn to do different things, and then to move to the triple-loop aspect of empowering the client to create a shift in their context or point of view so that they can learn to open up new possibilities and support them in fulfilling their potential. This approach uses the constructive orientation to learning that was discussed earlier in this chapter.

Similar to mentoring, coaching can provide training and development outcomes to both the coach and the client. The coach may develop additional skills and techniques related to coaching, while the client is supported in reaching their desired goals. Research has clearly shown that learning is much more likely to translate into on-the-job behaviors or performance change if the social context of the organization is receptive and favorable post-training conditions exist.

Leadership development

Management and leadership development, along with team-building programs and initiatives are important developmental areas. Included are on-the-job training, external short courses, special projects, residential courses and executive development courses (such as a company specific MBA). These development programs are delivered either through internal processes or externally by training companies, government bodies or universities. External programs can be designed specifically for the sport organization and its personnel, or the employee/volunteer may be integrated into 'open' programs that comprise participants from a range of organizations such as the Canadian Association for the Advancement of Women and Sport program. The Canadian Association for the Advancement of Women and Sport and Physical Activity's Women and Leadership Program consists of a series of professional development sessions that have been designed for women, by women, to prepare them for leadership roles in sport and active living communities. Their *Women on Boards: A Guide to Getting Involved*, was developed in partnership with 2010 *Legacies Now*, and provides practical resources to ensure strong representation and leadership from women at the board level (Canadian Association for the Advancement of Women and Sport and Physical Activity, 2013). Another development project – *The Women's International Leadership Development Program* – is a joint venture with national sports organizations from the Czech Republic, Denmark, Finland, France, Hungary, Italy and Sweden aimed at increasing representation by women in leadership positions in sport and building the competence and confidence of women in decision-making positions (European Women and Sport, 2014). The program is organized through the European Non-Governmental Sports Organisation (ENGSO) and funded through the European Commission's sport unit. The project offers women leaders across Europe the opportunity to learn skills together and create a pan-European network of women leaders.

Assessing the requirements of training and development of leaders and managers involves the complex task of identifying the competencies relevant to any given job and there are many instruments which aim to measure managerial and leadership behaviors and skills. As with all forms of training and development, programs which develop management, leadership and team capabilities should be undertaken with due consideration concerning how this development will enhance the organization's ability to meet its strategic objectives.

Career planning and development

'Effective career planning and development involves the alignment of individual employee development needs with the strategic capability requirement of an organization' (Watt, Bennett & Taylor, 2004: 372). Career development is a combination of career planning (which is the individual's responsibility) and career management (which relates to the organization's training and development requirements and initiatives). Career planning is the process that the individual undertakes to assess their strengths and development opportunities relative to the job they are currently performing and the future career that they aspire to. Career management refers to the support an organization affords an individual, through training and development and performance feedback, to assist in the implementation of the individual's career plan.

A supportive organizational infrastructure and culture can greatly facilitate effective career development. This includes devising processes to diagnose development needs, provision of the time and space to engage in development opportunities, monitoring and

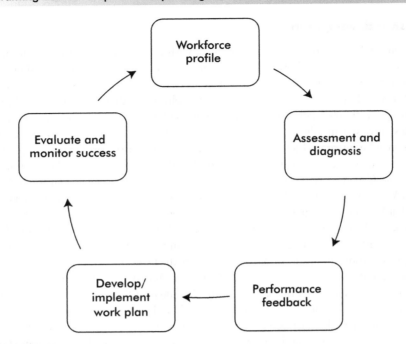

FIGURE 6.1 Developmental process

feedback systems, mentoring and coaching, and establishing a culture that values learning. The development process can be illustrated as a cyclical process as seen in Figure 6.1.

The first step in this process is the development of a *success profile* of competencies categorized under domains such as interpersonal, management or leadership skills. These are the competencies required to achieve individual and organizational goals and might include competencies such as decision making, negotiation and creativity. The success profile will change in response to demands of both the internal and external environment.

The next step is an *assessment* of the individual's current level of capability against the success profile. A wide range of assessment techniques exist and include testing, competency-based performance evaluations, and multi-rater surveys. Once assessed, *feedback* of the assessment results is provided to the individual. This should include provision of specific examples of the individual's behaviors that can be used to illustrate both his/her strengths and his/her areas for development.

Following the feedback session the individual should create a *development plan*, determine priorities and target two or three key areas to concentrate his/her efforts upon. The development plan should take into account the individual's learning preferences and should combine a variety of tools and learning techniques such as mentoring, coaching, special assignments or implementing tactical behavior changes in day-to-day tasks and responsibilities (Watt et al., 2004).

Finally, an individual and organizational level process for *measuring and monitoring* the success of the development progress should be instituted. This allows for periodic feedback and in some cases, rewards could be linked to the achievement of development plan goals. A re-evaluation should then occur for new developmental priorities for the next cycle.

Many sport organizations now provide a range of career development programs including pathway initiatives for athletes transitioning into the workforce. One such program is the *International Olympic Committee's Athlete Career Programme* that was designed to assist elite and Olympic athletes successfully manage the transition from sport to a new career through education, life skills training, professional development and job placement. The National Football League (NFL) *Transition Assistance Program* (TAP) has taken a unique approach and provides transitioning players and their significant others peer to peer support through relationships with trained NFL Transition Coaches (former players).The NFL states that inclusion of spouses and significant others is paramount given the role they play in the health and wellness of the family unit.

Step 5: Training and development evaluation

The evaluation of training and development activities should occur before, during and after implementation. The instructional objectives and training outcomes should be identified when the training needs are determined. For example, the needs analysis may have found that social media skills are needed for a range of positions within the organization. One consequent training objective might be that participants will know how to deliver social media content; and a training outcome could be that participants can embed social media within the organization's web pages from Facebook, LinkedIn, Twitter and Google. The evaluation process has been described as having four different levels, commonly referred to as the Kirkpatrick levels. Salas et al. (2012: 91) note that despite its widespread use, the Kirkpatrick hierarchy has limitations; however, they note that 'using it for training evaluation does allow organizations to compare their efforts to those of others in the same industry'. Furthermore, the latter clarify the purpose for evaluation and the evaluation measures and use precise affective, cognitive and/or behavioral measures that reflect the intended learning outcomes.

Learning criteria are designed to objectively measure the learning outcomes of the training on skill type tests, such as an ability to produce a financial plan, while behavioral criteria measure on-the-job performance. Reaction measures are widely used to evaluate training programs, despite the lack of any relationship between reaction measures and the other three criteria (Arthur, Bennett, Edens & Bell, 2003). Results and effectiveness criteria of the learning and behavior are measured by the impact of the training on organizational performance. Increases in efficiency or customer satisfaction would be examples of a positive return on investment. The evaluation undertaken should relate to the strategic goals of the organization. The choice of evaluation strategy will depend on the purpose of the evaluation.

Evaluation can occur prior to implementation of the training or development program through the assessment of the adequacy, scope and coverage of the proposed program. The aim is to assess any deficiencies and allow for corrective steps at an early stage, in other words is there evidence that the selected training and development methods will result in the knowledge and skills acquisition needed to complete the job task or role? During the course of the program the recipient may be asked about their perspective about the program as a form of evaluation.

Assessments conducted both prior and post the training and development can be used to measure the results of the intervention. Post-program surveys or interviews with participants are useful to gauge perceived outcomes and satisfaction with the program. Post-program monitoring of task and role performance will also assist with the evaluation process. The effectiveness of the training is best assessed after allowing sufficient time for participants to incorporate the developments into their job.

The trainer, coach or mentor should also be asked about the receptiveness of the participants and their developmental progress/outcomes. For training and development to be successful the employee or volunteer's motivation is critical. Motivation to learn has been related to the trainee believing that the training is relevant and therefore they are willing to exert effort in the training environment and it can influence the perseverance they demonstrate in applying skills on the job after training (Salas et al., 2012). However, it is not just openness to learning which is important for effective training and development. The training and development program and activities should be firmly positioned within the organization's strategic framework, be supported by top management, and be delivered with full awareness of cultural and situational contexts for maximum impact.

LIMITATIONS AND CONSTRAINTS TO TRAINING AND DEVELOPMENT

While the strategic human resource management literature expounds the virtues of strategic implementation of a systematic training and development process and the benefits of creating a culture that characterizes a learning organization, the reality of practice tells us a somewhat different story. Exemplary businesses exist, as evidenced in the proliferation of awards for being an 'Employer of Choice' for training support, but research suggests that a large number of organizations are less than strategic in the way they train and develop their staff (Gratton & Truss, 2003; McGraw, 2002).

Sport organizations have been found to have widely variable approaches to training and development, ranging from highly planned and strategic to completely ad hoc and reactionary (De Knop, Van Hoecke & De Bosscher, 2004; Taylor & Ho, 2005; Taylor & McGraw, 2006). In a study of 1,657 Flemish sport clubs, De Knop et al. (2004) noted that there was an inherent weakness in the strategic planning process of clubs, and training opportunities of administrators was limited. Taylor and McGraw (2006) concluded that within national and state sport organizations in Australia, the facilitation of employee development is not widely supported via formal systems of training. A further limitation to effective training and development relates to competing expectations of the various stakeholder groups. For example, Cuskelly, Taylor, Hoye and Darcy (2006: 158) found that management preferred highly formalized HRM practices, including training, do not always necessarily fit comfortably with the expectation of volunteers, 'viewing sport volunteers as an human resource tends to overlook the complexity of relationships between volunteers and CSOs'. The seemingly increasing pressure to professionalize sport organizations in terms of the qualifications and/or occupation of not just paid staff but also of volunteers is linked to quality human resources that strengthen an organization's competitive position. However, as Vos et al. (2012) caution, the drive for more efficiency and professionals in sports clubs could have unintended consequences in terms of a possible decrease in volunteers. These examples of competing expectations are derived from the different perspectives of different constituencies. Therefore, the challenge for sport organizations is to provide training and development programs that facilitate positive and motivating environments and do not unnecessarily compromise the mission and integrity of the organization, its employees and/or volunteers.

SUMMARY

Training and development are critical dimensions of a strategic approach to HRM. Attending to the learning requirements of employees and volunteers provides appropriately skilled and knowledgeable human capital that can effectively contribute to the attainment of organizational objectives. A supportive learning environment together with relevant training and development can lead to improved employee satisfaction, retention and motivation which in turn can create enhanced organizational performance.

Training refers to the acquisition of knowledge, skills and competencies as related to specific job or task requirements. Development is learning new attitudes and behaviors that will result in personal growth. Underpinning the concept of training and development is the premise of learning. The three key learning orientations, behavioral, cognitive and constructive, provide the basis on which to structure training and development initiatives. In the 'learning organization' training and development are strategically incorporated into the organization's culture as a form of learning. Employees and volunteers are encouraged and supported to learn, acquire new knowledge and skills, and disseminate this knowledge to others within the organization.

In this chapter the five steps to implementing a systematic training and development process were presented: (1) a training needs analysis is undertaken; (2) from this analysis training goals are established; (3) which are then used to inform the design of training or development programs; (4) these are consequently implemented; and (5) routinely evaluated. There is an increasing range of training and development methods that can be used to attain the organization's training goals and the employee or volunteer's career planning objectives. Effective training and development benefits the individual, other employees and volunteers and aligns with strategic directions of the organization.

DISCUSSION QUESTIONS

1   Conduct a SWOT analysis of a sport organization you are familiar with. What is the organization's vision? Where does it want to be in 3–5 years? What does this mean for its training and development needs? What training would you suggest they undertake?

2   List the different methods that can be used to deliver training and development. How do you assess which approach is the most appropriate i.e. what do you need to take into consideration?

3   Discuss the benefits and challenges for implementing a training and development program for employees and volunteers.

CHAPTER 7

Performance management

LEARNING OBJECTIVES

After reading this chapter you will be able to:

- Understand the basis of performance management
- Understand the factors that impact performance from a holistic perspective
- Outline a model of the performance management process
- Understand the benefits that may be achieved through effective performance management
- Explain potential sources of conflict in performance management at both a systemic and individual level
- Describe different performance appraisal methods and procedures
- Understand the good practice in relation to performance appraisal methods

CHAPTER OVERVIEW

Contemporary sport organizations face some major challenges in managing the performance of their staff and volunteers. Like many other organizations, sport organizations typically need to continually improve in order to survive in today's competitive world. Individual and organizational improvements in performance are key elements in continuous improvement. In order to understand how best to manage performance we first need to take a holistic view of the factors that impact upon it. We start by defining and outlining an approach to performance management that includes consideration of many parts of an organization's human resource (HR) system. Performance appraisal, a vital element of an overall performance management system, is also defined. Performance appraisal refers to the formal system that operates to set goals, monitor performance and establish consequences and improvement actions for organizational staff. The many benefits associated with effective performance management are described as well as some of the common systemic and operational problems that can occur. A sequential model of performance management is presented introducing key research findings relating to the effective management of both paid staff and volunteers in sport.

PERFORMANCE MANAGEMENT

The performance management system in organizations is a process through which managers translate, in dialogue with their staff, the strategic goals of the organization into more focused activities, behaviors and defined job outcomes for which they will be accountable. The performance management system in most organizations comprises a series of linked processes designed to elicit the highest levels of employee performance. Taking a holistic view, the process of performance management can be seen as involving a number of components including work and job design, reward structures, the selection of people to do the work, the training and development of those people as well as the formal system of management, and policies for rewarding and improving performance. From a strategic perspective the performance management system in an organization should stimulate the employees to produce high levels of discretionary effort and provide the linkage which translates the organization's broad goals into superior individual performance. In this way the performance management system in an organization is an essential component of the strategic human resource management (SHRM) approach discussed in Chapter 2 of this book and has elements of many other HR processes contained within it or linked to it.

As an example, a holistic performance management discussion might commence with a manager and staff member discussing performance improvements in the context of how work is structured and allocated between different members of a workgroup. The discussion may not only lead to further clarification of job roles for the staff member at an individual level but could also include issues around how the staff member interacts with other team members and how the team as a whole approaches their work. This in turn may lead on to the diagnosis of, say, leadership training for the individual staff member, training for the whole team and/or perhaps changes to the reward structure to reflect a more team-based approach to working. In this way a performance management process can lead to changes in individual jobs, interactions and relationships with other team members, training initiatives and the structure of rewards.

An illustration of the holistic approach to performance is provided in the article 'Scouting for the best athletes (or analysts): character vs. performance', in Box 7.1. This outlines how the Philadelphia Eagles look beyond performance on the field in selecting players and how team dynamics influence individual performance. The situation described in Box 7.1 reflects a number of aspects concerning the complex nature of stimulating performance in professional football clubs in the USA. First, the importance of selecting the right people in key roles is emphasized, a point discussed at length in Chapter 4. In particular, the importance of 'character' and 'winning attitudes' of players is stressed and, by implication, fit with other team members. Second, the critical role of the coach in working as a catalyst for team performance and getting the best performances from individual players is pointed out. Third, the importance of developing on-field leaders among the senior players is stressed. Fourth, we see the need for the managers of the clubs to manage the sometimes contradictory pressures of on-field success with shorter-term financial health of the club. Finally, the importance of intrinsic rewards as a motivational element in player performance is illustrated.

Performance appraisal, which is sometimes considered as synonymous with performance management, consists of only a subsection of the overall performance management system described above. Performance appraisal is a formal system for setting goals, assessing performance on an ongoing basis and rewarding the level of achievement while capturing all

---

BOX 7.1

Scouting for the best athletes (or analysts): character vs. performance

When the Philadelphia Eagles, a perennial contender in pro football, are checking out young prospects in advance of the annual NFL draft, they certainly look at the player's time in the 40-yard dash and contact his college coach – but the team is just as likely to talk to the guidance counselor or even the janitor at the young man's high school to see how he treated other people in his life.

That's according to Eagles owner Jeffrey Lurie, who said during a recent Wharton discussion on 'Leadership Lessons Learned from Sports' that character and on-the-field leadership qualities count for more than raw athleticism in putting together the Eagles roster. The Eagles, in building a team that has been to the playoffs six of the last seven seasons as well as the 2005 Super Bowl, use a battery of tests and evaluations in judging future draft choices that is more extensive than most Fortune 500 companies use when hiring MBAs.

The Eagles owner was joined on the panel – sponsored by the Wharton Sports Business Initiative as part of the recent 2007 Wharton Economic Summit – by several other team owners or executives with a background in sports, including Robert Castellini, CEO of the Cincinnati Reds baseball franchise. Although the wide-ranging panel touched on a number of topics, one central theme was this: What are the qualities that make someone a sports leader, especially on the playing field, and can the successful qualities of a winner in athletics be applied to the world of business?

In introducing the panel, Kenneth Shropshire, director of the Wharton Sports Business Initiative, invoked the increasingly popular science of analyzing the habits of highly successful coaches to see which of their leadership skills are useful away from the playing field. For example, championship basketball coaches Phil Jackson, Pat Riley and Mike Krzyzewski have all written books on leadership, while there is a cottage industry studying the wisdom of late football coach Vince Lombardi.

The panelists have hired or worked with some of the most accomplished names in sports, including Eagles coach Andy Reid and baseball manager Lou Piniella, now with the Cubs but a long-time friend of Castellini. Both Lurie and Castellini, in particular, described a similar model for constructing a sports team: Start with a foundation of players with personal character and a winning attitude, then hire coaches with the right kind of intelligence and the motivational skills to get the most out of them.

Lurie, in particular, quoted former Dallas Cowboy coach Jimmy Johnson, now a TV analyst, who said a successful player personnel director in the NFL is essentially 'a chemist … Football is such a team game, and so you need a mix of leaders, followers, people who will react well under stress.'

'The chemistry dynamic is very important,' agreed Gary Lieberman, president of West Side Advisors and part-owner of the New Jersey Nets basketball franchise. 'We try to think that if someone is a good guy in the locker room, so to speak, then he will do what's right for the team.'

If the general manager is a chemist, the head coach is the catalyst who makes the team perform well on the field. Lurie said that his 1999 hiring of Reid – a quarterback coach who lacked experience as a top assistant coach – was borne out of his desire to find a head coach who thought outside the traditional box and who would be an on-field innovator.

Lieberman agreed with the point. 'I was really surprised at the level of intellect' in the New Jersey Nets coaching staff, he said, adding that he expected them to be motivational 'rah-rah' guys or strict disciplinarians, but not as cerebral as they actually are. 'I would welcome the opportunity to work with them' – his coaching staff – 'in a different situation.'

Lieberman noted that the Nets have been under media and fan pressure this season to replace the current coach, Lawrence Frank, but that the owners believe the team's sometimes spotty performance has been, in part, the result of injuries and not due to a problem with Frank. 'He continues to be well-prepared, and he continues to motivate the players,' he said.

The Reds' Castellini added an important caveat to the discussion. 'Tommy Lasorda [the long-time Dodgers' manager] told me that while it's important to have chemistry in the clubhouse, if you don't have the talent, you don't win.' He also said a good manager helps to nurture two or three star players, such as a starting pitcher, as clubhouse leaders and role models. 'You pick people out to be leaders so that they can help you manage those 25 very individualistic people,' the ones who, 'let's just say, have a high opinion of themselves.'

Point guards, centerfielders

Several panelists said that while sports leadership skills are not easily learned, they can be transferred quite successfully to the business world.

Mark Fisher, founder of MBF Clearing Corp., the largest clearing firm on the New York Mercantile Exchange commodities exchange (NYMEX), told the panel that a disproportionately large number of the traders that he has hired for his firm have a background in college or professional sports. 'As a trader, I have found that the qualities that made the best traders are the ones that make the best athletes.' One reason is that athletes may have a losing day on the field just as a trader will make a bad trade, but the successful ones have the ability to move on.

A competitive nature is important, noted Fisher, who is a major supporter of youth basketball on Long Island. 'At the end of the day, you know how you did … There is no bureaucracy.' When hiring, he tends to focus on people who were in key on-the-field leadership positions – point guards in basketball or baseball centerfielders.

While there may be a lot of accountability on the playing field, there is less in the front office than one might expect. Castellini said he was surprised by the lack of any kind of evaluation system, similar to what might be found in the more traditional business world. He noted that when he arrived at the Reds' organization several years ago, the team was 29th out of 30 major league franchises in developing players through its own farm system, and that no one was deemed responsible for that failure. 'You might be paying a US$4 million bonus to sign a high school player, and so you had better be right,' Castellini said. 'And if you're not right, you ought to be held accountable.'

But that is only internally. Several of the attendees noted that the media attention a sports owner or general manager receives is comparable to just a few top superstar CEOs in other types of business. Castellini – who continues to manage Castellini Companies, a fruit and vegetable wholesaler, in addition to the Reds – said that he went to a kind of 'charm school' to learn how to deal with reporters. 'One little slip of the lip, and you are in trouble,' Castellini warned. What's more, both fans and journalists tend to have longer memories in sports than people do in the business world. One former sports owner who could attest to that is President George W. Bush, who, even after six years in the White House, still hears about the time his Texas Rangers traded away slugger Sammy Sosa back in 1989.

'Every decision that you make is really scrutinized, not just in the moment but for years to come,' noted Lieberman.

There is one other important issue that arises in professional sports as well as in business: finding a balance between the need to make a profit and the need to put a winning team on the field. As team executives such as Lurie and Castellini explained it, there is constant pressure and intense scrutiny – from both the fan base and from the hometown media – to win now, and to make short-term moves that might prove counterproductive in the long run.

'The fans want you to win, but you can't engage in a popularity contest or you will be in last place every year,' said the Eagles owner, who insisted that the best moves have tended to be the ones that were not popular with the fans. Although he didn't mention this at the Wharton event, Lurie may have been thinking of his 2004 signing of flamboyant wide receiver Terrell Owens, who was applauded in Philadelphia initially but who ripped the team apart with his antics a year later.

Owens may have been on the mind of one audience member who asked why more players didn't negotiate contacts with performance incentives, as is common with top executives in other businesses. Again, the answer was that such incentives didn't jibe with the type of winning, high-character athlete that these sports executives wanted. Said Lieberman: 'Fundamentally, players have to be motivated by more than money.'

http://knowledge.wharton.upenn.edu/article/scouting-for-the-best-athletes-or-analysts-character-vs-performance/

of these elements in a formal system. When employees and managers talk about performance management they may be referring to the appraisal system. This, however, provides a limited view of the broader performance management process. One way of thinking about the outcome of a performance appraisal discussion is to regard it as similar to a contract where the staff member and manager enter into a series of understandings about what each party is giving and what each is getting from the relationship. This involves both tangible aspects of the working relationship such as the level of measured performance and reward but also important elements of the 'psychological contract' (referred to in Chapters 5 and 8).

WHAT ARE THE BENEFITS OF PERFORMANCE MANAGEMENT?

Effective performance management systems should achieve a number of beneficial outcomes for sport organizations, as outlined below.

- Align people's behavior to achieving the organization's strategic vision and mission by translating the high-level strategic goals into individual objectives and job performance. This is often achieved by the 'cascading of objectives' down the organization from top to bottom with all managers translating and interpreting their personal goals into meaningful goals for their staff. In a performance discussion about multiple objectives a manager may help a staff member by clarifying expectations about which objectives should be given priority and by coaching the staff member in the areas of performance that need further development (see Chapter 6 on training and development).
- Align organizational and individual values by establishing clear behavioral norms for employees and volunteers. For example, a sport club which is based in the local community may promote values associated with respect for all community members. This may translate into codes of conduct for players concerning matters such as alcohol consumption in public places, dress codes on match days, racial vilification and devoting a certain percentage of time to charitable work in the community.
- Provide a fair and objective basis for rewarding the relative contributions of different staff to the organization. Thus, the performance appraisal mechanism should link to the reward system and provide financial incentives for employees to contribute high levels of discretionary effort (for more detail see Chapter 8 on rewards).
- Provide a basis for discussing the longer-term career development of staff. The performance management system also provides a framework for talented employees to be developed by identifying and preparing individuals for increased responsibilities (this is further elaborated upon in Chapter 3 on succession and talent management).
- Provide information which helps to evaluate the effectiveness of HR processes such as recruitment, induction, training and reward management. For example, in relation to training and development, performance review data might bring to light the fact that the organization is not using effective training methods (see Chapter 6).
- Provide an opportunity for managers to better understand the personal goals and concerns of staff members and volunteers.
- Provide a system of employee information so that organizations can meet minimum legal obligations concerning employment rights and responsibilities (this is addressed in further detail in Chapter 9 on employee relations).

This extensive list of potential benefits provided by performance management systems has led to a wide diversity of performance management practices and it is common for organizations to try to achieve multiple objectives with the use of one system (Armstrong & Baron, 1998). Looking at the list above, three broad objectives are in evidence. First, performance management can be a control and judgement system through which decisions are made about job responsibilities, pay and career progression. Second, performance management can be a developmental system through which decisions about training and development are taken. Third, performance management can be an information system which collects data on employee performance. While the broad nature of performance systems is a potential virtue, it can also lead to tension, particularly between judgement and motivationally orientated development processes. Sport organizations need to think carefully about their primary goal in using the system and potential unintended consequences from operating a system which tries to achieve too much. These potential problems will be discussed in a later section of this chapter.

A MODEL OF PERFORMANCE MANAGEMENT

A flow model of the performance management process is presented in Figure 7.1. Illustrative examples of the model are presented in the discussion of each stage which follows.

Stage 1

The first part of the model involves defining and agreeing on performance standards with the employee. Clearly the criteria for evaluation must first be established if these are to form the basis for the later discussion on actual performance. This part of the process can involve revisiting and, if necessary, amending the job description and defining agreed levels of performance outcomes. Many basic jobs have clearly defined task outputs and can be managed with rudimentary performance management systems as it is clear what has to be done and whether or not it is being done. For example, an office assistant in a state tennis association may be required to record, collect and dispatch mail, receipt all income, complete photocopying and printing as directed, and maintain office stationery. It is relatively straightforward to monitor the completion of these duties. In jobs where successful outcomes are more ambiguous and where employees have more discretion, outcomes cannot simply be listed as completion of a series of tasks and performance management becomes a more complex and important process. For example, the position description for a chief executive officer (CEO) of a national sporting organization designates the person in this role as responsible for the overall efficiency and effectiveness of all the organization's operations, including the management and development of all stakeholder and member relationships, and supervision of the strategic planning and marketing activities necessary to meet the organization's objectives. The position description also contains a section setting out the requirement for regular performance appraisals, against mutually established performance objectives. As the measurement of effective performance of these responsibilities is not necessarily obvious, it is critical that the objective-setting exercise is undertaken when the position is first filled, and then on a regular basis so that the CEO is clear about the measurements that will be used to judge his/her performance.

A common technique used with more complex jobs such as the CEO position noted above is to define job performance by the extent to which goals or key performance indicators are met. Developing criteria for performance appraisal and determining which aspects of a job are the most appropriate to use in measuring performance can be approached in a variety of ways. For example, research on how to measure the performance of sports coaches (MacLean, 2001) has defined performance in terms of behaviors (process and product) and designated categories relative to assessment. In this approach behavioral process factors are evidenced in job behaviors, including task and maintenance related factors. Behavioral product factors are the result of the process factors and are often quantifiable aspects measured by key performance indicators. MacLean and Chelladurai (1995) identified six

Stage 1

- Prepare/Revise individual job goals, accountabilities and relationships

- Agree with staff member on measures of performance for each accountability area
  e.g. Key performance indicators. Clarify values related to the job and behavioral
  dimensions of performance. Clarify reward expectations

Stage 2

- Remove barriers to job performance

Stage 3

- Ongoing assessment of job performance; provision of feedback

Stage 4

- Formal review of action on previous appraisal recommendations; appraisal of
  performance against goals

Stage 5

- Establish new goals; identify performance improvement action

Stage 6

- Assess future career potential; plan next career steps and individual training and
  development needs

- Implement performance improvement and career development strategies

Stage 7

- Recommend merit-based adjustments to remuneration

FIGURE 7.1 The performance management process

categories of coaching performance related to behavioral product and process factors. This scheme is outlined in Table 7.1.

In applying this framework to a golf club operations manager, we could designate task-related behavioral factors to a job-specific requirement to schedule and run club competitions, and maintenance-related process factors to issues such as liaising with corporate clients and other club personnel. The behavioral product factors for the golf operations manager may

TABLE 7.1 Measuring coaching performance		
Behavioral product factors	Team or athlete outcome measures	Personal outcome measures
	Number of competitions won	Receipt of coaching awards
	Improvement in placing over previous attempt	Upgrading of coaching qualifications
	Improvement in skill levels	Advice sought by other coaches
Behavioral process factors – task related	Direct task	Indirect task
	Application of strategies to enhance performance	Recruiting talented players
	Applying coaching knowledge	Maintaining and applying relevant statistics
	Effective communication	
Behavioral process factors – maintenance related	Administrative	Public relations
	Adherence to policies and procedures	Relationship with stakeholders
	Effective financial management	Liaison with community groups

(Source: adapted from MacLean, 2001; MacLean & Chelladurai, 1995)

relate to the number of players entered in competitions over a period of time or the amount of corporate sponsorship funding that the manager is able to secure for club competitions. Each of these factors could be assessed when undertaking a review of the golf operations manager's performance.

Defining complex, high-discretion jobs in terms of outcomes is entirely consistent with both the nature of the role and the fact that individual employees will have different approaches to achievement of set goals. Furthermore, clear and well-communicated goals provide direction to staff, encourage above the norm levels of effort and serve as a basis for appraisal feedback later in the process. The basis for effective goal setting is that goals should be specific, measurable, achievable, realistic and time bound (SMART). The more specific the goals, generally the higher the performance level, provided that the goals set are not only difficult and challenging, but also realistic. Participation in goal setting also enhances performance in that it generates increased understanding of goals, increases the likelihood of goal acceptance and increases commitment (Armstrong, 2006).

Also of relevance at this stage might be clarification of values that are important to the organization and the communication of clear expectations about these. Such values can be crucial to the identity of a sport organization and might include, for example, a commitment to a certain philosophy such as playing a sport in a particular way. To take an example from professional football in Europe, teams such as Manchester United, Real Madrid and Bayern Munich have been associated throughout their history not only with winning tournaments, but also with playing an attractive, adventurous and attacking style of football which have won them legions of fans around the world. Clearly part of the expectation of the coaching staff in such organizations is that they will continue in the club traditions which would form a component of their performance management. Many sport organizations seek to develop and maintain a high-performance culture and thus may expect employees to have a personal commitment to unconditional excellence.

Finally, during this stage there needs to be some discussion of the rewards that are to be forthcoming for performance at the desired level, especially if this is not already clear (reward is discussed in more detail in Chapter 8). A sport organization's rewards management system must outline the basis, level or rate and types of rewards available – including financial and non-financial extrinsic rewards. In general, individuals are motivated to perform to the extent that rewards are available that meet their personal needs.

Stage 2

The second stage in managing performance is to remove any barriers that may be inhibiting the performance. This may mean providing appropriate levels of resources for a position or simply providing adequate tools. In circumstances where adequate resources are not provided, employees have been found to become quickly frustrated and demotivated (Cascio, 1996). Take the case of the national program director of high-performance sport who is expected to create a world class performance environment, embracing, and supporting technical staff and personal coaches. If the director is not given the discretion to select appropriate technical staff or a sufficient budget to reward talented coaches the director may not be able to achieve the organization's goal of world class ranking.

Stage 3

The third stage in managing performance is to revisit performance on a regular basis and provide corrective feedback as required. Studies of coaching and provision of channels of feedback have conclusively shown that the feedback keeps goal-directed behavior on course and influences future performance goals by creating objectives for achieving higher levels of performance in the future (London, 2003). Providing corrective feedback is a vital stage in the development of performance. Giving feedback is an important managerial competency and the skillful manager knows how to blend positive and corrective (constructively critical) feedback, so that the outcome of the discussion remains positive and constructive.

However, the value of feedback is influenced by factors other than the skill of the manager. Two important moderators of feedback in performance management have been identified by London (2003). First, there is the individual's overall receptivity to receiving feedback. Important factors influencing receptivity are comfort with feedback, propensity to seek feedback, mindfulness with which feedback is processed, and sense of accountability to act on feedback. Second, there is the organization's feedback culture which will impact the quality of the feedback provided, the overall importance attributed to feedback by an individual, and the support available for processing feedback such as provision of coaching services.

It is important to note here that the feedback which is perceived as negative criticism has been found to have a demotivating effect on employees. In a seminal study at General Electric in the US (Meyer, Kay & French, 1965) it was found that:

- criticism had a negative effect on motivation and goal achievement;
- praise had little effect one way or the other;
- the average employee reacts defensively to criticism during the appraisal interview;
- defensiveness resulting from critical appraisal produced inferior performance;
- participation of employees in goal setting produced superior results;
- coaching by managers was most effective when done regularly.

There are two main approaches to overcoming the problems associated with the demotivating effect of negative feedback. The first involves getting feedback from multiple sources where feedback is more likely to be seen as objective and thus less of a personal attack. A version of this type of appraisal, 360-degree feedback, is discussed later in this chapter. A second approach involves giving feedback in a way which is less likely to generate a negative reaction. Research findings on the best way to give feedback are best discussed in relation to stage four of the model – the appraisal interview.

Stage 4

Stage 4 in the performance management process involves a formal review of the performance during the interval since the goal setting meeting. At the heart of this review is a conversation or appraisal interview during which the manager and employee discuss performance achieved relative to objectives. There are a number of key recommendations concerning how such interviews should be conducted, which are as follows.

1   Use a style of interview that encourages joint problem solving between the manager and staff member. This type of interview has the advantage of allowing opinions to be expressed which are less likely to be seen as judgements and is more likely to produce a mutually agreed outcome to which both parties are committed.
2   Encourage staff members to evaluate their own performance as a starting point and to find out as much as possible about how they see the situation. Research has shown that self-evaluation has the overwhelming advantage of getting staff to think about their performance and any shortcomings, which in turn leads to higher commitment to agreed improvement outcomes (Asmuß, 2008).
3   Focus on factual data wherever possible and use specific examples to illustrate optimal and sub-optimal performance. By focusing on objective data the manager can avoid being seen to make personal judgements about the character of the staff member and avoid defensive reactions to criticism of the type referred to above.
4   Use inclusive language wherever possible to depersonalize the discussion and reduce defensive behavior (e.g., 'what are we going to do about this' not 'what are you going to do about this').
5   Finally, it is recommended to hold the interviews in a private and neutral setting and allow enough time to properly deal with all the issues.

Stages 5 and 6

Stages 5 and 6 of the performance management process also most commonly occur during the performance appraisal interview. Stage 5 involves reaching consensus on any performance improvement actions that result from the review and setting new goals for the next performance period. Stage 6 involves a discussion about career planning and training stemming from Stage 5. Together these stages consist of the formal developmental component of the performance management process and are essential elements of an organization's SHRM strategy. A fuller discussion of training and development and its relationship to performance management can be found in Chapter 6.

Stage 7

The final stage of the performance management process is to determine and provide appropriate merit pay, financial bonuses or non-financial rewards, based on the formal review of performance. Rewards may be provided on a continuous (e.g., commission) or graduated (levels) scale, for individual performance or unit or organizational results. Performance-based rewards systems are described in more detail in Chapter 8.

Potential problems with performance management and appraisal systems

As performance management systems have the potential to achieve so many things, they are sometimes seen as a panacea for organizational problems that really should be resolved elsewhere. This is particularly the case when organizations too narrowly focus just on the control orientated aspects of the formal appraisal process. For example, in some sport organizations the formal performance appraisal system is used primarily to provide corrective discipline and collect data about employees that can be used to justify corrective or punitive action. The term 'performance-manage someone out of the organization' is indicative of this. While collecting data on inadequate performance is a legitimate use of a performance management system, a narrowly focused performance appraisal system used primarily for this purpose may not uncover the root of the problem or help identify its solution and may also generate negative assessments of the appraisal system. Therefore, when addressing problems with employee performance, managers should think beyond the narrow approach that is possible within the boundaries of the appraisal system. In order to improve their performance the staff may need (instead of more intensive performance appraisal):

- better tools, equipment and work methods
- more cooperation and support from co-workers or managers
- opportunities to demonstrate improvements
- a better understanding of their job-accountabilities, goals, priorities and performance measures
- new knowledge and skills (and opportunities to learn)
- incentives to improve
- a different job.

The above list of considerations illustrates the point made at the beginning of this chapter that performance management systems need to be broadly based within the sport organization, and able to diagnose fundamental causes of underperformance rather than provide mere evidence of such performance, which may be all that is captured in the appraisal process. Theoretically, performance appraisal is one of the most powerful tools that managers have to influence staff behavior, since it is the mechanism through which organizational rewards are administered. In practice, however, it can be disliked by both employees and managers equally and has the capacity to turn them into adversaries. The next section explores some of the reasons why performance appraisal can produce negative assessments and outcomes and suggests ways of avoiding these.

The first set of potential problems of poorly designed and executed performance appraisal processes can be termed systemic. As noted earlier, many appraisal systems attempt to achieve too much. There is an inherent underlying conflict between the judgmental and developmental components in the appraisal process for both managers and employees. First, managers have been found to dislike playing 'god' (McGregor, 1957) and often experience guilt about making negative judgments about others. Second, employees are unlikely to be completely open about their need for development when, as part of the same process, managers have to make judgments about their pay and promotion prospects. In order to overcome systemic conflicts such as those discussed above some sport organizations operate the judgmental and developmental components of appraisal as separate processes at different times of the year. An alternative and more radical way to overcome this problem is to use performance appraisal for only one purpose: either as a development process and part of the training and development system, or as a judgement process and part of the pay and rewards system – not both. It is also advisable to keep disciplinary and grievance issues separate from the performance management process wherever possible.

A second systemic problem might occur when there is poor integration between organizational strategy and the type of appraisal system used. For example, a sport organization might be trying to encourage team-based operating systems, but continue to evaluate and reward individual performance merit increases. Thus, football teams that reward individual players for the number of goals scored in a season need to be careful to also reward assists and other aspects of team play so as not to provide an incentive for players to pursue self-interest before that of the team. The well-known adage that 'what gets measured in an organization gets done' also needs to be considered. If the performance system is used to determine rewards it must try to fully capture all elements of performance if it is to avoid encouraging behavior only in the particular direction that is assessed.

Further systemic problems can occur if performance appraisal systems are not fully integrated into other HR systems. A common example of this concerns rewards where at the end of a complex appraisal system overall pay is capped within a narrow band due to wider cost containment initiatives in the organization. Such circumstances often lead to disaffection as the system is seen as lacking credibility by the staff and generating irrelevant workload by managers. Take for example, the Head Coach of a national volleyball association who has to manage day-to-day operation of the office, coordinate the development and maintenance of processes and procedures that ensure effective and efficient office administration, accept irregular and long working hours, and travel domestically and overseas for extended periods in return. Managing daily office operations and being away from the office for long periods of time may mean that achieving high performance across these two sometimes juxtaposed requirements may be difficult. Even if the coach is able to perform effectively, government funding limitations might mean that they receive a minimal pay increase. Therefore, in this instance the performance appraisal process should be flexible enough to deal with the issues identified above and align rewards with appropriate objectives for the coach. Additionally, there should be a clear indication of the range of salary increases, or alternative rewards, that can be provided and the level of performance required to attain these.

At the individual level between managers and employees the appraisal process may suffer from some of the same problems of subjectivity that were discussed in relation to the selection process in Chapter 4. These may include:

- 'halo' and 'horn' effects where managers are either positively or negatively over influenced by one staff member characteristic
- leniency/strictness effects – where different managers rate staff using varying standards
- recency effects whereby managers pay too much attention to a recent event rather than considering all events from the whole rating period
- central tendency whereby, when using a scale, managers will tend to mark towards the middle so as to avoid controversial decisions.

In order to minimize bias at an individual level it is recommended that managers:

- relate performance dimensions to a single activity (not groups of activities)
- avoid overall ratings
- observe job behavior regularly
- avoid ambiguous terms which can be liable to different individual interpretations (e.g., average)
- are trained to share a common frame of reference.

Notwithstanding any of these problems, performance appraisal remains not only an important part of an overall performance management system, but also a system which most modern sport organizations simply must have. Formal appraisal of performance provides the only rational basis for controlling behavior and distributing rewards and remains, when used well, a potent tool for creating meaning and higher levels of motivation for employees.

PERFORMANCE APPRAISAL METHODS

There are a range of performance appraisal methods and criteria which a sport organization can use. First, staff may be compared with each other or compared to some absolute standard. Second, performance can be measured on staff member attributes, behaviors or results. Third, staff may be measured by managers, themselves or a wider group of respondents. Different appraisal techniques combine elements of each of these approaches. Some of the more common ones are discussed in this section.

Comparative approaches vs. absolute standards

The simplest form of comparative approach uses a ranking methodology whereby staff members are numerically ranked from best to worst in relation to performance. Ranking has become popular again with many large corporate organizations adopting a forced distribution approach where employees are ranked in percentile groups around a standard statistical distribution. This technique has been widely adopted by organizations such as GE, where it is known as the 'vitality curve', in order to overcome the problems of managerial leniency and central tendency and literally force managers to make judgements about their best and worst staff. In many cases staff at the bottom end of such statistical distributions are 'managed out' of the organization on a yearly cycle and new staff are brought in to replace them. While this form of ranking has the advantage of providing a clear mechanism for distributing organizational rewards and punishments it often proves unpopular with managers and staff who feel uncomfortable with making the harsh judgements associated with such techniques.

A rating type approach is described by Lewis (2003) in the book *Moneyball*. The book is a case study of how one baseball team (the Oakland A's) used statistics on individual contributions to performance to build a successful team. Lewis provides some clear examples of how strong pressures on managers to succeed can be leveraged with a clear measure of efficiency (the number of games won divided by the team salary) to develop an effective performance management system.

The Oakland A's statistically based approach to assessing players became an exemplar of innovation and efficiency via good management. The relentless use of performance information and using such data gave the club a competitive advantage with its human capital (Lewis, 2003). Historically, baseball's conservative approach to methods of evaluating players' capacities and performance (i.e., using runs batted in [RBI] and slugging percentage) were not good predictors of team performance.

Using on-base percentage data for recruitment and strategy gave the A's a comparative advantage and this alternative criteria was not only better, but the players required to deliver it were also cheaper to bring in (Wolfe, Wright & Smart, 2006). Other teams were not using the right information, prompting Lewis to pen *Moneyball*'s first lesson: Data are not created equal.

Human resource management (HRM) must ensure that the categories within which data are collected and employees are evaluated are systematically consistent with corporate objectives. Lewis (2003) concludes that the success of performance management requires that managers whose concern for performance or financial necessity outweighs their attachment to traditional norms must overcome the tendency to overgeneralize from their own experience, or analyse recent performance rather than looking at performance in the long term. However, it should be noted here that while it is possible to isolate and measure an individual performance in professional sport, individual productivity is more difficult to isolate and measure in other sport workplaces.

In an absolute standards approach to performance appraisal the performance of an individual staff member is evaluated against specific dimensions of performance and these can be either qualitative or quantitative. These may vary from simple narrative reports to more complex rating systems of behavioral, attitudinal or results-based measures or some combination of all three. Rating systems comprise probably the most common types of appraisal and typically use a form in which the rater, usually the immediate manager, responds with a numerical score against a particular item. In this way an overall score can be derived and strengths and weaknesses are highlighted for the performance discussion. Systems using attributes and behaviors commonly measure items such as those illustrated in Figure 7.2.

Using the items in the rating scale, indicate your assessment of performance for each dimension by selecting the appropriate rating						
Performance item	Rating	Outstanding 5	Above standard 4	At standard 3	Below standard 2	Poor 1
Knowledge						
Communication						
Management Skill						
Teamwork						
Initiative						
Interpersonal Skill						
Creativity						
Problem Solving						
Willingness to accept responsibility						

FIGURE 7.2 Sample performance ratings scale combining attributes and behaviors

Who is involved in appraising performance?

Absolute standards-based systems may involve ratings by different people in the sport organization. The traditional method is appraisal by the immediate manager in the organization combined with an element of self-appraisal. Alternative approaches may use other respondents such as team members, peers in other parts of the organization, customers and sometimes subordinates. The use of multiple respondents from different parts of the organization is referred to as 360-degree feedback and is designed to eliminate subjectivity by aggregating multiple responses. These systems can provide the person being appraised with an authentic and powerful insight into how they are perceived by various organizational stakeholders and can provide a good foundation for development. However, they should be implemented mainly to assist with employee development rather than rewards and should be maintained with appropriate support mechanisms, such as follow-up coaching, for the person being appraised. Further, these assessments should be avoided in environments where they can be abused due to excessive peer rivalry or when radical changes such as downsizing are occurring.

Management by objectives

Most forms of managerial appraisal usually combine some component of management by objectives (MBO) which has existed in some form or other since the 1950s. MBO commences with the formulation of the sport organization's strategic objectives by the most senior managers, usually the Executive Committee. These managers then formulate goals with their direct subordinates and the process is repeated at each successive level down the organization. The MBO system consists of four steps: goal setting, delegating, ongoing feedback and overall evaluation. As strategic goals are cascaded down the organization they are contextualized at each step for individual managers. Although the system is inherently top down in character, MBO emphasizes joint determination of actual objectives followed by joint evaluation of performance to allow situational variability and contextual limitations to be built into the system.

Research on the effectiveness of MBO shows that it usually increases productivity (Rodgers & Hunter, 1991), although care must be taken to avoid some well-known problems. First, MBO can lead to breakdowns in interpersonal and inter-group cooperation if groups and individuals set their goals without reference to the goals of others. This problem is often overcome by having liaison meetings between the various parts of the organization that need to coordinate their activities to ensure goal congruence and having high levels of cooperation built into the goals for each section. Second, comparative assessment of different staff can be difficult with MBO since each staff member is working on unique goals. This problem is typically overcome by combining an MBO system with some degree of attribute or behavioral rating in a hybrid system. Such a hybrid also has the benefit of ensuring that the behavioral standards are maintained and MBO systems do not degenerate into systems where goal achievement is the only thing that matters.

Performance management and appraisal alternatives

From the brief description of common appraisal methods in this section we can see that sport organizations have alternatives from which to choose when building a performance management system. There is no system which is necessarily better than others in all circumstances. The best system at any given time will be contingent on what an organization considers the most important goal to achieve through the operation of the performance management system. Emphasizing different criteria might yield a different system. Is the main focus developmental or evaluative? Should the system be economical to introduce and operate or error free? Is it more important to emphasize strategic goals or behavior and values? What is the right balance between a simple scheme which has user acceptance and a complex scheme which captures all of the information that the organization requires?

Baruch, Wheeler and Zhao's (2004) research into the Shanghai Sports Technical Institute (SSTI) performance management system provides an interesting case to illustrate some of these contingencies. In 1985 the Chinese government attempted to develop an incentive reward system to motivate professional sports players, resulting in schemes linking pay to performance which have now become widespread in Chinese professional sports. (See Chapter 8 for a review of the nature and motivational aspects of reward systems.) The SSTI developed a scheme that aimed to motivate sports players, deliver a positive message about performance expectations, focus attention and drive on key performance issues, differentiate rewards to sports players according to their competence and contribution, reinforce a culture of high levels of performance, innovation, quality and teamwork, and link pay to team performance (Baruch et al., 2004).

The researchers found that when pay had high valence, with clearly established links to well-defined goals and objectives, improvements in performance were likely to be the result. Also, clearly established individual performance standards were highly related to improvements in individual performance levels, but negatively related to team performance. Further, clearly defined team performance standards were related to team performance, but not to individual improvements in performance. This indicates that organizations need to determine carefully whether individual or team performance is the most critical, so that the appropriate emphasis on establishing clear individual or team goals can be established.

For competitive professional sports, core values and objectives relate to the need for continuing short-term individual and team performance. A reward structure that establishes performance goals with clearly communicated links between performance and rewards would be consistent with these core values. The nature of competitive professional sports, with an emphasis on personal abilities, objective measures of performance, and an emphasis on continuing short-term performance is particularly suited to a performance-related system of rewards (Baruch et al., 2004).

Incentive-based systems have been found to be a useful tool for competitive professional sports in the USA. Becker and Huselid (1992) examined the effects of the tournament system with racing drivers. They found that large prize differentials between those finishing at the top compared to those finishing lower had incentive effects on individual performance. They also reported that such a spread in the size and availability of prizes could encourage dysfunctional behavior, some of which could be reckless and potentially harmful, in an attempt to claim the prize.

For volunteers in sport organizations, performance management has become an increasingly important area. Research by Cuskelly et al. (2006) in community sport organizations found that formal practices related to the performance management of volunteers were not commonly used. This is not surprising given that these sport organizations are largely run by volunteers. Thus, one set of volunteers would need to be monitoring, providing feedback and addressing the performance problems of other volunteers. Formalizing performance management may also weaken such an organization's ability to meet the social needs of the volunteers and may increase the level of bureaucracy and perception of compliance control, thus likely detracting from the volunteer experience (Seippel, 2002). By contrast, interviews with community sport volunteers (Taylor, Darcy, Hoye & Cuskelly, 2006) revealed that many volunteers desired feedback on their performance and clearer guidance about the organization's expectations of them. This suggests that while community sport volunteers should not be treated in the same way as employees, many would appreciate relevant performance appraisals.

Notwithstanding the need to build a performance system that relates specifically to the objectives and characteristics of individual organizations, certain key points emerge from studies of effective performance management systems. These include the need for the following.

- Top management commitment to performance management.
- Use of multiple raters to reduce subjectivity.
- A self-assessment component to increase employee engagement.
- Compatibility between job design and appraisal method.

- A system tailored to organizational strategies, culture, tasks and workforce.
- A structured process of performance appraisal to assist managers.
- Clear performance measures.
- Ongoing feedback during the performance cycle.
- Recognition of organizational obstacles to effective performance.

SUMMARY

This chapter has provided an overview of performance management and performance appraisal. Managing staff for the highest levels of performance requires a broad approach involving concerted action in many HR systems including those relating to recruitment and selection, the analysis and design of jobs, training and development and rewards. Performance appraisal has been defined as an important component of performance management that deals with the formal system of goal setting and review and consequent action to influence behavior in the desired direction. The benefits of effective performance management have been outlined as well as some of the more common systemic and operational problems. A stage model of performance management has been presented as well as key research findings relating to the effective management of both paid staff and volunteers in sport.

DISCUSSION QUESTIONS

1 What are some of the key differences between performance management and performance appraisal? Discuss any experiences that you have had of either.

2 What are some of the benefits that can be expected from a well-developed performance management system? How might they help a staff member? A manager? The organization?

3 Explain the terms judgemental and developmental in relation to performance appraisal. Why might these two processes be in tension with each other?

4 Explain some of the things a manager should and should not do when giving feedback to an employee.

5 Think of your favorite sports team. How do they manage the performance of their playing squad? What are the best and worst features of the performance management system? What would you change if you were the manager?

6 Design a performance management system, including a detailed performance appraisal process (what is assessed, by whom and how), for each of the following positions:
   a retail staff at a sporting goods store
   b athletic therapists in a sports medicine clinic
   c head coach of a national swim team
   d supervising manager of fitness club employees.

CHAPTER 8

Motivation and rewards management in sport organizations

LEARNING OBJECTIVES

After reading this chapter you will be able to:

- Explain the role of rewards in employee and volunteer motivation
- Describe different types of intrinsic and extrinsic rewards
- Describe the components of a financial compensation plan
- Recognize job design as part of a rewards management system
- Understand the importance of volunteer recognition

CHAPTER OVERVIEW

The purpose of rewards management is to attract, motivate and retain valuable employees and volunteers. Reward strategies should support an organization's corporate agenda and its human resource plan in order to ensure their success. What gets rewarded will be the focus of employees' attention in the workplace, therefore it should be consistent with what an organization is trying to accomplish and how. A basic understanding of human motivation will help in the selection and design of an effective rewards management system. The first part of this chapter reviews several theories that explain motivation in general and in the workplace in particular. The second part of this chapter looks at rewards management, beginning with a review of the different types of rewards that can be made available. The focus is on more than financial compensation for work, although that is a large and critical part of rewards management. Rather, consideration is given to the place of intrinsic rewards as well as extrinsic financial and non-financial rewards in strategic human resource management. This chapter reviews the components of a compensation plan, including pay structure and benefits, as well as considering job design and volunteer recognition as important elements of a sport organization's overall rewards management system.

THEORIES OF MOTIVATION

Motivation is defined as the 'inner desire to make an effort' (Mitchell & Daniels, 2003: 226). It is not the effort or behavior itself; rather, motivation is a psychological state that describes one's drive to engage in a particular behavior. This inner drive is believed to be critical to individual performance in an organization. It is motivation that may distinguish the behavior of two individuals who have similar skill sets – for example, if an organization has two volunteers with the same abilities, greater effort can be expected from the one who has a stronger inner desire to make a difference. Motivation to exert effort is further characterized by the direction of that intended effort (what), the intensity (how hard) and persistence (how long). Given that, it is important to understand what factors affect an individual's inner drive. Sport organizations should be concerned with what will motivate someone to accept a job, to exert effort and to remain with the organization.

People are motivated to fulfil unmet needs. They work because they need money, they enjoy social interaction, feel good about helping or serving others, or want to challenge themselves. If an individual determines that a particular job can help them satisfy any number of needs, he or she will be motivated to apply for that job and accept the job if it is offered. Furthermore, if the individual perceives that certain behaviors on the job (e.g., doing what is expected, performing quality work, leading a group, going above and beyond what is asked) will result in rewards that will help satisfy certain needs, he or she will be motivated to engage in those behaviors. The strength of an individual's need (e.g., for money, for recognition, personal growth) will determine the strength of his or her desire to exert effort in a given direction for a given period of time. Of course, the desire to exert effort may not be translated into behavior or performance. Even skilled and motivated workers may encounter conditions beyond their control that will impede their work – for example, budget restrictions that do not permit sport program ideas to be put into practice, delayed arrival of sports equipment for instructional activities, or the lack of motivation or ability of other workgroup members.

Content or need theories

It is helpful if an organization can understand what individuals' particular needs are, and thus provide opportunities (rewards) to satisfy those needs so that individuals are motivated to join, work hard for, and remain with, the organization. Content theories of motivation attempt to explain *what* motivates individuals. Three classic theories are examined here: Maslow's hierarchy of needs theory, Herzberg's motivator–hygiene theory and McClelland's three needs theory.

An early and seminal framework is Abraham Maslow's (1943) hierarchy of needs theory. This theory contends that there are five progressive levels of needs that every human experiences, as follows.

1 Physiological needs (e.g., food, shelter, clothing).
2 Safety needs (e.g., security, stability, health).
3 Belongingness needs (e.g., affection, acceptance, friendship).
4 Esteem needs (e.g., self-esteem, confidence, respect by others).
5 Self-actualization (e.g., personal growth, morality).

The first three levels comprise lower order or basic human needs – that is, the need for food and water, for health and safety, and for social interaction. The last two levels are regarded as higher order needs that reflect an individual's need for growth beyond those basic needs – that is, the need to feel valued and to develop to one's potential. Maslow's theory contends that a person may have unmet needs at all five levels; however, one of the levels will be predominant at a given point of time and will thus determine the primary direction of that person's efforts. For example, if an individual does not have the resources to acquire food and shelter, he or she will be driven to find a job with adequate compensation to satisfy that basic need. The theory also argues that there is a satisfaction-progression process, such that once needs are met at one level, the individual's predominant driving need will then be at the next level. An individual can remain at the top level of self-actualization, unless a lower level need becomes predominant (e.g., because of job loss, personal bankruptcy, some critical incident that has compromised one's self-esteem or confidence). For example, a recent sport management graduate may be motivated to find a decent-paying, secure job where he feels he belongs and will be respected for what he can contribute. Maslow's theory would argue that one of those needs will be predominant, perhaps in this case a need to pay the bills, and will largely dictate the kind of job the individual will look for and ultimately accept. Once the recent graduate has secured a job with adequate compensation and his basic physiological needs are being met, he will likely evaluate whether there is sufficient security in the job to meet his subsequent need for a stable environment. If this need is met, then the individual is likely to stay and consider whether his need for a sense of belongingness can be met and so on. If the recent graduate determines that there is not sufficient security in his new job to meet his need for stability, then he is likely to try and secure an adequate paying job elsewhere.

Maslow's theory directs our attention to the concept of levels of human needs, and the notion that one level of needs will be predominant and dictate inner drive at a given point in time. However, critics argue that human needs are more dynamic and complex than Maslow's hierarchical levels allow, and that the model is too inflexible to adequately explain motivation, particularly in the workplace (McShane & Steen, 2012). Nonetheless, the theory provides a solid foundation for subsequent need theories.

Frederick Herzberg's (1968) motivator–hygiene theory presumes that only higher order needs will be motivating in the workplace, thus inciting effort there. His theory is derived from research on workers who were asked to describe when they were most satisfied (i.e., their needs were being met) and most dissatisfied (i.e., their needs were not being met). Herzberg found that the workers tended to describe aspects of the job itself (work content) when talking about satisfaction – for example, having responsibility on the job, achievement, recognition and personal growth. He subsequently argued that only those things associated with satisfaction could be motivating and these he called motivators. In contrast, Herzberg found that the workers in his sample tended to describe aspects of the workplace (work context) when talking about dissatisfaction – for example, company policies, relationship with supervisor and pay. He labeled these hygienes, and argued that individuals will not be motivated by these factors; rather, they are necessary elements in the workplace to keep the organization running and to ensure employees are not dissatisfied. The motivators tend to align with Maslow's higher order needs, while the hygienes tend to align with the lower order needs in his theory.

Herzberg's findings and conclusions were not definitive such that some of the hygiene factors were reported to contribute to satisfaction (e.g., pay) and could therefore presumably be motivating, while some of the motivators were reported to contribute to dissatisfaction (e.g., recognition). Particularly noteworthy to this chapter is the contention that pay is primarily a hygiene factor and thus, by definition, cannot be motivating. In fact, pay is a source of satisfaction, and thus motivating, when it is perceived as a form of recognition for achievement (Milkovich, Newman & Gerhart, 2011). The implication of this theory is that management must be concerned with improving hygiene factors in order to avoid employee dissatisfaction – for example, by providing adequate and fair salary and wages, and job security, and ensuring effective supervision. However, to increase motivation management must focus on providing opportunities for employee's achievement, recognition and growth. These opportunities can be provided through job design that focuses on maximizing the motivating potential of a job (see Chapter 3 and below for a fuller description of job design). As an example, staff at a sport facility may expect to receive decent pay with good benefits and work in a safe environment. According to Herzberg's theory, these factors alone will not be sufficient to motivate staff to exert extra effort in the workplace (although, according to Maslow's theory, they may attract someone with predominant lower order needs to consider working there). Rather, it is the responsibility in their jobs, the opportunity to achieve something, to be recognized for it, and to develop personally and professionally, that will incite staff to give greater effort. It is the work itself, rather than the workplace, that is the source of motivation.

A final content theory to consider is David McClelland's (1961) three need theory. This theory argues that individuals have secondary needs in addition to their primary or basic needs for such things as shelter and security. These secondary needs are learned and reinforced over time rather than being instinctive. This notion has important implications for organizations to try to cultivate or at least reinforce certain needs in employees that support corporate strategy. McClelland contends that secondary needs for achievement, power and affiliation can help to explain what motivates employees beyond financial compensation or security in the workplace.

- *Need for achievement*: a desire to accomplish reasonably challenging performance goals, be successful in competitive situations, assume personal responsibility for work (rather than delegating it to others), and receive clear feedback and recognition for success.
- *Need for power*: a desire to control one's environment, including people and material resources. Individuals with a high *socialized power* need to seek power to help others, either in the workplace or in society in general. Those with a strong *personal power* need seek control over their environment in order to benefit themselves.
- *Need for affiliation*: a desire to gain approval from others by catering to their wishes and expectations, and avoid conflict and confrontation, and projecting a favorable image of oneself. People with a strong need for affiliation want to form positive relationships, even if this results in lower job performance.

(McShane & Steen, 2012)

McClelland's theory argues that individuals may have some need for achievement, power and affiliation; however, one of these needs will be predominant. Further, an individual will be motivated by the opportunity to satisfy that predominant need – for example, by leading a group (need for socialized or personal power), accomplishing challenging tasks (need for achievement) or developing positive relationships (need for affiliation). Again, it is important for a manager/supervisor to try to recognize an individual's predominant need and provide an opportunity for it to be met – by providing leadership opportunities, challenging but attainable goals or opportunities to work with others – as this is what will motivate an individual in the workplace. It is equally important, though, for a manager to guide the direction of an individual's efforts; thus, opportunities for achievement, power or affiliation should be consistent with the organization's overall strategic plan. The strength of a person's need for achievement, power or affiliation will determine the intensity with which he or she pursues and engages in behavior that can help to satisfy that need.

Consider Box 8.1, which outlines the case of Ellen Anderson and her decision whether to continue volunteering with the local cycling club or take the offer to move to the state cycling association.

BOX 8.1

Will she stay or will she go?

Ellen Anderson was a volunteer with a local competitive cycling club for eight years. She had served in various positions on the club's board of directors, including Vice President for the last three years. The volunteer board of the local cycling club saw itself as a social group as much as a decision-making body, and the directors had been friends for many years. This atmosphere certainly contributed to the continuity and cohesion among the directors.

In her role as Vice President, Ellen had responsibility for communicating between the club head coach and the board. This involved keeping the board up to date on what the coach was doing with the training and competition program, and bringing the coach's budget requests to the board. Ellen had a good rapport with the coach and the board. The board wanted Ellen to move into the President's position for a three-year term. The President was essentially responsible for chairing meetings and determining the decisions of the board with regard to any issues that arose (e.g., fundraising, budgeting, hiring coaches). While Ellen appreciated the importance of a board whose members got along well, she found it frustrating that they often spent more time chatting than working. She wondered if she could make a difference in the position of club President.

At around the same time, the state cycling association (located in the same city as the local club where Ellen was volunteering) contacted Ellen to invite her to assume a position on its volunteer board of directors. Each director had responsibility for managing a particular portfolio and subcommittee (e.g., marketing, state race series, junior development). Each director was also responsible for overseeing a particular geographic region of the state. The board would meet every two months to receive reports from the various directors and their respective subcommittees.

Ellen knew she had to make a decision between staying with the local cycling club, with which she had been involved for some time, or moving to the state cycling association where she felt she could make a real difference in the cycling world.

For discussion

Use McClelland's three need theory to describe Ellen's motivation to remain with the local cycling club vs. her motivation to become involved in the state cycling association. What needs could be met in each organization? Where do you think she ended up and why?

This discussion of content theories presumes that individuals are motivated by unmet needs. Punnett (2009) noted that needs, and thus the motivating effect of particular rewards, may be very different in a cross-national context. This has implications for SHRM in multinational corporations such as Nike, Adidas and IMG where managers need to be aware that what is generally valued in one national culture or society may be of less importance in another – for example, financial versus intrinsic rewards, individual versus group rewards, and private versus public recognition. Nonetheless, the notion of motivation based on unmet needs is universal (Punnett, 2009), and the content theories imply that, to increase work motivation, the organization should provide a variety of jobs and rewards that can be matched with members' needs (McShane & Steen, 2012). While these theories help to explain *what* motivates individuals, they do not elaborate on the mechanisms by which individuals determine whether to exert effort, in what direction or for how long. Process theories attempt to provide further insight into these issues.

Process theories

While content theories help to explain *what* motivates individuals, process theories help to explain *how* they are motivated – that is, the cognitive process that individuals go through that explains how a felt need can result in certain behavior. There are a number of motivation process theories; however, this chapter will focus on two classic theories that have direct implications for rewards management: equity theory and expectancy theory.

Equity theory extends the content theories of motivation by proposing that individuals will be motivated, not just by a given reward, but by whether they perceive the reward situation to be equitable and fair. Specifically, equity theory contends that individuals will evaluate a given reward according to whether they feel it is proportionate with their own efforts (Jaques, 1961) and whether it is equitable to the efforts and rewards of others (Adams, 1965). According to Adams' classic model, 'people will evaluate the fairness of their situation in an organization based on a comparison of the ratio of their own inputs and outcomes with some referent's ratio of inputs and outcomes' (Mitchell & Daniels,

2003: 242). When the ratios are unequal then individuals are motivated or driven by a need to rectify the perceived inequity by: (1) modifying their own input (effort) to outcome (rewards) ratio; (2) changing their referent other and focusing instead on another person's ratio of inputs and outcomes; (3) distorting their perceptions; or (4) quitting (Mitchell & Daniels, 2003). Research indicates that the effect of lowered effort to correct negative equity (i.e., when an individual feels under-rewarded in comparison to others) is felt more in an organization than any increased effort to correct positive equity (i.e., when an individual feels over-rewarded in comparison to others) (Mitchell & Daniels, 2003). Thus, organizations should be aware of the risks associated with under-rewarding staff and volunteers.

A telling example of equity theory to explain individual behavior is the situation with professional athletes' salaries. It may be difficult to comprehend why a player (or his agent) will hold out for another 5 per cent of a multi-million dollar contract, particularly if that player has publicly indicated his desire to stay in a particular city and play with the team there (see Box 8.2, which gives the example of National Hockey League (NHL) player Ryan Smyth). Does that individual really have a need for a further 5 per cent in salary? Equity theory may be able to help explain this situation and others like it. The player (or his agent) is likely not willing to 'settle' for less, or even the same, as what is being paid to players he (or his agent) consider to be of equal or lesser ability. The individual will be motivated to reduce any perceived inequity (i.e., under-reward) – in this case, moving to a different organization where he perceives he will be rewarded more fairly.

BOX 8.2

A matter of equity in professional sport salaries

In February 2007, NHL player Ryan Smyth was traded from his beloved Edmonton Oilers to the New York Islanders. 'Captain Canada', as he was known, grew up in Banff, Alberta only a few hours from Edmonton. He was drafted in 1994 and played all 12 years of his professional career to that point with the Edmonton Oilers, a team he had idolized as a child. The Oilers star had reportedly sought a five-year deal from Edmonton worth US$5.5 million a season, but it could not be arranged. Smyth denied reports that he and the Oilers split because of a mere difference of US$100,000 per season. His agent, Don Meehan, claimed that he and the Oilers tried to find some common financial ground but could not make that happen. According to Meehan, 'both sides compromised throughout this process, but not to the degree where we both felt comfortable that we could come to a deal' (cbc.ca/sports). Smyth shed tears during a press conference at the Edmonton airport as he was leaving town to head to New York.

With information from Wikipedia.com,
ESPN.com and cbc.ca/sports, retrieved on 15 March 2007

On a smaller scale financially, one research study revealed that 90 per cent of administrators in the professional sport, fitness and parks and recreation sectors used external referents when considering how satisfied they were with their pay (Smucker & Kent, 2004a, 2004b). The majority of those (73 per cent) made comparisons with individuals working in other organizations in the same field, followed by comparisons with others in their own organization (62 per cent), and past jobs (47 per cent). The authors suggested that this 'market' comparison may explain the tendency of employees in the sport industry to be neutral or dissatisfied with their level of pay, particularly when making comparisons with those who are in fact in a more favorable position. Equity theory appears to provide a useful explanation of individual's motivation with regard to given rewards. Sport organizations should recognize that staff and volunteers are likely to rationalize whether the available rewards are worth their perceived effort.

Expectancy theory is another approach that describes the cognitive process individuals go through when determining whether to exert effort. Expectancy theory, which originated with Vroom (1964), assumes that individuals are rational beings who think about possible outcomes before they engage in behavior: 'Can I do this? And, if I do this, what will I get out of it, and do I care?' Rewards play a key role in the model as they are the potential outcomes of behavior – 'What will I get out of it?' A key aspect of the model, and a key factor in effort, is the intrinsic value of the reward to the individual. The motivation to exert effort is a function of an individual's perception that, if he or she engages in a particular behavior (e.g., takes a job, performs one's tasks at a minimum level or beyond) it will be acceptable and rewarded, and that those rewards will be of personal value. The content theories described earlier help explain what may be valued in the organization. If any part of this cognitive process is compromised, then motivation and hence effort will be compromised. For example, if an individual feels she cannot do what is expected in a job and so will not be rewarded, her motivation is diminished; if she feels she can do a job and will be rewarded but does not value the reward, then her motivation is compromised. If an individual feels he can do what is expected in a job but will not be rewarded, then his motivation is diminished; similarly, if the individual feels he cannot do what is expected but he will be rewarded anyway, motivation to exert effort is diminished, because he will be rewarded regardless of his performance.

A key tenet of expectancy theory is that rewards must be tied to behavior or performance for there to be motivation. It assumes that individuals are most motivated if they know they will be rewarded for their work; motivation is unaffected, or is diminished, if the individuals know they will be rewarded just for showing up. Another key tenet is that rewards must be valued. It is unlikely that financial rewards would be seen as anything but positive; however, non-financial rewards may have different value to different individuals. For example, the outcome of acceptable task performance by an individual may be a promotion to leader of a workgroup (think back to Box 8.1 – the example of Ellen Anderson and her involvement in the local cycling club). Even though one has done very well at a given job, he or she may not want to be – in fact may fear being – the leader (although this did not seem to be the case for Ellen). According to expectancy theory, if the outcome of expending effort and doing acceptable work is being asked to take on a leadership role, the individual may be disinclined to expend the effort in the first place and avoid the perceived risk of being seen as a leader. The personal value of a particular outcome or reward is a direct function of an individual's needs. Thus, a person who perceives he can do an acceptable job and receive valued rewards in return (e.g., a commission on sales), will likely have a greater force of effort to engage in the behavior. An organization can use rewards to strengthen an individual's motivation or force of effort by providing valued rewards in return for acceptable performance that the individual feels he or she can accomplish.

Content and process theories of motivation help to explain what motivates employees and volunteers in the workplace, and the thought process they go through in determining whether to engage in a particular behavior. Organizational rewards are a critical component of individual motivation as they are a means by which unmet needs can be satisfied, and thus a basis of individual motivation to exert effort. The next section discusses the rewards management system, beginning with a description of different types of rewards in the workplace, followed by a review of the compensation plan, the role of job design in managing rewards, and volunteer recognition and rewards.

TYPES OF REWARDS

Rewards are the 'return' individuals receive for doing the work of an organization. While rewards tend to have a positive connotation, we cannot assume that various types of rewards an organization offers carry the same value for all staff and volunteers. This in itself may be the most challenging part of rewards management; providing rewards that are valued enough by staff and volunteers that they are attracted to join the organization, motivated to put in a good effort there and committed to staying. As noted above, rewards are valued to the extent that they help an individual to meet a felt need (e.g., need for financial security, need for social interaction, need for personal challenge), and are seen to be fair (i.e., adequate and equitable compensation for the work that is done). The role of intrinsic as well as extrinsic financial and non-financial rewards in the total rewards management system is considered here.

Individuals may receive both intrinsic and extrinsic rewards in the workplace. Intrinsic rewards are those that an individual receives directly as a result of performing his or her job – for example, a sense of achievement, feeling of competency or personal growth. Again, these may hold different value to different individuals, depending on their needs. Intrinsic rewards, by definition, are not something that can be given to staff or volunteers. Rather, intrinsic rewards presume that there can be value in the task itself and, thus, the organization can structure the workplace (e.g., job design) so that the individual has a greater chance of experiencing these rewards. Intrinsic rewards are particularly critical for volunteer management, as extrinsic financial rewards are not, by definition, part of the compensation volunteers may expect to receive. The role of rewards in volunteer recognition is discussed below.

Extrinsic rewards can be distinguished as financial or non-financial. Direct financial rewards include salary or wages, incentives or bonuses, and cost-of-living adjustments that the individual can use at his or her discretion. In contrast, indirect financial rewards are employee benefits (e.g., dental plan, pension contributions, life insurance, paid vacation) that have a monetary value that can be accessed only through the use of these benefits. Indirect financial rewards also include benefits in the form of reimbursement for expenses (e.g., car allowance, skills upgrading). Some individuals may see this form of compensation as a perk of the job and a very attractive component of the compensation package, depending on the value they attach to it. The organization, on the other hand, can use these benefits as a way to facilitate the work it wants to have done. Although volunteers typically do not receive direct financial compensation, they too may receive indirect financial rewards in the form of reimbursement for expenses (e.g., travel, telephone) or costs of training courses, conferences or seminars.

Non-financial rewards are things provided by an organization that do not have specific monetary value to the individual, but may be highly valued nonetheless. Examples range from a pat on the back for a job well done, to a key to the executive washroom or promotion to group leader (with no additional financial compensation). In the sport setting, it may be common, and fairly easy, to provide benefits such as complimentary tickets to sporting events or team merchandise. Non-financial rewards are an important means of recognizing the effort and contributions of volunteers. These can range from an informal or formal thank you, to more material rewards such as team clothing or trips to national and international competitions. Volunteers are unlikely to cite these non-financial rewards as a reason for being involved, although some are likely to value the recognition that accompanies them.

It can be expected that the various financial and non-financial rewards that are made available will have different worth to recipients, and as such it is important for the organization to understand what rewards are valued. Providing rewards that are not valued can be expected to have little impact on motivation. Furthermore, linking valued rewards with effort and performance can be expected to motivate employees to exert effort and perform at a higher level, yet providing rewards that are not commensurate with one's perceived effort can be expected to detract from work motivation.

THE FINANCIAL COMPENSATION PLAN

Financial compensation is one part of the total rewards management system. Direct financial compensation includes the base pay structure, incentives or merit pay and cost-of-living adjustments. Indirect financial compensation comprises employee services and benefits, such as paid vacation, medical and dental insurance, and pension contributions. In designing a compensation plan, it is important to determine the objectives of that plan; in other words, what does the organization want to pay for? What does it want to reward? This should be consistent with its corporate strategy and human resource plan. For example, the objectives of a sport organization's compensation plan may be to facilitate organizational efficiency and effectiveness by cost effectively attracting and retaining competent employees, as well as rewarding their contributions and performance (Milkovich et al., 2011). These objectives have several implications for the basis upon which pay and incentives will be awarded, which are considered below.

Pay structure

Milkovich et al. (2011: 69) define pay structure as 'the array of pay rates for different work or skills within a single organization. The *number of levels*, the *differentials* and the *criteria* used to determine those differences describe the structure' (italics in original). Three principles guide the establishment of a pay structure: internal alignment or equity, the external market and employee contribution (Milkovich et al., 2011). The importance of perceived equity to employee motivation was described earlier. Similarly, internal equity in determining pay structure refers to the principles of: (1) comparable pay for comparable content of work; (2) comparable skills that are required; and (3) comparable contribution of the work or skills to the objectives of an organization. Internal equity calls for consistency within the organization.

The external market principle refers to positioning an organization's pay structure, indeed its overall compensation plan, relative to what competitors are paying their staff. For example, pay levels may be set higher in order to attract and retain the best applicants. Alternatively, pay levels may be set lower; however, better benefits or greater job security may be offered relative to the competition. Consider Boxes 8.3 and 8.4, the cases of the YMCA (USA) and Sport Chalet, which promote their employee benefits to potential recruits.

BOX 8.3

YMCA employee benefits

Believing that people deserve the best, YMCAs offer competitive wage and benefit packages. Each YMCA is unique in its benefits offered, but most offer all or a combination of the following.

- Health and dental insurance.
- Disability and life insurance.
- Funded retirement plan.
- Flexible work schedule.
- Subsidized childcare.
- Free YMCA membership.
- Tuition reimbursement.
- Discounted programme fees.
- Time-off benefits (vacation, sick days and holidays).

YMCA, 2012

BOX 8.4

Employee benefits at Sport Chalet

Sport Chalet is a specialty sporting goods store with outlets in southwest USA. It offers both traditional and specialty merchandise and services for sport enthusiasts in such activities as rock climbing, hiking, cycling, skiing and dive/SCUBA. It claims that, 'At Sport Chalet, we are end users of the products we sell and believe in the services we offer.' In line with that, benefits for store-level teams (sales staff) include:

- competitive salary
- generous employee discount
- selling incentives
- flexible schedules for students
- fun, hands-on comprehensive training
- discounted scuba lessons
- free or discounted ski lift tickets
- free equipment rentals
- 'extreme discounts' from vendors.

Full-time employees are offered paid vacation, company-sponsored life insurance, adventure leave and a diverse benefits package with medical, dental and vision. Salaried management teams are also eligible for quarterly incentives.

Sport Chalet, 2014a, 2014b

Where actual pay levels are set will depend on the need to control labor costs; however, the external market principle directs management to establish a competitive (and equitable) compensation package in order to attract and retain competent staff.

The principle of employee contribution refers to the relative emphasis in a pay structure on compensation by: (1) job level; (2) skills; (3) seniority; or (4) performance – or some combination. Again, it is important to remember that what is rewarded will be the focus of employees' attention. We consider these four bases of financial compensation in more detail below.

With a job-based reward system, the pay structure is determined according to the type of work and its value to the organization. Criteria for determining the levels of pay include task difficulty, responsibility for supervising others and decision-making responsibility (McKenna & Beech, 2002). For example, it is likely that, among sport facility staff, the marketing director will be paid more than the sales staff, who will be paid more than the ticket takers at an event. The marketing director's position has more responsibility than staff at the lower levels, and involves more challenging tasks. The same may be said for sales staff in comparison to ticket takers. In a job-based reward system, compensation is for the position rather than the individual and what he or she accomplishes or their worth to the organization. What is involved in a job can be known from a description of the duties and responsibilities, as determined through job analysis (see Chapter 3). With this type of reward system individuals doing the same type of work with the same requirements, get the same level of pay, regardless of performance. This system is consistent with the principle of internal equity; however, alone it is not likely to foster motivation for employees to work any harder than what is necessary to keep their job, as rewards are linked to the job rather than the individual's behavior or performance.

With a skills-based reward system, the pay structure is determined according to the skills and qualifications required for the job – for example, a certain level of education, skills, years of experience or certification (McKenna & Beech, 2002). It is not unusual for job- and skills-based rewards to be closely linked. That is, particular skills are required for a given level of job. However, one purpose of the skills-based system is to encourage employees to upgrade their skills and qualifications, with the assumption that it will pay off for the organization to have more highly skilled workers. This rewards system supports an organization's training and development initiatives (see Chapter 6). Thus, an individual with higher qualifications will typically be compensated more than someone with lower qualifications. This compensation may be in the form of moving up the pay scale through a merit increase or from a one-time financial bonus.

Consider an example of a job in the sport sector where the pay structure may dictate that an individual with a post-secondary degree will get paid more than someone with a high school diploma. The assumption is that the university graduate is more highly qualified and knowledgeable, and therefore is compensated at a higher level. As another example, a collegiate sport coach may receive an increase in base pay for acquiring higher levels of coaching certification or a financial bonus for taking the time to apprentice with a master coach. A system that rewards skills may be expected to motivate employees to improve themselves or at least demonstrate to the organization that they have the desired skills. This effort can be expected to have a positive effect in the organization.

With a seniority-based reward system, the pay structure reflects longevity in the organization. The assumption is that employees should be rewarded for staying with the organization because they have acquired skills and knowledge over time that are valuable to the organization. For a staff member, there may be motivation to join and stay with an organization that provides financial security. With this type of system, an employee knows there will be incremental pay increases over time and this kind of security can be very attractive to staff. It is also a relatively easy system for an organization to administer, and labor costs can be forecasted. However, there may be no further motivation to work hard because longevity rather than behavior or performance is linked to compensation. A simple example of a seniority-based system is found in the pay structure for Game Staff and Minor Officials hired for intercollegiate athletic competitions at one Canadian university. The 2013–2014 pay rates started at C$11/hour, and increased by C$0.50/hour for every year that returning staff had been in that position (increase of C$1.00/hour for those in supervisory roles). Thus, individuals in their first year as a Game Staff or Minor Official were paid the basic rate of C$11/hour, while those in their third year in one of those positions were paid C$12.50/hour. This presumably provided some incentive for these staff and officials to return to the job each year.

Finally, with a performance-based reward system, the pay structure provides compensation in return for acceptable results or behavior. Rewards may be provided on a continuous scale where the better one performs the better the rewards or on a graduated scale where there are set levels an individual must reach in terms of performance before the next level of rewards is provided. Providing rewards for *individual results* is synonymous with a commission system, where compensation is directly linked to the quantity of the employee's output, such as number of units sold. Compensation by results is not uncommon for employees such as sporting goods sales staff or personal trainers at a fitness club. As well, a winning season may be the basis for determining whether a collegiate coach can expect a raise in pay, or a financial bonus or to keep his job! An example of performance-based pay with professional athletes was reported in Chapter 7 as an aspect of performance management. With this system the employee is presumably motivated to work harder because pay is directly tied to productivity. The rate of compensation based on results is typically established by determining an acceptable level of performance at an expected level of effort, so that compensation is considered fair.

Rewards in a performance-based system may also be given for *workgroup, department or organizational results*, which is synonymous with profit sharing. With this type of system employees are presumably motivated to work harder when they know that their efforts may lead to direct compensation in the form of an increase in base pay or a one-time financial bonus. Profit-sharing systems may distribute rewards to employees soon after profits have been determined (e.g., quarterly or annually), rewards may be deferred until retirement, or both strategies may be used (Milkovich et al., 2011). Profit sharing has the potential to increase employee motivation and effort in the workplace, and directly benefit the organization, if rewards are tied to what is considered to be desirable behavior and performance. Consider Box 8.5, an example of profit sharing at a UK-based sportswear retailer.

BOX 8.5

Profit-sharing at Sports Direct

In 2009, Sports Direct launched a bonus scheme to all full-time staff who had been employed with the company for at least one year. The premise of the scheme was that if profit targets were reached, and the employee stayed with the company for the next four years, the employee would be given free shares in the business worth 25 per cent of his or her salary.

When this scheme was devised, Sports Direct's share price was £1.00. By 2013, the company had experienced huge profit increases with share prices reaching £6.60. That meant 2,000 employees shared in the value of 21 million company shares, which translated to, for example, an employee earning £20,000 salary receiving a pay-out worth about £79,000, on the basis of receiving 12,000 shares.

The scheme significantly reduced staff turnover. Before the scheme was introduced, one in three staff had resigned annually. Within a year of introducing the profit-sharing scheme, the staff turnover rate was reduced to one in five. The success of the program led to Sports Direct introducing a similar scheme in 2011 to be paid out in 2015.

Sports Direct's Chief Executive Officer, Dave Forsey, said: 'The share scheme glues this company together. These schemes are typically only for executives, but this goes deep into the company. I'm surprised more businesses haven't adopted something like this sooner' (Neville, 2013).

Information from Neville (2013) and Ruddick (2013)

Instead of relying on discrete results, compensation may also be based on *individual behavior or performance* that has been evaluated through performance appraisal. With this system, an increase in base pay or a financial bonus is linked to an individual's behavior and accomplishments. For example, if the marketing director of a professional sports team is evaluated positively on, say, his group leadership, ability to deploy personnel in the marketing department, planning and budgeting for the unit, and sponsorship acquisition, he is likely to be rewarded. The presumption is that the marketing director will be motivated to be effective in these areas when compensation is a direct outcome of his behavior and accomplishments.

A sport organization may implement a compensation plan that is based on a mixture of job-based, skill-based, seniority-based and performance-based reward systems. For example, in a fitness club, instructors' wages may be based on a given dollar amount for the number and level of classes taught (job-based), with an annual percentage increase of a given amount based on cost-of-living increases, as well as a small increase in their base salary for every year they continue to work at the club (seniority-based). The instructors may also have the opportunity to earn a financial bonus each year for outstanding performance as determined through performance appraisal. It is important for an organization to understand the bases of its compensation plan because employees will pay attention to what is rewarded. Consider Box 8.6, an example of a compensation plan for limited hourly employees at a municipal recreation department.

BOX 8.6

Compensation plan for limited hourly employees of a municipal recreation department

Definition: The City defines a limited hourly employee as one who works full time or part time on a temporary basis, on-call basis or hourly basis in a specified seasonal program such as a summer camp. Limited hourly employees work less than 1,000 hours per fiscal year.

Salary and classifications: The City's intent is to compensate limited hourly employees at a similar rate of pay to that of regular employees performing similar work. The City stipulates that limited hourly employees are to be hired at a level or 'step' that is closest to a corresponding classification for regular employees in terms of both level of work performed and rate of pay.

Salary increases: Limited hourly employees may receive a salary step increase after 700 hours or 6 months, whichever occurs first from the date of hire, if they demonstrate continued development and efficient and effective service, as reflected in their performance appraisal. A limited hourly employee must receive a 'meets requirements' rating in order to be considered for a salary increase. A limited hourly employee who demonstrates exceptional leadership ability and job performance may also be given a merit raise, upon written justification and departmental approval.

Sample job classifications and salary

Administrative Specialist I: This position requires advanced skills or knowledge that enables an individual to perform administrative work in support of a department/division or program.

Step 1	*Step 2*	*Step 3*	*Step 4*	*Step 5*
$20.52	$21.72	$22.98	$24.30	$25.72 per hour

Administrative Specialist II: This position requires advanced skills or knowledge that enables an individual to perform more complex work in specialized software programs and data analysis and in the specialized areas that support a department/division or program. The position also requires two years of experience equivalent to an Administrative Specialist I.

Step 1	*Step 2*	*Step 3*	*Step 4*	*Step 5*
$24.51	$25.93	$27.43	$29.02	$30.71 per hour

Instructor II: This position requires that the individual, with limited supervision, prepares classes, programs and camp curriculum, presents classes and field trips and provides assignments to instructor aides and volunteers. The position requires previous teaching experience and in-depth knowledge of the topics to be taught. The position also requires two years of experience equivalent to an Instructor I.

Step 1	*Step 2*	*Step 3*	*Step 4*	*Step 5*
$23.62	$25.10	$26.44	$27.97	$29.60 per hour

Recreation Leader II: This position requires a minimum of one season of experience and the requisite certifications for Sports Camp Leaders (CPR, First Aid), Sport Officials (CPR, First Aid), Assistant Pool Manager, Senior Swim Instructor/Lifeguard (Lifeguard training, CPR, First Aid), Summer Camp Assistants, Coaches.

Step 1	*Step 2*	*Step 3*	*Step 4*	*Step 5*
$12.60	$13.33	$14.10	$14.92	$15.78 per hour

Based on information from the City of Palo Alto Compensation Plan, retrieved from http://www.cityofpaloalto.org/civicax/filebank/documents/6942 and Labor Agreement, retrieved from www.cityofpaloalto.org/civicax/filebank/documents/6949

Discussion questions

1   What is the basis, or bases, of the rewards offered in this compensation plan?
2   What effort or behavior might the City expect from its limited hourly employees as a result of this compensation plan?

Another potentially valued and therefore important component of an organization's compensation plan is indirect financial rewards. Indirect financial rewards like pensions, or life or medical insurance plans, are available as employee services or benefits. These may take a variety of forms and have different value to different employees depending on whether they address important needs. Employee benefits may be particularly important to an organization's reward management system if they make up for relatively lower financial compensation for employees. Consequently, a 'cafeteria style' or flexible benefits system may be most attractive to employees and recruits. A flexible system lets an employee, or group of employees, pick and choose which benefits are most needed (up to a maximum value that is the same for everyone) and, as such, optimizes the compensation received. In other words, employees are not receiving rewards that they are not likely to use and which have little value or attraction (e.g., childcare when one has no dependents, life insurance when one is already covered through a spouse's plan). In some instances, additional salary may be taken in place of the value of certain benefits. Benefits can be an important part of a total compensation plan that helps to attract and retain valued staff.

To conclude, consider Box 8.7, an example of how rewards are managed at the sports-based Camp Pinnacle, including the compensation plan, extrinsic non-financial rewards that are available, and intrinsic rewards that may be experienced.

BOX 8.7

Motivation and rewards management of sport staff at Camp Pinnacle

Canadian families have a host of options when it comes to summer opportunities for children and youth. Residential (overnight) camps are only one of the activity possibilities for children. Camp Pinnacle, a summer sports camp, experiences substantial competition not only for customers (campers), but for staff as well. Camp Pinnacle uses a finely tuned system to motivate staff and create incentives for high performance.

Motivating employees begins in the recruiting process, when potential staff members are introduced to Pinnacle's purpose, expectations and culture. Like many residential camps, Pinnacle is a non-profit organization whose mission – creating a superior sports camp experience for underprivileged youth – is a unifying and motivating factor for staff. The Camp believes that serving the mission of the camp will be a source of intrinsic motivation for staff.

The Camp has a graduated pay structure in which all summer employees earn the same base salary, with increases awarded to returning staff members for each year of experience. In addition to their base salary, all staff receive a stipend of C$40/week for 'living expenses' (i.e., laundry, sundries, a treat in town on their day off). Staff are also eligible to be reimbursed for the cost of upgrading their qualifications in Camp Pinnacle's instructional areas – for example, staff can get back up to 100% of the costs of advanced training in kayak or high-ropes instruction certification, and lifeguards can be reimbursed for up to 50% of certification costs per year.

While Camp Pinnacle is focused on motivating staff through rewards, like many summer camps it has limited financial resources to compensate staff. Thus, the organization invests creatively in other non-financial reward systems. At the end of each two-week camper session, there is a gathering of all staff. At this time the senior management team recognizes one member of the seasonal staff team from each camper age group and activities area (e.g., water sports, land sports) with a 'Reaching for the Pinnacle' award for exceptional job performance. The selection is based on performance appraisal of each seasonal staff member by the section head for each age group and activities area. Though there is no financial component to these awards, they are highly regarded by staff members, who wear their special edition 'Reaching the Pinnacle' T-shirts with pride.

Another rewards strategy utilized by Camp Pinnacle is job scheduling. Senior management must schedule staff for days off as well as special assignments throughout the season. They recognize that different members of staff may perceive a certain cabin assignment, a particular day off or a specific out-trip responsibility to be a meaningful perk. To capitalize on these preferences, Camp Pinnacle has created the 'Excelections' system. Staff members submit their preferences for assignments, housing or days off to their supervisor, who then does the scheduling giving priority to those employees with the highest performance appraisal scores from the previous camp session.

Discussion questions

1   What is the basis, or bases, of rewards at Camp Pinnacle?
2   What other rewards (intrinsic or extrinsic) could Camp Pinnacle use to attract, motivate and retain staff?
3   Based on your understanding of motivation theory, what factors might staff take into account in their decision whether to return the following summer?

Prepared by Katie Misener based on information about Camp Pinnacle

JOB DESIGN

This chapter discusses in further detail the motivational approach to job design that was outlined in Chapter 3. According to De Cieri, Kramar, Noe, Hollenbeck, Gerhart and Wright (2005), the opportunity to fulfill individual needs can be built into the design of a job, and thus increase its potential to motivate employees and volunteers in the workplace. As indicated earlier, typical motivating elements of a job are autonomy (level of independence in carrying out job duties), intrinsic job feedback (from the work itself), extrinsic job feedback (from others), social interaction (through group work and customer-service), task variety, task identity (involvement in a complete or identifiable piece of work), skill/knowledge requirements (level of challenge in the task), task significance (interconnected with other work, impacts others inside and outside the organization), growth/learning (challenging work, support is provided) and recognition (acknowledgement of good work). A job can be designed to increase the likelihood that an employee or volunteer will experience one or more of these rewards, and will thus be motivated by such a job to the extent that the rewards are of personal value.

The work of Hackman and Oldham (1980) supports the notion of job design (or redesign) on the basis of the task itself being intrinsically rewarding. Their job characteristics model of motivation is consistent with Herzberg's (1968) contention that it is the aspects of the work content (i.e., the job itself) that will be motivating. According to Hackman and Oldham's model, five core job characteristics – skill variety, task identity, task significance, task autonomy and job feedback – contribute to employees' sense of the meaningfulness of their work, responsibility for the outcomes of their work and knowledge of the results of their work. These three 'critical psychological states' are the intrinsic rewards for doing one's job, and thus are instrumental to one's motivation in the workplace. An organization can manipulate, through job design, the variety of skills and activities required in one's job, the extent to which a job involves a whole, identifiable piece of work (e.g., a project or major piece of project from start to finish), and the importance of the particular job to the organization (or its clients). These three job characteristics are proposed to impact directly on an employee's experienced meaningfulness of the work. Further, an organization is able to increase the autonomy or decision-making discretion one has in a job, thus enhancing his or her sense of responsibility. And an organization is able to design a job so that an employee receives feedback directly from the job itself on how he or she is performing, thus increasing the direct knowledge of results.

There are four important considerations for enhancing the meaningfulness, responsibility and direct feedback in one's work through job design – that is, the 'motivating potential' of a job (Hackman & Oldham, 1980). First, the employee himself or herself must perceive there to be sufficiently high levels of the core job characteristics for there to be an adequate sense of meaningfulness, responsibility and knowledge of results for the job to be motivating. Second, an individual must be willing to accept a job that has been designed to be more motivating; in other words, these intrinsic rewards must have personal value to the jobholder. Third, designing – and particularly redesigning – a job so that intrinsic rewards are more available may impact on the design of someone else's job. For example, to increase skill variety and task identity in one person's job may mean reducing skill variety and task identity in someone else's job. This can reduce the motivating effect of that individual's job. Fourth, a redesigned job that has, say, increased skill requirements and autonomy, may dictate moving the job to a higher level on the pay scale with financial implications for the organization. Thus, the effect of job design may be felt beyond its potential to increase employee motivation, and not necessarily in positive ways.

Job design may be particularly challenging for workgroups, where the motivating potential of each group member's role needs to be considered. However, Campion, Medsker and Higgs (1993) noted that all of Hackman and Oldham's (1980) job characteristics are applicable at the group level. We can expect that individuals will be aware of their own skill variety, task identity and significance, autonomy and feedback within the group, *and* aware of those characteristics with respect to the group's work as a whole. The four considerations for enhancing the motivating potential of a job outlined earlier also apply to redesigning group work.

Job design as a strategy to create (more) motivating positions is not limited to the paid staff; it applies equally well to volunteers, particularly given sport organizations' heavy reliance on intrinsic rewards as the basis of volunteers' motivation for being involved. In a study of volunteers involved with the 2008 European Football Championship, Neufeind, Güntert and Wehner (2013) examined the effect of job characteristics on the event volunteers' satisfaction with their experience. Hackman and Oldham's (1975) Job Diagnostic Survey was used to assess the volunteers' perception of skill variety, task significance, task identity, autonomy and feedback in their volunteer role with the championship event. They found significant differences in the motivating potential of various roles – for example, volunteers at the helpdesk reported a relatively high motivating potential score while those attending the parking lot reported a very low score. The investigators also found some differences in the impact of various job characteristics for different types of volunteers: Skill variety was most important to the satisfaction of individuals who volunteered for the first time; task significance and feedback were most important for individuals who had some volunteer experience in the past; and, task identity and autonomy were the strongest predictors of satisfaction for individuals who were currently volunteering elsewhere as well. The findings highlight the potential complexity of job design as a motivating force.

The intrinsic benefits that may be accrued through job design are certainly not the only means by which volunteers are rewarded. We turn now to a consideration of the use of rewards for recognizing volunteers.

VOLUNTEER RECOGNITION AND REWARDS

Intrinsic and non-financial rewards are the types of incentives that sport organizations have to entice individuals to volunteer. Sport organizations rely heavily on volunteers' attraction to helping out in sport because of a desire to help others, the social benefits of interacting with others, and the personal rewards of contributing one's skills and making a difference (Cuskelly, Hoye & Auld, 2006). These may be classified as: (1) normative incentives, where the sport volunteer is motivated by the opportunity to help a cause such as a sport program which he or she may feel is important for children and for a community as a whole; (2) affective incentives, where the sport volunteer is motivated by the opportunity to work with others, develop friendships, and identify with a group; and (3) utilitarian incentives, where the sport volunteer is motivated by the opportunity to use his or her skills or sport background, to develop new skills and work experience, to network in the community, and to help his or her child participate in sport (Cuskelly et al., 2006). Research further suggests that the importance of these incentives varies by sport volunteers' age (Doherty, 2005a). Older adults (60 years or older) are more likely to be motivated by normative incentives and social benefits, younger adults (less than 35-year old) are more likely to be motivated by utilitarian incentives relating to their own personal development, while those in the middle (35–60-year-old and most likely to have children participating) are likely to be most motivated by utilitarian incentives followed by social benefits. Kim, Zhang and Connaughton (2010) also found differences in the motives of volunteers according to whether they were involved with international (mega) sport events, national sport organizations and local sport clubs. They concluded that each type of event or organization was presumed to offer different perceived benefits. To attract, motivate and retain volunteers, sport organizations must ensure that individuals have the opportunity to realize important, valued intrinsic benefits through their involvement in the work of the organization (Ringuet-Riot, Cuskelly, Auld & Zakus, 2014; Welty Peachey, Lyras, Cohen, Bruening & Cunningham, 2013).

Sport organizations also rely fairly heavily on non-financial extrinsic rewards as a form of volunteer recognition and appreciation (Doherty, 2005b). Where extrinsic (direct) financial rewards are not, by definition, provided to volunteers, non-financial rewards can be an important symbolic expression of appreciation for contributions and performance. Perhaps it is the very fact that financial rewards are not handed over that sport organizations are concerned with providing some kind of alternative recognition. Indeed, Kim et al. (2010) noted that small appreciative gifts may be valued by volunteers who are motivated by the opportunity to make a difference and experience personal growth, while Østerlund (2013) found that sport organizations' volunteer recruitment efforts were enhanced by the provision of such perks and material incentives. It is important to understand that 'recognition stems from genuinely valuing volunteers … rewarding volunteers takes recognition a step further, by providing something tangible and extrinsic to the act of volunteering itself' (Australian Sports Commission [ASC], 2000: 15). Recognition and rewards for volunteers vary in terms of their formality, cost, individual or group focus, and public or private nature. Box 8.8 lists the potential rewards that may be used to recognize volunteers.

BOX 8.8

Ideas for recognizing and rewarding volunteers

- Celebrating achievements and effort (e.g., a successful season, effective fundraising or well-organized event).
- Offering personal praise to the volunteer while on the job.
- Acknowledging efforts during committee meetings.
- Allocating noticeboard space to acknowledge volunteer achievement.
- Writing letters of thanks.
- Presenting volunteer awards at the annual general meeting.
- Presenting awards for years of service.
- Holding social events in honour of volunteers.
- Giving identification pins, badges, shirts or caps.
- Providing complimentary tickets to special events and functions.
- Arranging discounts at recreation and sport stores or restaurants.
- Recommending volunteers to prospective employers.
- Providing letters of reference.

Information from Australian Sports Commission (2014b)

Discussion questions

1   With reference to the various content theories discussed earlier in this chapter, consider what needs may be met by the different rewards.
2   What can sport organizations do to help ensure that volunteers' higher-order needs (Maslow), motivators (Herzberg), and the needs for power, achievement and affiliation (McClelland) can be met through volunteering? Give specific examples in addition to those listed above.

Decisions regarding the nature of extrinsic rewards for volunteers should take into consideration what is of value to different volunteers, as well as what the organization is able to spend in terms of time and money. Some volunteer coaches may relish quite public acknowledgements of their involvement or success, while others will shun the limelight and prefer that their athletes receive any accolades that may be due. Some board members may expect team merchandise, while others may prefer the money to be spent on programs for the participants (Doherty, 2005b). While many volunteers would say they do not expect extrinsic rewards for their efforts, equity theory suggests that individuals will compare the rewards they receive (both intrinsic and extrinsic) with the effort they give, and will further compare that to what other volunteers contribute and receive. If volunteers perceive inequity, then they may be disinclined to continue their involvement. Similarly, if they perceive they are being more than rewarded for their efforts, then they will be more inclined to continue. Along with intrinsic rewards derived from volunteering itself, extrinsic rewards may be a meaningful component of what the volunteer perceives he or she gets back from volunteering, and should be managed carefully.

SUMMARY

Theories of human motivation are fundamental to understanding the impact of rewards systems on individuals' intent to take a job, exert effort and remain with an organization. Content theories (e.g., Maslow's hierarchy of needs theory, Herzberg's motivator–hygiene theory, McClelland's three need theory) explain what motivates employees and volunteers, while process theories (e.g., equity theory, expectancy theory) explain how they are motivated.

Rewards management systems must include potential for intrinsic rewards from the job itself as well as extrinsic financial and non-financial rewards that are given by the organization. Financial rewards include direct (i.e., pay, bonus, cost-of-living adjustment) and indirect (e.g., reimbursement of expenses) elements. Non-financial rewards are things that have no financial value, yet may be highly valued by an employee or volunteer (e.g., team clothing, national team travel, complementary sport event tickets).

The financial compensation plan is one part of the total rewards management system. The establishment of a pay structure must account for internal equity, external market forces and employee contributions. The basis of the pay structure may be job level, skills, seniority, individual, group or organization performance – or some combination of these.

Job design is an important element of rewards management. It is a tool that can be used to increase the motivating potential of a job by increasing task variety, task identity, task significance, autonomy and direct feedback – all of which provide an employee or volunteer with an increased sense of the meaningfulness of their job, responsibility for the outcomes of their work and knowledge of results of their contributions.

Volunteers by definition do not receive extrinsic (direct) financial compensation, therefore the organization must rely on the intrinsic rewards of the volunteer role itself to ensure their needs are met. Sport organizations also tend to rely on extrinsic non-financial rewards as more tangible tokens of recognition and appreciation. The provision of these rewards requires careful consideration as they can be costly in terms of time and expense for the organization.

DISCUSSION QUESTIONS

1   Consider your most recent job (full-time, part-time, summer employment). What aspects contribute(d) to your satisfaction in the organization? What aspects contribute(d) to your dissatisfaction? Are these things consistent with Herzberg's (1968) motivators (satisfying) and hygiene factors (dissatisfying)? If not, why not? (Consider whether you are/were motivated by higher- or lower-order needs.)

2   List and describe all the intrinsic and extrinsic (including direct and indirect financial and non-financial) rewards you receive(d) in your most recent job.

3   Consider your most recent job or volunteer experience. Using Hackman and Oldham's job characteristics model, describe whether the five core job characteristics are/were low, medium or high in that job. Consider how this impacts or impacted your sense of meaningfulness of your work, responsibility for outcomes and knowledge of results. If several job characteristics were rated low to medium how could the job be redesigned to be more motivating? (Describe how the job characteristics could be improved.) What impact, if any, would this have on others in the organization, including the motivational design of their job?

CHAPTER 9

Sport organizations and employee relations

LEARNING OBJECTIVES

After reading this chapter you will be able to:

- Explain the meaning of employee relations in sport organizations
- Outline the different forms of organizational justice in the workplace
- Describe employee involvement through effective communication and participation in decision making
- Describe the concept of trade unions and the collective bargaining process
- Understand the bases and process of workplace grievance
- Describe the importance and management of health, safety and employee wellness in the organization
- Consider the nature of volunteer relations in the sport organization
- Understand the bases and process of employee termination

CHAPTER OVERVIEW

Employee relations refer to the activities and processes designed to maintain a productive workplace while satisfying the needs and legitimate interests of employees and managing within the law (Suffield, 2005). This chapter considers employee relations in a broad sense, rather than limiting the presentation to labor relations, which focuses specifically on the union–management relationship. The employee relations approach, with its focus on building a committed and high-performing workforce, is more consistent with strategic human resource management (SHRM) than the traditional industrial relations approach. The latter tends to focus on interactions between management and workers, and there is a connotation of an adversarial (us vs. them) relationship (Lewis, Thornhill & Saunders, 2003; McKenna & Beech, 2002).

Organizational justice or the perception of fairness in workplace decisions and practices is a basis of effective employee relations. Another basis is employee involvement, where people have a voice in decisions about their working environment (e.g., pay, workload, task, conditions). Consequently, organizational communication and employee participation in decision making are key elements of employee involvement.

Participation through trade unions is one mechanism for employee involvement. The union represents a collective voice for employees in negotiations about labor issues such as pay and workload. The result is a collective bargaining agreement (CBA) that pertains to all employees. This agreement is analogous to an individual employee's contract in a non-union workplace. When an employee, or groups of employees, perceives that the contract or collective agreement has been violated, it becomes grounds for grievance. The formal grievance procedure gives an employee recourse to resolve a formal complaint and is a critical part of effective employee relations.

Working conditions may be a basis for grievance. In addition to contractual obligations, an employer has a moral and legal obligation to provide a safe and healthy working environment. This chapter examines hazards and risks at work that impact on workplace safety and employee health. Increasingly, organizations are proactive about employee health and wellness, with the intent of supporting a productive work environment and workers. These important elements of employee relations are considered here.

A productive and mutually satisfying relationship between the sport organization and its volunteers is just as, if not more, important than with paid staff. While many of the same principles apply, this chapter examines the specific nature of volunteer relations in the sport organization.

The employee–organization relationship will inevitably end at some point. This chapter closes by considering various forms and bases of termination. Exit interviews to determine reasons for employee resignation are also discussed. Exit interviews, when conducted properly, can be an important feedback mechanism for improving overall human resource management (HRM).

EMPLOYEE–MANAGEMENT RELATIONS

The employee relations approach focuses on communication, liaison with individuals, and policies and practices that are directed to the individual in the workplace. This approach does not necessarily replace interactions between management and the group or union with regard to pay systems or workplace conditions. However, in comparison to traditional industrial relations, 'HRM approaches based on employee relations have sought to broaden the involvement of employees and take a more participative approach to management through increased communication' (McKenna & Beech, 2002: 255).

The relationship between management and employees must be based on exchange (i.e., the organization provides valued rewards in return for staff performance), and the organization's social and moral obligation to treat its workers well (Chelladurai, 2006). The organization must reward its employees fairly, provide a safe and non-threatening working environment and provide support for them to do the work of the organization. In turn, employees have an implied duty to:

- be ready and willing for work
- take reasonable care and skill in performing the job
- obey the employer's lawful orders
- take care of the employer's property
- act in good faith.

(Lewis et al., 2003: 11)

These mutual expectations form the basis of the employee's psychological contract, a concept that was introduced in Chapter 5.

ORGANIZATIONAL JUSTICE

A key principle underlying employee relations, organizational justice is defined as the perception of fairness in all decisions and practices (Greenberg, 1987). From an SHRM perspective this includes the processes of recruitment and selection, staffing and task assignment, training and development, performance appraisal and rewards management. Organizational justice is a reflection of the organization's social and moral obligation to fairness. According to Chelladurai (2006: 122), 'managers should realize that they themselves are the guardians of justice within their organization'. There are also economic and legal rationales for ensuring justice in the organization, given the potential economic fallout of unjust practices from customer boycotts and employee withdrawal of services, and the notion that 'justice in the workplace is fast becoming an arena for legal actions' (Chelladurai, 2006: 123). Most importantly, it is the employees' *perception* of justice that is critical to the role of organizational justice in maintaining a productive workplace while satisfying the needs of employees (Lewis et al., 2003; Suffield, 2005).

There are three basic forms of organizational justice – distributive, procedural and interactional – each with implications for managing employee relations. Distributive justice refers to the fair and just allocation of resources and rewards in the organization to people and to programs or units. For example, lifeguard staff at an aquatics facility may question the fairness of pay increases to management, when the guards are the front line workers who have the responsibility of serving the public directly. As another example, coaches of what may be described as lower profile intercollegiate sport teams (e.g., gymnastics, wrestling and field hockey) may wonder about budget cuts to their programs while higher profile sports get an even bigger piece of the pie. These employees may perceive that an injustice has been done, which can ultimately affect their attitude towards the organization. Distributive justice is not limited to economic goods such as pay to individuals or budget allotments to groups. It also concerns the fair and just distribution of conditions and goods that affect psychological, physical, economic and social well-being (Kabanoff, 1991). You may recall the importance of different types of intrinsic and extrinsic rewards in the workplace presented in Chapter 8. The distribution of any type of reward, condition or good is subject to perceptions of justice and injustice.

There are three bases of distributive justice: (1) equity, which is distribution based on members' contribution to the organization (recall the equity theory of motivation presented in Chapter 8); (2) equality, which is equal distribution to all members, regardless of contribution; and (3) need, which is distribution based on identified individual or group needs (Chelladurai, 2006). Any one of these bases of distribution may be used by the organization, as deemed appropriate to the decision and the situation. Again, the critical implication for employee relations is whether employees perceive the decision as fair and just. For example, if the lifeguards noted earlier recognize that management has taken on additional responsibilities with the recent expansion of programs or personnel, the decision to increase their pay may be deemed to be equitable, and just and fair. Or, if the lifeguards learn that management has not had a pay increase in 10 years, and that the organization risks losing some outstanding leaders, they may acknowledge the need to provide better compensation to those individuals. In the example of intercollegiate coaches given above, these employees may perceive an injustice in the unequal distribution of resources to higher profile sport teams. The outcome of distributive injustice may be reduced job performance, reduced cooperation or withdrawal behavior. Not all employees will agree with the basis of a decision all the time, and perceived distributive injustice is not uncommon. An understanding of how the decision was made may help to restore employees' sense of fairness in the organization.

Procedural justice refers to fair and just procedures for determining the distribution of resources and rewards. In other words not only making a fair decision, but being seen to make a fair decision through the use of proper procedures. When decisions are based on procedures that are considered to be fair and transparent, they are more likely to be accepted by the individuals or groups they affect, even when those decisions have adverse implications such as increased workload, limited or no pay raise, or even dismissal (Folger & Cropanzano, 1998). Employee involvement in the decision-making process is linked to perceptions of fairness (Lewis et al., 2003). Other examples might include the right to a 'fair' hearing and 'right of reply' when allegations of misconduct are made or the right of appeal in relation to some organizational decisions. For example, if sales staff have at least some input in determining the commission rate in their fitness club or sporting goods store, they are more likely to perceive that the final decision is fair, even if it was not as high a rate as they were hoping for.

Interactional justice refers to the fair and just communication and explanation of distributive and procedural justice; in other words, 'this is the decision, and this is how we made it'. It is based on both interpersonal justice, or whether information was communicated in a respectful way, and informational justice or whether adequate information was provided to explain and justify the decision (Chelladurai, 2006; Lewis et al., 2003). Interactional justice is an important consideration in managing employee relations, particularly when individuals are not formally involved in decision making. Employees may perceive their lack of opportunity to be involved as a procedural injustice. For example, fitness club staff may feel that they should at least be consulted regarding a new pay structure that includes commission rates. If the club's management is able to clearly explain the basis for the decision on the new pay structure, in a way that demonstrates respect for staff knowledge and expertise in this area, this will increase the chances that staff will perceive they have been treated fairly. Another example is the decision to eliminate programs or staff, or both, from a public community fitness center like a YMCA. Staff may feel they should have been consulted in the decision process at least regarding what programs to reduce or eliminate. Interactional justice can help to re-establish a sense of fairness if staff are fully apprised of the basis for the decisions in a respectful and sensitive manner (Lewis et al., 2003). While interactional justice can be critical to effective employee relations, it should not be a substitute for the opportunity to have employees involved in organizational decisions.

EMPLOYEE INVOLVEMENT

Employee involvement is the principle of engaging staff in the organization through various processes and mechanisms. From an SHRM perspective, the intent is to foster their understanding and support of, and commitment to, the organization's objectives (Lewis et al., 2003). Employee involvement is also associated with trust in management, increased job performance, job satisfaction and intent to stay (Boxall & Macky, 2009; Cropanzano & Greenberg, 2001; Jones, Kalmi & Kauhanen, 2010). Jones et al. (2010: 1) note that 'participatory work environments' can be meaningful even for low-skilled employees and those who do simple tasks. The focus here is engagement that is management-directed, where the organization determines how, when and to what degree staff are involved in the organization. This is in contrast to employee involvement through participation in trade unions, which is discussed below. Staff may be engaged through communication, decision making and even financial investment (see the example of employee profit sharing as a form of compensation in Chapter 8; Lewis et al., 2003). We turn now to a discussion of employee involvement through communication and participation in the workplace.

Communication

Employee involvement starts with internal communication. Employees can only be involved in the organization if they are kept informed. Effective communication, where the intended message is received and understood, keeps employees informed about such things as the organization's mission and objectives, organizational and HR policies, expectations for and evaluation of performance, and change in strategic direction (Booth, Fosters, Robson & Welham, 2004; McKenna & Beech, 2002). Such communication may be one-way and downward only, through team briefings, corporate newsletters, and email or social media announcements; the intent is to provide information and in this case involvement is relatively limited (Lewis et al., 2003). Two-way communication, in contrast, gives employees the opportunity to communicate with management about such things as the direction of the organization, the best ways to get there, and obstacles to performance and goal achievement. This may take place through briefing groups that include feedback and managerial response and even joint employee-management consultation teams (Lewis et al., 2003). The opportunity for two-way communication is related to the degree of employee participation in organizational decision making.

Participation in decision making

Employee participation is a specific form of employee involvement which includes 'direct involvement of individuals in decisions relating to their immediate work organization and … indirect involvement in decision making, through representatives, in the wider socio-technical and political structures of the firm' (Brannen, 1983: 16). Not only is such involvement expected to generate employee trust and commitment, the organization hopes to tap into the valuable insight employees may have regarding the production or service process that management does not have (Appelbaum, Bailey, Berg & Kalleberg, 2000). The direct and indirect involvement of employees in organizational decision making, including policy and direction, and such processes as hiring, evaluation and rewards, and working conditions, involves a shift in the 'location and nature of power' in the organization (McKenna & Beech, 2002: 285). Although it may be difficult for management to relinquish control, doing so promotes employee involvement. Østerlund (2013) found that voluntary sport organizations whose boards tended to involve others in major decisions and tended to delegate decision making were more attractive to volunteers. There is likely some variation in the degree or depth, scope, level and form of employee (or volunteer) involvement (Lewis et al., 2003).

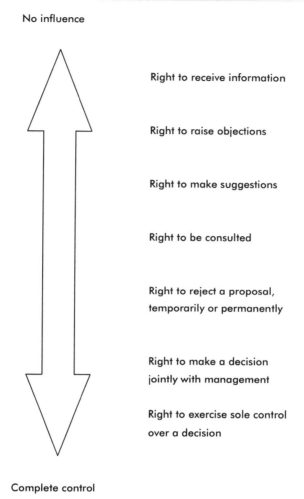

No influence

Right to receive information

Right to raise objections

Right to make suggestions

Right to be consulted

Right to reject a proposal, temporarily or permanently

Right to make a decision jointly with management

Right to exercise sole control over a decision

Complete control

FIGURE 9.1 A continuum of employee influence over organizational decisions (Lewis et al., 2003)

Degree of participation refers to the extent of employees' influence over a particular decision, ranging on a continuum of no influence to complete control. Figure 9.1 illustrates the possibilities for influence that lie between these two extremes, from the 'right to receive information … to [making] a decision jointly with management, and exercise sole control over a decision' (Lewis et al., 2003: 252). For example, a media relations officer with a professional sports team or intercollegiate athletics program may only receive information about organizational strategic planning, or she may be consulted about certain aspects that pertain to her area of expertise (e.g., developing a corporate brand), or she may be involved in making a joint decision with management regarding the direction of the organization. The extent to which an employee has influence in decision making may be a function of the type of decision. In general, the greater the degree of influence, the greater the sense of opportunity for involvement (whether staff take advantage of that opportunity or not).

The scope or types of decisions over which employees have some degree of control is a key indicator of employees' participation in the organization. Decision types can be distinguished as strategic (what the organization is doing), operational (how it is doing it), and individual task (what each person is doing as part of operations). At the least, staff should have some degree of influence over their own job tasks. Staff may be further involved in operational and even strategic decision making, directly or through a representative. To be able to participate further in operational and strategic decision making can be very rewarding for staff, because of the responsibility, challenge and even recognition it brings. At the very least, indirect participation through a representative can promote a sense of procedural justice. Using the example of employees at a golf club (e.g., grounds crew, sales staff, 'pro shop' staff), participation can provide at least some influence over decisions regarding their own job, operations in general, and even the strategic direction of the club.

The type of decisions in which employees usually participate depends on the level of the decision and their position within the organization. That is, they are more likely to be involved in decisions that are taken at lower levels of the organization and those that have an immediate impact on their day-to-day work such as individual task decisions. They are less likely to be involved in strategic and even operational decisions that are typically taken at the top management or board level. However, there are a number of exceptions to this that will determine employee involvement. As suggested above, employees may be represented by a delegate to board-level meetings, thus giving them indirect involvement at higher levels. For example, a coach's representative may sit on an intercollegiate athletics advisory council. As well, a macro-approach to strategic and operational decision making entails organization-wide involvement (McKenna & Beech, 2002) – for example, a company-wide planning retreat. In smaller organizations, such as an independent fitness club, there may be a monthly or semi-annual meeting of all club staff and management where employees have an opportunity to provide input and vote on organization-level issues. Of course, employee participation in higher level decision making may be restricted to only certain decision areas (e.g., health and safety, workload, performance appraisal policies and processes), depending on where upper management wants employee input, and where they are willing to concede control. Furthermore, Lewis et al. (2003) note that the participation of employees in decision making at the strategic level tends to be limited in practice because of logistical and attitudinal problems. Specifically, 'greater management familiarity with, and in-depth knowledge of, strategic matters, as well as their control over information, gives them a significant advantage over employee representatives' (Lewis et al., 2003: 254–255). Effective employee involvement through decision making relies on effective communication and shared influence. Finally, typically higher-level decisions may be brought to lower levels with a micro-approach (McKenna & Beech, 2002), whereby decisions are delegated to units or individuals. For example, municipal recreation department staff members responsible for a given sector of the community (e.g., seniors) might be given free reign to design and implement programs and a marketing strategy for that particular sector.

A fourth consideration in employee participation is the form of that involvement. As already noted, it may be in the manner of direct involvement in decision making, or indirect involvement ranging from the provision of feedback to representation by an elected or designated member of formal decision-making bodies. The trade union is one form of representation and is discussed in more detail below. The opportunity for indirect employee participation in decision making through a trade union is dependent on the presence and strength of the union in the workplace, and by the scope of decisions on which it is able to negotiate (Lewis et al., 2003). A formal consultation arrangement is an alternative to the trade union. However, with this form of involvement, participation is typically restricted to consultation rather than negotiation where employees actually have control in the decision-making process. The lesser influence in a consultation arrangement is likely due to the level of decisions and managerial attitudes towards employee participation in decision making and the associated power sharing that must be realized (Lewis et al., 2003).

TRADE UNIONS AND COLLECTIVE BARGAINING

Unions are one way employees have formal involvement in the decision making of the organization. A union is defined as 'an organization of employees that has the objective of improving the compensation and working conditions of [unionized and non-union] employees' (Suffield 2005: 40). In the majority of countries the right of an individual to join a trade union is enshrined in law. The primary function of a trade union is regulating the employment relationship (Lewis et al., 2003). The underlying premise of unionization is that individual employees have little voice or power when dealing with their employer, but they can increase their power as a collective group or union (Suffield, 2005). Consequently, laws such as the National Labor Relations Act in the USA give employees the right to self-organization, the right to bargain collectively, and the right to engage in activities for the mutual assistance or protection of employees (including the right to strike) (Gallant, Remick & Resnick, 2005). A union is a formal body established by a vote of organizational members to represent their interests in organizational decision making related to work. Local labour laws dictate the formation and nature of unions, but they are typically potentially powerful forces in an organization, to the extent that members are united in their support of the union that represents them. Union members' involvement, or at least representation, in organizational decision making is mainly through collective bargaining, although unions can also represent individual members in connection with grievances.

There are several notable differences in the employee–management relationship in union and non-union organizations (Suffield, 2005). In a unionized organization, the legal basis for the employment relationship is a collective agreement which has been negotiated by the union. The basic terms of employment are identical for all employees in a given job category that is covered by the collective agreement – for example, the standard players' contract in the collective bargaining agreement (CBA) of North America's National Hockey League Players Association (North America's National Hockey League Players' Association [NHLPA], 2013). In a non-union organization, the legal basis for the employment relationship is individual contracts which have been negotiated individually by the employees themselves. The terms of employment may be variable and unique for each employee.

The existence of unions in the sport industry is variable and depends on the segment or the job category. For example, unions are prominent in professional sport leagues, for both players and officials. It is also possible that only certain types of employees within a sport organization will be members of a union – for example, trades people, machine or equipment operators, or concessions staff at sport facilities. Unions are less likely to be found in small sporting goods retailers or sport marketing agencies, and in non-profit, voluntary organizations which are prominent in the sport industry (i.e., non-governmental community, state and national sport organizations). We tend to think of the role of unions in advocating for, establishing and monitoring workplace conditions for their members. However, professional players' associations are an example of unions that go beyond ensuring fair salaries and benefits. Consider Box 9.1, which gives an example of the Australian Football League (AFL) Players' Association.

BOX 9.1

AFL Players' Association supporting careers and lives

In the 2012 *AFL Players' Development & Wellbeing Report*, the General Manager of Player Development highlighted the goal of the AFL Players' Association as ensuring 'all of our players ... achieve successful careers and lives through football'. Mr Brett Johnson noted the Association's focus on sporting excellence and long-term personal growth and wellbeing, and outlined several successful initiatives in that regard.

- The negotiation of several player welfare, education and personal development initiatives as part of the new Collective Bargaining Agreement (CBA).
- Development and delivery of the Next Goal Education Pathway program that equips players with the knowledge and skills needed to develop their career outside of football.
- Roll-out of the Players' Association's wellbeing program pilot in 15 clubs.
- First phase of a research project aimed at producing evidence to better support clubs and players in an inclusive environment that values personal development.
  Information from the Australian Football League Players Association (2012)

Discussion questions

1   Identify similar initiatives in other professional sport players' associations, and their CBAs.
2   Discuss why players' unions devote time and resources to developing these aspects of their CBAs. Why might these things be important to players? How do such initiatives impact employee relations between the players and their teams?

Table 9.1 provides a brief overview of players' unions in the professional sport industry, with the example of the four major sport leagues in North America. There are several similarities and differences between their respective CBAs. For example, the collective agreements in all four players' unions are characterized by a free market system and the certification of player agents. They differ in that two unions have a hard salary cap or limit on total team payroll (NHLPA and National Football League Players Association [NFLPA]), while the National Basketball Players Association (NBPA) has a soft cap with several concessions. The Major League Baseball Players Association (MLBPA) has no salary

TABLE 9.1 An overview of players' unions in the North American professional sport industry

Union	National Hockey League Players' Association (NHLPA)	National Basketball Association Players' Association (NBPA)	Major League Baseball Players' Association (MLBPA)	National Football League Players' Association (NFLPA)
Year established	1967	1954	1885, 1966	1970+
Current CBA	2012–2022	2011–2021	2011–2016	2011–2021
Key features of CBA	• Hard salary cap • Revenue sharing across lower revenue teams • Player compensation floor (minimum) • Rookie compensation (maximum) • Free market system, players can move to any team when their contract expires • Players share 50% of league revenues • Regulation of player agent certification	• Soft salary cap (ceiling with several exceptions) • 'Luxury tax' for excess payroll penalty (distributed to teams with lower payrolls) • Player compensation floor and ceiling; Rookie compensation sliding scale • Free market system • Players share 50% of league revenues • Regulation of player agent certification	• Rookie salary cap only • 'Competitive balance tax' for surpassing threshold (to lower revenue teams) • Player compensation floor • Free market system • Lower revenue teams share 30% of league revenues • Regulation of player agent certification	• Hard salary cap • Fines paid to NFL and distributed to NFL-related charities • Player compensation floor • Free market system • Players share 47% of league revenues • Regulation of player agent certification

(Source: adapted from Hornby, 2012; MLBPA, 2012; NBPA, 2012; NHLPA, 2013)

cap; however, it has a payroll threshold beyond which teams must pay a competitive balance tax to lower revenue teams. All four unions have a player compensation floor or minimum salary level; however, the NHLPA also has a compensation ceiling for entry level players, while the NBPA has a ceiling for all players (to try to control what are the highest salaries in professional sports in North America). One thing the four unions have in common is the method of collective bargaining. We turn now to a review of this form of employee involvement.

Collective bargaining

Collective bargaining is a process of negotiating a labor contract that is acceptable to both management and unionized employees. In this process, the trade union negotiates on behalf of its members on issues such as pay, benefits, workload and working conditions. Local and national labor laws dictate what issues can be addressed through collective bargaining. These can be distinguished as substantive issues (e.g., pay, hours of work, holidays, health and safety, pensions and training) and procedural issues (e.g., negotiation or bargaining, grievance and arbitration, and disciplinary action) (Lewis et al., 2003). The CBA is the union contract which spells out the details of these issues for a given time period, after which time the contract expires. If the union and management cannot come to a new agreement before the contract expires, employees are said to be 'without a contract', although the terms of the previous agreement are held over until a new agreement is reached. Nonetheless, being without a contract, or sensing that the collective bargaining process may fail to establish a mutually agreed upon contract, can be the basis for industrial or 'strike' action where workers walk off the job (in essence breaking their contract with the organization). Although there is variation in national and local labor laws, typically union members vote on whether they are willing to go on strike, and ultimately vote (or let their union representatives vote) on strike action.

Collective bargaining between the professional sport leagues and their players' unions presented in Table 9.1 is an interesting case. Within each league, the team owners and management negotiate collectively with the players' union in order to reach a contract agreement. The negotiated agreement applies to each team and all players must abide by the actions of their bargaining unit (Gallant et al., 2005). The collective bargaining process in professional sports tends to be unlike the negotiations that take place in labor industries. Given the relative power of the players' unions in the professional sports industry, collective bargaining 'has been described less as negotiating over working conditions than as "two mega-corporations talking to each other about mergers or splits or sales" (Chass, 1994)' (Kovach, Hamilton & Meserole, 1997: 13).

The context for collective bargaining in professional sport is characterized by a relatively closed and sheltered labor market where only a very small percentage of athletes are likely to make it to 'the big league' (Kovach et al., 1997). Players' unions bargain collectively, but not for union-wide wages like their industry counterparts, although entry level salary floors (NBPA and NFLPA) and ceilings (NHLPA) have been introduced. Rather their focus tends to be on the rules governing the league, such as team salary caps, player-free agency and salary arbitration (Kovach et al., 1997) – that is, procedural vs. substantive issues. The issue of pay is negotiated between the individual (or their agent) and the team. The mutual interest of players' unions and the team owners is to gain what they each see as their share of the revenue pie. It is generally recognized, however, that revenues can only be maintained or increased if there is competitive balance among teams, game outcomes are fairly unpredictable, and hence fan interest continues. The collective bargaining process in professional sports is one of finding a mutually agreeable system of player mobility and salary restrictions, with the intent of balancing teams and limiting spending (Kovach et al., 1997).

Organizations often resist the idea of unionization, because of the inevitable shift in power, and what many deem to be a much more rigid and less managerial decision-making structure (Lewis et al., 2003). On the other hand, sometimes organizations embrace unions because they simplify the bargaining process because the workforce speaks with 'one voice' and managers have only one bargaining unit to deal with. Furthermore, to the extent that 'management and unions have learned to cooperate more effectively in the negotiation process, CBAs have become an important tool for ensuring positive relations between employees and the organization, and for making workers and the workplace more productive' (Covell & Walker, 2013: 332). Also, unions give employees a voice where they otherwise might not have one. Where employees do have a voice, through both macro- and micro-level participation, they may be generally content with the employee–organization relationship and less likely to feel the need for the formal collective voice of a union.

GRIEVANCE

Despite an organization's best attempts to provide a workplace that is productive for the organization and rewarding to employees, dissatisfaction is inevitable. This can occur if an individual's needs are not met, their formal or psychological contract is violated or they have a sense of unfair or poor treatment in the organization. When dissatisfaction is expressed overtly, the organization needs to be prepared to address the employee(s) concerns. Just as providing a positive working environment is critical to employee relations, so too is providing a mechanism for expressing concerns about that environment. At a basic level, a complaint is a 'spoken or written [dissatisfaction] of which supervisors or managers are made aware' (Lewis et al., 2003: 282). Further to that, a grievance is a complaint that is 'presented formally to management or a union official through the use of a recognized procedure' (Lewis et al., 2003: 282). The grievance procedure is reviewed here.

An employee, or group of employees, may have a grievance in relation to: (1) the conditions of employment (e.g., pay, physical conditions, job design); (2) ideology in the workplace (e.g., person-organization goal conflict, perceptions of inequity); and (3) relationships (e.g., employee–management, union–management, discrimination, harassment) (Lewis et al., 2003). The latter group constitutes the most common basis of grievance (Lewis et al., 2003).

An organization must have an effective grievance procedure in place so that employees feel they have a viable mechanism for dealing with contract violations and unfair treatment (Booth et al., 2004). A formal grievance procedure is typically built into the CBA of any trade union. However, an organization need not rely on a union to establish a process for dealing with formal complaints in a fair and timely way.

There are several basic steps and elements in any grievance procedure, which are as follows.

1 Attempt informal resolution first. A complaint is more likely to be resolved amicably or in a collegial fashion at an early stage. According to Booth et al. (2004: 102), 'mediating between two aggrieved individuals is often far quicker and easier than immediately suggesting they turn to the [formal] grievance procedure to resolve their differences'. However, a formal process must be available at any point if an employee is not comfortable with an informal discussion, perhaps because of a power differential or the nature of the ill treatment, or feels he or she is not being taken seriously.

2 If informal resolution is unsuccessful or inappropriate, there is a move to formal resolution. This involves the following.

   a The complainant or griever provides a written submission to his or her supervisor (or higher if the supervisor is directly involved in the complaint) or union outlining the issue.

   b An initial meeting is held, with subsequent meetings as necessary, to investigate the grievance. The complainant is able to be accompanied to any grievance meeting by a colleague or union representative.

   c Specific timelines for a decision on the grievance are communicated.

   d A decision is rendered by the organization, which may or may not be acceptable to the complainant.

3 If there is no resolution, the grievance may move to arbitration, where an independent body renders a final decision.

In any grievance procedure the following considerations should be taken (Booth et al., 2004; Lewis et al., 2003).

- Attempt to deal with grievances quickly and fairly, 'before they develop into major problems and possibly collective disputes' (Lewis et al., 2003: 286).
- Make all employees and management aware of their right to grieve, and the grievance procedure in the organization. This includes informing the employee of his or her right to appeal the decision, and potential disciplinary action if the grievance is upheld (e.g., formal apology, transfer, termination).
- Maintain written records of all formal interactions during the grievance process, in support of interactional, procedural and, ultimately, distributive justice.

Members of a union are bound to a formal grievance procedure for their own protection. If any steps are not followed by either party (employees or management) it amounts to a breach of contract, with further consequences for employees or management. A formal grievance process may be challenging in a small sport organization – for example, a private fitness or sports club where there are relatively few staff and the owner is the supervisor, or there is one manager below the owner. In this case the head of the organization has an obligation to deal with the situation as impartially as possible.

HEALTH, SAFETY AND WELLNESS

Every sport organization has a moral and legal obligation to provide a safe and healthy working environment. We begin this section by considering hazards and risks at work, and conclude with a review of employee assistance and wellness programs.

Workplace hazards and risks

A safe workplace is one that is relatively free from hazards and risk. A workplace hazard is 'any source of potential damage, harm, or adverse health effects on ... someone under certain conditions at work' (Canadian Centre for Occupational Health and Safety [CCOHS], 2009: para 3). Hazards may be classified as biological (e.g., bacteria, viruses), chemical, ergonomic (e.g., repetitive movements, improper workstation), physical (e.g., radiation, electric shock, lighting, noise, temperature), psychosocial (e.g., harassment, violence) and safety (e.g., slipping, equipment malfunction) (CCOHS, 2009). In the sport organization setting, hazards may include substances or materials such as pool chemicals or cleaning agents, workplace conditions such as wet floors, excessive noise or overcrowding, and certain job practices such as outdoor adventure instruction, race car driving or fitness class instruction.

Risk is the 'probability that a person will be harmed or experience an adverse heath effect if exposed to a hazard' (CCOHS, 2009: para 8). For example, we can expect that the risk of harm or adverse health effect in the form of fatigue or injury increases in direct relation to the number of fitness classes an instructor teaches back to back, and the level of those classes. The chance of harm to lifeguards is inherently high because of their workplace conditions (i.e., wet floors, proximity to a body of water).

While some hazards cannot be eliminated, the risk of harm or adverse effect can be controlled. It is incumbent on the organization to ensure that the employees are aware of the hazards and risks of a job, and of the procedures the organization has in place to minimize the risk or potentially harmful effect of the hazard. Employees must in turn take some responsibility for being aware of their working environment, and adhering to safety procedures and standards. A job safety analysis, similar to a job analysis described in Chapter 3, is a systematic way to identify potential accidents or hazards associated with a particular job, and to design appropriate preventative measures (CCOHS, 2008). There are four basic steps in a job safety analysis (CCOHS, 2008), listed below.

1   Select the job to be analyzed (priority may be based on frequency/severity of accidents and new/modified jobs where hazards are unknown).
2   Break the job down into a sequence of steps.
3   Identify potential hazards (consider what could happen for any given work step).
4   Determine preventive measures to overcome these hazards (eliminate or reduce the hazard, revise work procedures, reduce exposure).

The analysis should be conducted by directly observing the employee doing his or her job, with follow-up discussion to ensure all steps or activities have been accounted for. For example, a supervisor can analyze the job hazards experienced by a gymnastics coach by observing that person as he or she conducts classes or training sessions. The supervisor can pay attention to what the coach does to prepare him or herself for the physical work involved, the actual tasks involved, time on task, rest periods and so on. The coach can then discuss what he or she considers to be hazardous and risky activities. The job safety analysis may be most relevant for employees who do physical work in potentially hazardous conditions. However, workstation design can also be critical to the health and safety of office workers (e.g., gym club receptionist, sports information officer, sports team head office staff).

Hazards and risks can be controlled by: (1) elimination of the hazard from the workplace (e.g., removing asbestos, eliminating outdoor adventure classes); (2) engineering controls, which involves re-designing the workplace so that the hazard or risk is reduced (e.g., improved ventilation, reconfiguring equipment or workstations); (3) administrative controls, which involves altering the way the work is done (e.g., shift length, program scheduling) and work practices standards (e.g., training, personal hygiene); and (4) personal protective equipment worn by employees to reduce the risk of harm (e.g., water shoes for lifeguards, sun hats for camp counselors) (CCOHS, 2006).

Consider Box 9.2, which outlines the phenomenon of sexual harassment as a workplace hazard for female sports writers, editors and columnists.

BOX 9.2

Sexual harassment: a workplace hazard for women in sport print media

Sport media is an industry that continues to be dominated by men. A US study reported that over 90 per cent of sports editors, assistant sports editors, columnists and reporters were men (Lapchik, 2008), and as a result women may be perceived as intruders (Claringbould, Knoppers & Elling, 2004). Pederson, Lim, Osborne and Whisenant (2009: 337) further noted that 'one outcome of the intrusion of women into these historically male dominated institutions is the subjection of women to harassment in the workplace'. They examined the extent to which women in sport print media have encountered sexually harassing behaviors. Title VII of the US Civil Rights Act of 1964 and the subsequent Equal Employment Opportunity (EEOC) guidelines define such behavior as,

> Unwelcome sexual advances, requests for sexual favors, and other verbal or physical conduct of a sexual nature [that] is made either explicitly or implicitly a term of condition of an individual's employment … is used as the basis for employment decisions affecting such individual, or … unreasonably [interferes] with an individual's work performance or [creates] an intimidating, hostile or offensive work environment.
>
> (Pederson et al. 2009: 337–338)

In a study of over 100 women employed as sport print media professionals, 51 per cent reported encountering some form of sexual harassment in the workplace in the previous 12 months (Pederson et al. 2009). The harassing behavior was from a variety of individuals with whom the women came into contact while employed, and most often co-workers (31 per cent), other sport media professionals (22 per cent), athletes (18 per cent), coaches (15 per cent) and immediate supervisors (9 per cent). The most common form of sexual harassment reported by these women was verbal incidents (50 per cent), followed by unwelcome sexual advances (26 per cent), incidents of physical conduct of a sexual nature (13 per cent) and requests for sexual favors (10 per cent). The women believed that in at least one-third of the incidents the behavior was intentional.

Pederson and colleagues (2009) reported that almost half of the women suffered adversely as a result of the harassing behavior, including 11 who actually changed jobs because of it. However, just over half indicated that they either directly addressed the sexual harassment or certainly did not tolerate it. Several women noted that organizational policies and guidelines provided some clarity and support in that regard. Pederson et al. (2009: 356) subsequently encouraged sport print media organizations to (continue to) work to 'prevent or at least reduce' sexual harassment in the workplace by adopting several strategies including '(1) developing and publicizing a sexual harassment policy ... (2) developing and publicizing a grievance procedure to resolve sexual harassment complaints ... (3) conducting periodic sexual harassment sensitivity training sessions ... and (4) surveying employees to determine if sexual harassment is occurring'.

Employee stress

The organization also has an obligation to provide a workplace where employees are not at risk of, and do not suffer from, excessive levels of stress (Booth et al., 2004). Stress has physical, psychological and behavioral ramifications, ranging from headaches and sweating to anxiety and job dissatisfaction, to reduced performance and turnover (Langton, Robbins & Judge 2010). Understanding what contributes to stress in the workplace can help to alleviate or avoid it. Stress is a condition caused by an individual's inability to cope with constraints or demands (Langton et al., 2010). The more important and uncertain the outcome of a given situation, the more stressful is that situation. For example, a tournament organizer will be more stressed by the demands of getting the event ready to go if she is very committed to the event, but is uncertain whether it will go well. A tournament organizer in a similar situation will be less stressed if he does put a high priority on the event and/or is fairly confident everything will go well.

The hazards and risks presented earlier can be a source of stress in the workplace. Work-related factors that are most likely to lead to stress are 'poor internal communications, lack of resources, and a decrease in staffing resulting in an increase in workload' (Booth et al., 2004: 96). However, stress is not caused by work factors alone. Non-work stress is believed to contribute to an overall level of personal stress that has implications for employee satisfaction and performance at work. Organizations must try to prevent or at least reduce workplace stress by managing the above-noted sources of stress and controlling workplace hazards. In addition, employee assistance programs (EAPs) exist to help staff deal with stress resulting from various sources (Booth et al., 2004).

Employee assistance and wellness programs

Employee assistance is a general term that refers to a variety of confidential counseling services that are made available to employees (McKenna & Beech, 2002). EAPs are an employer-sponsored, non-financial extrinsic benefit or reward (see Chapter 8 for a review of rewards). The intent of an EAP is to help an employee whose job performance may be adversely affected by personal problems. Services can include support pertaining to mental health, substance abuse, marital problems, parenting problems and financial management. Many of the problems that affect an individual's work performance are in fact not work related. However, it is in the organization's best interests to provide support to help its employees deal with any issues that may ultimately impact productivity and employee satisfaction. In-house EAPs, where counseling is provided on-site, tend to be found only in very large corporations. Instead, it is more common to outsource employee assistance services, which also has the advantage of a greater sense of confidentiality and impartiality.

The elements of EAPs tend to be fairly standard across all types of organizations, with some variation in the extent of services supported, and some variation in organization-specific services that may be included. For example, the EAP in several of the CBAs in the professional sports industry reviewed in Table 9.1 focus on support for recreational and performance-enhancing substance abuse.

A more proactive approach to a healthy workforce is the concept of employee wellness programs. The recent attention to employee wellness in and beyond the workplace is a result of the acknowledged impact that overall physical, mental and emotional health can have on employee attendance, performance, and retention, with potentially substantial savings to the organization. Thus, the wellness approach to employee health 'focuses on preventing accidents, injuries or illnesses before they happen' (Covell & Walker, 2013: 331). This proactive approach encourages employees 'to engage in a range of behaviors and activities associated with better health' (Covell & Walker, 2013: 331), including regular exercise and better nutrition, regular medical examinations and financial planning. In-house or outsourced educational seminars on a variety of topics related to a healthy lifestyle complement counseling services offered through an EAP, all in support of a productive workforce. Employee assistance and wellness programs come at a (sometimes great) cost to an organization. Yet, 'these expenses are generally found to be much lower than the potential productivity gains from a healthy work force' (Covell & Walker, 2013: 331). In addition, the wellness program may add to the attractiveness of the organization as a place to work and might be used in recruiting new staff and as a point of differentiation from the benefits offered by competitor organizations.

VOLUNTEER–ORGANIZATION RELATIONS

Many of the employee relations principles and practices that have been outlined in this chapter are equally relevant to ensuring a productive and mutually satisfying relationship between the organization and volunteers: the sport organization and its volunteers have reciprocal obligations, which are described below; volunteers may be expected to equally value justice in the organization's practices and processes; and volunteer involvement is critical as one of the main reasons they contribute their time and effort is to make a difference in the organization (Cuskelly, Hoye & Auld, 2006). Although communication with volunteers may be more challenging than with employees who have a more regular schedule and contractual link with the organization, it is equally important that volunteers are kept informed. Volunteer involvement is also enhanced through participation in decision making, with consideration for the degree and scope of that influence, and level and form of involvement. As noted earlier, voluntary sport organizations whose boards tended to involve others in major decisions and tended to delegate decision making were more attractive to volunteers (Østerlund, 2013). Further, in a study of community sport club volunteers, Egli, Schlesinger and Nagel (2014) found that volunteers could be grouped according to their expectations of the club. Notably, 'participation and communication' (Egli et al., 2014: 12) were particularly critical to older volunteers (41 years and older) and those who had been volunteering less than five years. These volunteers 'had above-average expectations [for] informed about important decisions in their club and expected a constructive exchange of knowledge and experience' (Egli et al., 2014: 10).

The health and safety of volunteers is also of critical importance to the organization. In addition to the hazards and risks noted earlier, volunteers may be susceptible to liability in certain sport-specific situations, and the organization has an obligation to offer legal protection. For example, the majority of volunteer coaches work with children and youth who are a vulnerable population. While the sport organization needs to protect its participants, it also needs to protect the volunteers who provide programming and services to those participants.

As with employees, the relationship between the organization and its volunteers must be based on exchange, where volunteers receive valued intrinsic and sometimes non-financial rewards as a result of their involvement and contributions to the organization. The organization also has a social and moral obligation to treat its volunteers well (cf. Chelladurai, 2006). The Australian Sports Commission (2014c) outlines a list that indicates that volunteers have the right to:

- orientation to the [organization] and their role
- a clear job description
- support and respect from the [organization], no matter how small their role
- guidance from a supervisor or club member in charge
- access to training
- insurance and feeling safe while volunteering
- know who they are accountable to and have clearly defined communication channels
- know what is expected from them.

In turn, sport volunteers have an obligation to honor their commitment to the organization by undertaking their responsibilities in a timely and conscientious manner, and with respect and integrity (Volunteer Canada, 2006). Again, positive volunteer relations are based on practices and processes that engender a productive working environment that is satisfying to sport volunteers.

TERMINATION OF EMPLOYMENT

A final consideration in employee relations is the termination of the employment relationship. The employment, or volunteer, relationship ends because of dismissal, resignation or retirement. When an employee resigns or a volunteer leaves, a sport organization may wish to conduct an exit interview or survey to determine why the individual chose to terminate the relationship.

Dismissal

An employee's employment may be terminated because of dismissal by the employer, defined as an involuntary requirement for the employee to leave the organization. 'Fair' reasons for dismissal include: (1) conclusion of a fixed-term contract; (2) gross misconduct; (3) lack of capability or qualifications for the job; or (4) redundancy through organizational downsizing (Lewis et al., 2003). A volunteer is most likely to be 'dismissed' because he or she has reached the end of a fixed term on a sport organization's board of directors.

Gross misconduct can be distinguished from general and serious misconduct. General misconduct can be characterized by such things as absenteeism or poor performance, while serious misconduct may be characterized by unaccounted absences or a refusal to perform. In contrast, gross or severe misconduct is defined by particularly serious offences such as theft or fraud, violence or abusive behavior, deliberate damage to company property, significant incapability or severe insubordination (Lewis et al., 2003). In law, such gross misconduct represents an immediate repudiation of the contract by the employee and usually confers the right on the employer to move to immediate dismissal. Repeated acts of general misconduct may constitute serious misconduct, and repeated acts of serious misconduct may constitute gross misconduct. However, usually (or ideally), disciplinary action is taken by management before behavior escalates to gross misconduct. Progressive discipline (Government of Canada, 2013) may begin with speaking to the employee and providing a verbal warning, while allowing for two-way communication, with the hope that behavior improves and the problem is solved. Failing that, a written warning about possible suspension is given. If behavior is still unchanged then a suspension is given. Ultimately the employee is dismissed if the problem remains unresolved.

Lack of capability or qualifications is a fair grounds for dismissal 'if an employee lacks the skills, aptitude, physical health or correct qualifications to carry out the duties of the job' (Lewis et al., 2003: 349). This may be due to long-term illness or a series of short-term illnesses or an inherent inability to do the job (Lewis et al., 2003). The latter may be realized because of ineffective hiring, but it may be more likely to occur when one's job has changed to include tasks that the employee is not capable of undertaking. For example, an administrative officer of a growing private sports club who was hired when all tasks were done manually finds himself increasingly being asked to work with different data management software and he is not keen to learn how to use these applications. If he is unwilling to upgrade his skills to handle this new aspect of his job, he may have to be dismissed and replaced with someone who has the capability and aptitude required in this changed job role. Progressive 'discipline' (Government of Canada, 2013) to deal with incompetence parallels the performance management process discussed in Chapter 7. It begins with clarifying job expectations and providing training and supervision as required, allowing the employee the opportunity and time to improve his or her job performance, providing written warning of consequences if work does not improve, and eventually a performance review. If performance does not improve and the problem is not solved then continued incompetence is a fair grounds for dismissal.

A third 'fair' reason for dismissal is redundancy because an employee's job no longer exists. This could be the case with the administrative officer in the example above, if the position itself was deemed to no longer exist (rather than just being redesigned). Redundancy occurs when positions are eliminated and resurrected in different forms (as could happen with a renaming of the administrative officer position) or are eliminated altogether because of downsizing. For example, a fitness club may dismiss one or more instructors if the classes they teach are discontinued.

We have focused on reasons for 'fair' dismissal, which presumes there can be 'unfair' dismissal. In most developed countries, the law prohibits employers from unreasonably, harshly or unfairly dismissing workers and sets out legal remedies should this occur. Specific potential reasons for claims of unfair dismissal are on grounds of gender or racial discrimination, joining a trade union, pregnancy or childbirth, taking or seeking parental leave, taking action to ensure health and safety standards are observed, retail employee refusing to work on Sundays, and taking lawful organized strike action (Lewis et al., 2003). Employees have recourse to claim compensation from the employer for unfair dismissal. Employers may also 'wrongfully' dismiss workers in which case an employee can sue for damages under common law as a civil remedy. The typical basis for a claim for wrongful dismissal is where an employer has improperly terminated a fixed-term contract. This circumstance is one that may apply to players contracted to professional sports clubs who are terminated before the expiry of the contract. If there is not a clause in the contract allowing this, or if the termination is not on contractually specified reasons, then the player may have grounds to claim 'wrongful dismissal'.

Resignation or retirement

Alternatively, an individual's employment may be terminated because of resignation or retirement, or voluntary departure. As noted earlier, volunteers may be dismissed from their role when their fixed term, such as on a board of directors, comes to an end. However, they are most likely to end their relationship with a sport organization because they choose to resign or retire from their position. Employee resignation or retirement may be due to age or health-related reasons, taking a job elsewhere, or following a spouse or partner to a different geographical location (Lewis et al., 2003). Resignation may also be due to breach of contract by the employer. Also known as 'constructive dismissal', this form of resignation involves the employee terminating the contract (resigning) because of the employer's conduct with regard to changing the terms or conditions of employment without the employee's knowledge or consent (e.g., reduction in pay, change in position, work location or hours) (Lewis et al., 2003). If a sporting goods retailer decided to eliminate the sales staff's salary and put them on commission-only wages, they could claim constructive dismissal upon resigning from this less than desirable situation if they did not consent to the new pay structure. In the example of the administrative officer of the private sports club, if he decided to resign his position he could claim constructive dismissal as the basis for his resignation if he did not agree to the position changing to include different duties. Another grounds for constructive dismissal is harassment or abuse by the employer (Government of Canada, 2013).

Termination and severance pay

As a last gesture of the employee–management relationship, an organization may be required to provide termination pay, which is compensation in place of sufficient termination notice. Some employment standards laws exclude employees who are dismissed because of misconduct from receiving termination pay (e.g., Ontario Ministry of Labour, 2013a). Termination pay is usually a 'lump sum payment equal to the *regular wages* for a *regular work week* that an employee would otherwise have been entitled to during the written notice period' (Ontario Ministry of Labour, 2013a: 5, italics in original). In contrast, severance pay may be provided to employees to compensate them for loss of seniority and job-related benefits when their employment has been 'severed'. Employment is considered to be severed if the employee is dismissed, laid off for an extended period (e.g., at least 35 weeks in a 52-week period; Ontario Ministry of Labour, 2013b), or laid off because the organization's business is permanently discontinued. Labor laws in different countries and regions dictate who qualifies for severance pay (e.g., minimum length of employment with an organization), and what organizations are obligated to provide such compensation (e.g., based on minimum payroll). To illustrate, a sales associate with a sporting goods store that is part of a national chain should receive termination pay if he or she is dismissed immediately without written notice. That same sales associate should also receive severance pay if he or she has been with the organization for a minimum period of time (e.g., five years) (Ontario Ministry of Labour, 2013b).

Exit interviews

When an employee resigns or a volunteer leaves, a sport organization may choose to undertake an exit interview or survey. The purpose is to try to understand, and identify patterns in reasons for resignation. For example, are staff leaving because of pay levels, working conditions, the job or task itself (e.g., challenge, responsibility, boredom), the supervisor and his or her leadership style, relationships with colleagues, and so on. A sport organization may be inherently curious to know why an employee or volunteer chose to leave, with the understanding that it might try to do something to improve on particularly problematic areas. However, Torrington, Hall and Taylor (2002) suggest that the data collected through exit interviews may not be very accurate. If an employee has already secured a new job, he may be not be able to clearly recall why he really left his original job – for example, if a coach is getting a higher salary at a new club, he may indicate that he left the last club because of low pay, when the primary reason was really because of lack of autonomy with respect to handling his team. Also, a former employee may still be hoping for reference letters from the organization, and so will be reluctant to say what she really thinks about the workplace. Nonetheless, the exit interview can provide the departing employee or volunteer with 'a chance to give some constructive feedback, and to leave on a positive note, with good relations and mutual respect' (Chapman, 2005: 1).

The exit interview may be conducted face-to-face, by phone or as a survey which the departing employee or volunteer completes on-site or at home (either a pen and paper or online survey). The focus of an exit interview is typically on reasons for leaving, reflections on the positive and negative aspects of the organization, level of satisfaction with various aspects of the workplace (e.g., pay, workload, safety, training, promotion opportunities, leadership), the individual's job and the organization in general. It may consider some of the very elements of SHRM considered in this book: HR planning, recruitment and selection, orientation to the organization (depending on length of tenure with the organization), training and development, rewards, employee relations and management of diversity. Table 9.2 provides a sample of questions from an exit survey that is conducted with former

TABLE 9.2 Sample questions from an exit interview for departing staff of a fitness club (rating scale of 1 Unacceptable to 10 Perfect)

1. How would you rate the resources available to you to do your job?
2. How would you rate how well you were appreciated and thanked for your work?
3. How would you rate the skill development and training opportunities available to you?
4. How would you rate the level of teamwork, and people available to turn to for help?
5. How would you rate the flexibility of your work schedule, and/or work arrangements?
6. How would you rate the level of trust and respect you had for your manager?
7. How would you rate the career opportunities available to you?
8. How would you rate your salary or hourly wage?
9. How would you rate the commission and bonus portion of your pay?
10. How likely are you to recommend this club to your friends and/or family as a place to work?

staff of a fitness club chain. Ideally, the individual would have an opportunity to elaborate on his or her answers, allowing that person to reflect on each aspect and providing the organization with more in-depth information. However, it can be a challenge to recruit departing employees and volunteers to take part in this voluntary process.

SUMMARY

Employee relations are defined as the activities and processes that maintain a productive workplace while satisfying the needs of employees. Employee–management relations are based on mutual obligations, which are reflected in the employee's psychological contract with the organization. Critical to positive employee relations is a sense of organizational justice. Staff and volunteers alike need to perceive that their working environment is characterized by distributive, procedural, and/or interactional justice. In general, the principles and practices associated with employee relations apply to volunteer relations with the organization as well.

Central to positive relations is the strategic process of employee and volunteer involvement. Effective communication and participation in decision making are two critical mechanisms for promoting employee involvement. Trade unions are another mechanism for employee involvement, as union members have a collective voice when negotiating or bargaining with the organization over working conditions such as pay, benefits, workload and grievance procedures.

Formal grievance procedures in the union and non-union environment provide employees with the opportunity to seek recourse for what they perceive to be breach of contract or ill treatment. The grievance process must be well laid out and communicated to employees and volunteers, so that they know there is a fair and just mechanism in place for handling formal complaints.

A safe and healthy workplace must be provided to employees and volunteers. This means that the working environment must be relatively free from biological, chemical, ergonomic, physical and psychosocial hazards. Controlling the risk of harm or adverse health effects due to hazards is the mutual responsibility of the organization and its employees and volunteers. Employee assistance and wellness programs may be instituted to help staff deal with non-work personal problems that may affect their performance in the workplace.

The employee relationship will end with dismissal, resignation or retirement. Grounds for employee dismissal may be the conclusion of a fixed-term contract, gross misconduct, lack of capability or qualifications, or redundancy. When an employee resigns, the organization may conduct an exit interview or survey to attempt to understand the reasons for the departure, as well as to gather any insight into the former employee's positive and negative experiences in the organization.

DISCUSSION QUESTIONS

1   Refer to an organization for which you have worked or volunteered. What efforts are there to promote employee or volunteer involvement, if any? (Consider communication, participation in decision making or any other forms of involvement.) Is employee or volunteer involvement effective in that organization? How could it be improved?

2   Using the example of employees at a private golf club, design a plan to involve different types of staff in different types and levels of decisions. How much influence should they have (see Figure 9.1)?

3   Take a look at the CBA of one or more professional sport players' associations. Many are publicly available on the World Wide Web. What particular aspects of the CBA stand out for you? What is the strategic rationale behind the key features of each CBA?

4   Think of a sport organization with which you are most familiar. Describe various types of work hazards in that organization. What is the risk associated with each of those hazards (noting any variation by job type)? What does the organization do, if anything, to reduce the hazards and the risk of harm or adverse effect?

5   Look up the employment standards act in your state, province or country. How is dismissal defined? What is the legal procedure for fair dismissal by an employer?

6   Design an exit interview or survey for volunteer coaches. What questions would you ask? What form would it take (personal or phone interview, pen and paper survey, online survey)? How would you encourage departing coaches to provide the desired information?

CHAPTER 10

Sport organizations and diversity management

LEARNING OBJECTIVES

After reading this chapter you should be able to:

- Explain factors contributing to workplace diversity
- Describe the benefits and challenges of diversity in a sport organization
- Discuss the strategic management of workplace diversity

CHAPTER OVERVIEW

People differ in many ways and this has implications for workplace interactions. Diversity management refers to managing differences to capitalize on the benefits of diversity and to minimize its potentially negative consequences. This chapter examines the nature and extent of diversity in the workplace, and identifies various forces that contribute to that diversity. The challenges of a diverse organizational workforce and the potential for positive and negative impact are considered. This is followed by a discussion of strategies for managing diversity to ensure the fair treatment of all employees and volunteers, and recognizing the complexities of diversity in the workplace.

DIVERSITY IN THE WORKPLACE

The nature of diversity

Diversity is defined as a variety, assortment or mixture. Here we are interested in the nature and impact of a variety or mixture of personnel in sport organizations, and implications for strategic human resource management (SHRM). Cunningham (2007: 6) defines diversity in the workplace as *'the presence of differences among members of a social unit that lead to perceptions of such differences and that impact work outcomes'* (italics in original). A key element of this definition is that diversity is a perception and thus differences are in the 'eye of the beholder'. A group of male community sport club coaches may view themselves as very similar because they are all male, or very diverse if they are from different racial backgrounds or some are single parents while others are not. Diversity is a significant issue in sport and sport organizations today as changing demographic trends in many countries and legal mandates (e.g., Title VII Civil Rights Act in the US) are combined with the perceived value that diversity can bring to the workplace (Cunningham, 2009).

Perceptions of diversity may be based on demographic or surface level differences, and psychological or deep level differences among individuals (Harrison, Price & Bell, 1998). Surface level differences are found in personal attributes such as sex, age, race or physical disability – characteristics which may be readily detectable by others. We may also include such personal demographics as sexual orientation, socioeconomic status or religion in our description of surface level differences. They represent social categories that can be used to differentiate between people. These personal attributes contribute to individuals' perceptions that they are with others who are similar or different to themselves at least at a surface level.

Deep level differences are found in underlying psychological characteristics such as values, beliefs and attitudes. Deep level differences may also be found in cognitive skills and abilities, including knowledge and experience (Jackson, May & Whitney, 1995; Milliken & Martins, 1996). These attributes are less readily observable and for the most part can be known only through extended interaction with others. Thus, diversity based on deep level differences may only become apparent after individuals or the workgroup have had some meaningful interaction.

We can expect deep level differences to have the greatest consequences for workplace outcomes, because they reflect diversity in the values and attitudes that inform people's decision making and behavior (Adler, 1997). However, diversity based on surface level features may generate anxiety among staff and volunteers about possible differences among individuals, given the unknown, uncertainty and even prejudice that may accompany the perception of diversity. These can have a considerable impact on workplace outcomes as well. Nonetheless, research indicates that, as people continue to interact with one another in the workplace, differences in surface level attributes become less important than deep level attitudinal diversity (Harrison et al., 1998).

Considering again the example of the community sport club coaches, they may either appear on the surface to be a diverse group because of differences in race, or parental status or both, or perceive themselves to be a homogeneous group because they are of the same sex. In fact, any diversity within the group may instead be a function of deep level differences in values regarding community level sport and how it is played. Some of the coaches may feel that it is most important for all kids to have a chance to play; others may feel it is most important for the team to experience success, perhaps at the cost of having lesser skilled players spend more time on the bench. This diversity in perspectives may be expected to be more critical to the coaches' effort and performance, and the outcomes of the organization as a whole, than any surface level differences such as race or parental status. Nevertheless, the example suggests a link between deep and surface characteristics – for example, it may be the parents who value all children playing. We can in fact expect a link between deep and surface level attributes (Doherty & Chelladurai, 1999; Cunningham, 2007). Individuals will possess any or all of the values, beliefs and expectations, as well as the customs and behaviors, of various groups of others who have similar surface characteristics (e.g., parents) to the extent that they identify most closely with those various characteristics (e.g., a coach may identify most strongly as being a parent, a male, an African-American and/or a Christian). However, we risk inaccurate and harmful stereotyping if we assume that someone with a given surface level characteristic possesses the underlying values and beliefs of that group (Johns & Saks, 2011). Only through interaction can we know an individual's deep level attributes and understand whether we are similar or different in that regard.

Several factors contribute to workplace diversity. Changing population demographics, legislation regarding hiring practices, proactive hiring to increase diversity in the organization in order to capitalize on potential benefits, the nature of work that continues to reflect a team-orientated approach where interdependence and interaction is intensified, globalization, and changing attitudes in society and the workplace towards differences that lead to an increased awareness of diversity all contribute to the increasing perception and reality of differences among staff and volunteers in sport organizations (Cunningham, 2007; Johns & Saks, 2011). We consider each of these factors further.

Changing population demographics

Changing population demographics has a direct influence on the makeup of the workforce in general, which translates to diversity in the workplace. Two population changes that are particularly notable with regard to the workforce or employment pool are an aging population and immigration. A report from the Population Division of the United Nations Secretariat (United Nations, 2013) projects that, between 2013 and 2050, the proportion of the world population under 15 years of age will drop from 26.2 to 21.3 per cent; the proportion of what is defined as working age (15–59 years) will drop from 62 to 57.5 per cent; and the proportion of the population aged 60 years and over will increase from 11.7 to 21.2 per cent. Table 10.1 provides details for several countries. With an aging population we can expect greater age diversity as organizations, including sport organizations, increasingly rely on older workers and volunteers to meet their needs.

Immigration makes a substantial contribution to population growth in many Western countries. This can have a major impact on the proportion of racial or visible minorities in the workforce (immediately and through subsequent generations), as well as increasing

TABLE 10.1 Projected population figures (per cent) of selected countries

Country	2013			2050		
	Under 15 years	15–59 years	60 years and over	Under 15 years	15–59 years	60 years and over
Australia	19.1	61.2	19.8	17.9	54.4	27.6
Canada	16.4	62.3	21.2	16.5	52.8	30.7
China	18.0	68.1	13.9	14.7	52.5	32.8
Japan	13.1	54.6	32.3	12.5	44.8	42.7
New Zealand	20.2	60.5	19.3	17.0	54.1	28.8
United Kingdom	17.6	59.2	23.2	16.6	52.6	30.47
USA	19.5	60.7	19.7	18.2	54.8	27.0
World	26.2	62.0	11.7	21.3	57.5	21.2

(Source: United Nations, 2013)

the ethnic, language and religious diversity. For example, in Canada, visible minorities comprised 16.2 per cent of the population in 2006 (Malenfant, Lebel & Martel, 2010). This figure is expected to almost double to one-third (32 per cent) of the population over a 25-year period. During that time, the population will be particularly bolstered by Canadian-born visible minorities – the children of immigrants – as well as continued immigration particularly from China and South Asia. The sharpest increase is expected to be among Arab and West Asian immigrants. India continues to be the top source country for permanent migrants to Australia, with China and the United Kingdom ranked second and third respectively (Australian Government, 2013). Immigration is expected to continue to make a substantial contribution to the projected 40 per cent increase in the population of Australia through to 2051, largely because of its 'non-discriminatory immigration policy' (Andrews, 2006: 1). Diversity in the workforce as a result of increasing immigration will continue to be manifested in sport organizations as well. The Coaching Association of Canada is one sport organization that is aware of changing population demographics with respect to immigration. It commissioned a study entitled 'Engaging new Canadians in coaching' the purpose of which was to determine recent immigrants' motives and barriers to getting involved in coaching (Coaching Association of Canada, 2006).

Demographic changes obviously vary from country to country. As noted earlier, many Western countries are experiencing low birth rates and aging populations. This is in contrast to numerous emerging economies and developing nations where the youth population is dominant. In Asia, countries such as China introduced measures such as the one child policy to mitigate their massive population growth.

Legislation

Diversity in the workplace may be attributed in large part to legislation protecting the rights of individuals in the recruitment and selection process. Sport organizations are held to local, regional and federal government statutes that are in place to ensure equity and equality in hiring. Civil and human rights legislations and equal opportunity laws make it unacceptable and illegal to discriminate based on sex, age, race, disability and so forth. The Australian Human Rights Commission Act (1986), Disability Discrimination Act (1992), Sex Discrimination Act (1984) and Racial Discrimination Act (1975), the Canadian Charter of Rights and Freedoms (1982) and the Canadian Human Rights Act (1985), the American Civil Rights Act (1991) and Americans with Disabilities Act (1990), and the United Kingdom's Disability Discrimination Act (1995) are some of the laws that protect prospective employees in these countries. In civil law, the EU legal system offers protection against harassment and discrimination on the basis of ethnic origin. The Racial Equality Directive (Council Directive, 2000) covers the area of employment (including selection criteria and promotion or membership in any 'organization whose members carry on a particular profession'), but also many other areas of life. The result is increasing diversity based on surface level characteristics that were a traditional basis for discrimination in hiring. See the case in Box 10.1.

Affirmative action is government policy stemming largely from human rights legislation that actively seeks to redress past employment discrimination by increasing the representation of certain disadvantaged groups, particularly women and racial minorities. It is manifested in organizations through initiatives ranging from encouraging members of

BOX 10.1

Title IX and gender diversity in sport leadership

Title IX of the Education Amendments Act (1972) in the USA is a law that prohibits sex-based discrimination in educational programs that receive federal government funding. While the legislation is not specific to sport, it likely impacts sport more than any other law (Cunningham, 2007). It requires that males and females be given equal opportunities to participate in federally funded activities, which includes athletics programs in high schools, colleges and universities.

Title IX has had a major impact on the growth of female participation in sport, particularly in high schools where girls comprised only 5 per cent of high school athletes in 1972 and 41 per cent in 2002 (Acosta & Carpenter, 2005). At the collegiate level, the average number of women's teams per institution rose from 2.5 in 1972 to 8.73 in 2012 (Acosta & Carpenter, 2012).

Despite, or perhaps because of, the increased support for girls' and women's athletic programs as a result of Title IX, there has actually been a decrease in the proportion of women in coaching and administrative leadership. Ninety per cent of coaches of women's collegiate teams in 1972 were women, which dropped to around 43 per cent by 2012 (Acosta & Carpenter, 2012). In 1972, 90 per cent of administrators of women's athletics were women, and in 2012 women comprised only 36 per cent of athletic administrative staffs.

There are several explanations for this dramatic decline in the participation of women in sport leadership, including individual and structural factors that influence women's interest and opportunity to be involved. Another explanation is that leadership opportunities in well-supported and increasingly prestigious women's programs are an attractive option for men, who are more likely to be hired in those positions than women (Cunningham, 2007).

In the end, this legislation, which has been successful in its mandate to ensure equal opportunities for male and female participation, has likely had a negative impact on the participation of women leaders in high school and collegiate sport organizations, and reduced the level of diversity there.

underrepresented groups to apply for jobs, to the establishment of quotas for the hiring of individuals from particularly disadvantaged groups. The intent of affirmative action is to correct the imbalance of underrepresented groups of employees in an organization that have historically faced employment discrimination. Yet affirmative action is not without its critics, who claim that it is in fact reverse discrimination, contravening human rights legislation as it gives preferential treatment to one group over another. Consequently, affirmative action policies and programs have generally evolved to include an 'all things being equal' clause, where an individual from a targeted group is selected if all bases for selection are considered equal among all candidates. Affirmative action is a factor affecting increased diversity in sport organizations. The examples on Box 10.2 illustrate the positive effect of affirmative action in sport organizations.

BOX 10.2

Affirmative action in sport organizations

The Fédération Internationale de Football Association (FIFA) adopted the Buenos Aires Resolution against racism, in which the delegates 'noted with deep concern the current infiltration of racist elements into football stadiums and other activities connected with football' (Fédération Internationale de Football Association [FIFA], 2001: para 5). The resolution required 'all football bodies at all levels to ensure racial equality in the employment, appointment and election of individuals in all areas of activity and to work with ethnic groups to involve them more closely in football activities' (FIFA, 2001: para 20).

In order to increase the number of women occupying leadership and administrative positions in Olympic sport, in 1997 the International Olympic Committee (IOC) set a target for National Olympic Committees (NOCs), International Sports Federations (IFs) and sports bodies belonging to the Olympic Movement to have at least 20 per cent of the positions in all their decision-making structures held by women by the end of 2005 (IOC, 2006). This objective was not achieved. In 2013 the IOC reported that 11 NOCs were headed by female presidents, 24 females served as secretaries general and several more as vice-presidents, deputy secretaries general, treasurers and deputy treasurers in the executive committees of the 204 NOCs (IOC, 2013d). IOC recognized International Federations were noted to have 26 per cent female representation on their Executives (IOC, 2013d).

Beyond beginning to redress gender imbalance, further apparent benefits of the IOC's affirmative action initiative are consistent with the diversity strategy of proactive hiring, which is discussed shortly. We have also discussed this matter in other chapters of this book in relation to human resource (HR) planning, selection, orientation, training and development, and succession and talent management.

In our discussion of various forces that influence workplace diversity, we should take a moment to consider the degree of diversity found in sport organizations.

How diverse are sport organizations?

The Institute for Diversity and Ethics in Sport at the University of Central Florida produces a comprehensive dataset in The Racial and Gender Report Card (RGRC). This scorecard is an assessment of hiring practices of women and people of color in a selection of professional and amateur sports and sporting organizations in the United States. The report considers the composition – assessed by racial and gender make up – of players, coaches and front office/athletic department employees in the country's leading sports organizations, including the National Basketball Association (NBA), National Football League (NFL), Major League Baseball (MLB), Major League Soccer (MLS) and Women's National Basketball Association (WNBA), as well as in collegiate athletic departments. The data is updated on an annual basis and the most recent reports can be found at www.tidesport.org/racialgenderreportcard.html.

Consider Box 10.3, a 2013 news report in *Forbes* magazine (Forbes, 2013).

BOX 10.3

Diversity management in the NFL

By failing to hire any minorities to fill eight head coaching and seven general management vacancies following the conclusion of the 2012 NFL regular season, the NFL made it abundantly clear that diversity management remains a serious challenge. This is very concerning when you consider that in 2003, the NFL specifically established the Rooney Rule to ensure that minority coaches were considered for senior level coaching positions. This is yet another example of how diversity is managed as an initiative, rather than a best practice. However, unlike America's corporations and political parties that tend to hide their diversity management problems – and in many cases 'cut checks' to keep minority group activists quiet – the NFL is taking responsibility and holding themselves accountable for these recent hiring actions.

After NFL teams decided to pass on minority candidates, NFL Executive Vice President of Human Resources Robert Gulliver stated, 'While there has been full compliance with the interview requirements of the Rooney Rule and we wish the new head coaches and general managers much success, the hiring results this year have been unexpected and reflect a disappointing lack of diversity' (Forbes, 2013: para 2).

Diversity remains an issue, not just with paid employees, but also within the ranks of sport volunteers. Across a number of countries, including Canada, Australia and England, the profile of community sport volunteers is fairly narrow, suggesting a relatively homogeneous rather than diverse volunteer workforce with regard to certain surface level attributes. According to a report from Canada, the 'typical' community sport volunteer

BOX 10.4

Discussion question

What might hinder diversity among volunteers in community sport organizations (consider any of the factors that promote diversity as factors that may, instead, limit diversity – e.g., available workforce, hiring, societal expectations)?

is male (64 per cent), 35–44 years of age (41 per cent), a college or university graduate (53 per cent), married (73 per cent) with dependents at home (62 per cent), employed full time (82 per cent), with a household income of $60–99,000 (Canadian) (43 per cent) (Doherty, 2005a). Coaches are an even more similar group, where 73 per cent are men (Doherty, 2005a). Data from Australia and England reveal similar profiles of sport volunteers (Cuskelly, Hoye & Auld, 2006) and coaches specifically (Dawson, Wenner, Phillips, Gastin & Salmon, 2013).

Proactive hiring and inclusive culture

The potential for increasing gender and racial diversity may be attributed to employment legislation, affirmative action or both. It may also be the result of proactive hiring. The strategic objective of proactive hiring is to actively increase diversity in the organization in general or with respect to a particular surface level attribute (e.g., gender, age, race, physical ability), with the intent of capitalizing on the potential benefits of a diverse workplace. These benefits include increased creativity and improved problem solving because of the diversity of values, perspectives and attitudes that are presumed to be brought to the table by people who differ from each other. Another potential benefit of diversity is increased understanding of the marketplace, which allows the organization to better serve different customers, and to further develop services and marketing strategies targeted to a broader (more diverse) customer base. A diverse workforce may also enhance an organization's corporate image and reputation, and help position it as an employer of choice to attract skilled workers (Worman, 2005).

Box 10.5 illustrates a preliminary proactive hiring initiative to increase diversity in NASCAR (National Association for Stock Car Auto Racing, Inc.) organizations.

BOX 10.5

Diversity internships at NASCAR

The National Association for Stock Car Auto Racing Inc.'s (NASCAR) long-running Diversity Internship Program provides opportunities for qualified candidates to work with NASCAR's sanctioning body, NASCAR sponsors and licensees, NASCAR teams and track, and other motorsports-related companies.

College/university students are employed in a 10-week summer program designed to introduce them to the world of NASCAR and the exciting career opportunities available throughout the motorsports industry. The program is designed to support deserving students with an interest in the motorsports industry who are of Alaskan Native, American Indian, Asian/Pacific Island, African-American, Hispanic or other racial minority descent.

For more information about the NASCAR Diversity Internship Program visit www.findinternships.com/2013/03/nascar-diversity-internship-program.html

The nature of work

As organizations continue to structure their work around teams (Langton, Robbins & Judge, 2010; Johns & Saks, 2011), employees continue to work more interdependently and interactively with others. It is not uncommon, for example, that a national sport organization will create committees to work on various initiatives (rather than assigning the task to individuals), such as developing a coaching education program. Such a committee may comprise individuals with surface and deep level differences. A 'team' of lifeguards at an aquatics facility may be established to improve communication, generate cohesion among the staff and commitment to the organization, and increase efficiency in scheduling. Given demographic changes in the workforce and changing attitudes towards diversity in the workplace (see later), we may expect some degree of diversity in this workgroup. Through workgroup or team member interaction, surface and deep level differences become apparent and are reinforced through continued interaction (Harrison et al., 1998).

Globalization in the sport industry and its impact on sport organizations may be reflected in the diversity it creates in the workplace. Examples of workplace diversity created through the ever-increasing connection between people, cultures and economies around the world include the composition of international sport governing bodies (e.g., IOC), the staffing of multinational sport corporations such as Nike with local employees, parent-country nationals and third country nationals, and the international movement of athletes and coaches (e.g., approximately one-third of players in North America's National Hockey League (NHL) who typically come from more than 15 countries outside of North America). A global workforce requires employees and volunteers to interact with others from different national cultures and backgrounds.

Changing attitudes towards diversity

Changing population demographics, human rights and employment legislations, proactive hiring and the very nature of work have brought us face to face with people who are different from ourselves. The increasing level of diversity, but particularly its increasing acceptance in society and in the workplace, has heightened our awareness of differences. Employees and volunteers cannot be expected to completely set aside their values, lifestyle preferences, and even customs when they join an organization (Robbins & Langton, 2004). It has made us more aware that we are different in many ways. As noted earlier, diversity in the workplace is really a function of the perception of diversity – whether we see differences among ourselves or not. Therefore, diversity in sport organizations, as in all organizations, is also affected by our increasing awareness of differences (both surface and deep level). To the extent that diversity is beneficial in the organization, the organization will benefit from increasing awareness about differences among people.

THE IMPACT OF DIVERSITY IN THE WORKPLACE

Diversity in the workplace is a critical concern for SHRM because of its potential impact on workplace outcomes. SHRM is concerned with aligning an organization's human resources with its strategic goals and initiatives. A diverse workforce creates certain challenges that can both threaten and enhance organizational effectiveness. We now discuss the potential positive and negative ramifications of diversity at work.

Benefits of diversity

In general, diversity is assumed to be beneficial to an organization because of the different values and perspectives it brings to the workplace. Most of the research on organizational diversity has focused on surface level differences, such as gender, race and age. Thus, it is important to bear in mind that when we talk about the benefits, and challenges, of workplace diversity we are generally referring to surface level differences and the deep level diversity that implies.

As noted earlier, the benefits of diversity in the workplace may include increased creativity and improved problem solving, and greater marketing insights that may be available from diverse employees (Chelladurai, 2005; Johns & Saks, 2011). These insights and different perspectives (deep level diversity), as a function of diverse backgrounds and experiences, are what contribute to increased creativity and innovation, a broader range of alternatives and higher-quality ideas in a diverse workplace. Diverse individuals and groups may be expected to 'generate unique alternatives and challenge old ideas and standard ways of doing things' (Doherty & Chelladurai, 1999: 284). In this way, diversity can be a source of constructive conflict in the group or organization such that higher-quality decisions are the result.

The benefits of diversity depend on the extent to which individuals work on complex tasks where there is discretion in decision making and new ideas are expected and valued (Doherty & Chelladurai, 1999) – for example, event planning, policy development or marketing strategy. Benefits are also more likely to accrue when diverse individuals work interdependently with others on tasks that require interaction and collaboration (Doherty & Chelladurai, 1999). Thus, diversity will be more or less meaningful in different situations. It can be expected to be less beneficial, and less detrimental, where people work on simple, standardized tasks, or have little need or opportunity for interaction with others in the workplace or both – for example, a parking lot attendant at a sports facility, ticket takers at a sports event and even sales associates at a fitness club or sporting goods store, where the tasks are very standardized and scripted. In the latter case, however, a diverse staff who mirror the (current and potential) customer base may be very beneficial to the organization.

The potential benefits of diversity do not come without a cost. In addition to the challenges of workplace diversity, which we will discuss shortly, research indicates that a diverse group is likely to take longer than a more homogenous group to complete its problem-solving tasks (Cunningham, 2007). It takes time to overcome some of the challenges created by the interaction of diverse individuals. Nonetheless, the outcome of that interaction (idea generation, decision making) can be expected to be superior to that of groups of individuals who are similar to each other. Efficiency may be sacrificed for the effectiveness that comes from workplace diversity.

The case in Box 10.6 provides an illustration to let us consider how workplace diversity can benefit a sport organization.

Challenges of diversity

One of the basic challenges of a diverse workforce is the anxiety and even fear that it can generate among employees and volunteers who are faced with the unknown. When someone is different from us, in either surface or deep level characteristics, it creates some uncertainty about what to expect from that person. For example, if a woman joined the all

BOX 10.6

The Original Gus Macker 3-on-3 Basketball Tournament

Gus Macker 3-on-3 basketball has grown from a driveway game in Lowell, Michigan in 1974 to the Macker Tour which hosts indoor and outdoor tournaments in over 75 cities across the US (and one in Canada). More than 200,000 players and 1.7 million spectators take part in 3-on-3 competitions every year. Local hosts partner with the national organization to operate the tournaments. There are competition categories for men and women, boys and girls, catering to almost every age and ability level. Participants are very diverse; the only thing they may have in common is their love of street basketball! In addition to the basketball action, the organizing committee of each tournament donates a portion of the proceeds to a local charity(s).

The six basic objectives of Gus Macker are as follows.

1   A wholesome, family orientated event.
2   A tournament designed by players for players.
3   A value to sponsors.
4   An outstanding fundraising event for the local community.
5   A major media sporting event.
6   Entertaining for the spectators.

The national organization is focused on the long range success and continued growth of the Gus Macker 3-on-3 Basketball Tournament.

Information from www.macker.com

For discussion

Consider (with specific examples) how surface and deep level diversity could help the national organization (and local hosts) meet these objectives and continue to grow.

male group of community level coaches described earlier in this chapter, her presence may create some anxiety on the part of the group because of the surface level perception of her being different from the other coaches, and thus an unknown entity with regard to coaching. Some members of the group may have concerns about her ability, interests and intentions with regard to coaching. Uncertainty and anxiety may be heightened when one or more persons in the group is diverse from the others in several respects – for example, with regard to gender, age, sexual orientation and race. Multiple differences may intensify the sense of the unknown and the associated discomfort. When members of the community level coaching group get to know the new female coach, through personal and group interactions, they will become aware of her deep level attributes (including her ability, interests and intentions with regard to coaching). This increased understanding may reduce, or further increase, perceptions of diversity and associated uncertainty.

Diversity can also create barriers to effective communication, such that the intended message is not received or is not understood by the intended recipient. Potential barriers to communication among a diverse workforce include language that is not understood well by the receiver (e.g., too sophisticated or technical, not the receiver's first language), and 'noise' in the communication channel caused by biases and prejudice on the part of the sender or receiver (McKenna & Beech, 2002). Communication is critical to carrying out the work of the organization. As noted in Chapter 9, it is also key to involving employees and volunteers in the organization and promoting positive employee relations. Diversity training, which is discussed later in this chapter, is aimed at reducing the biases that compromise communication by educating and enlightening employees and volunteers about the nature of differences in the workplace. English-as-a-second-language (ESL) training is another example of attempts to reduce barriers to effective communication among a diverse workgroup by promoting a common language in a country where the first language is English. Barriers to communication can, of course, intensify the unknown and uncertainty associated with diversity in the workplace, where different individuals are not hearing or understanding each other.

Prejudice is a key barrier to communication and workplace relations, and may be heightened where there is diversity. It is defined as an unfavorable attitude towards a group, and by extension anyone who is perceived to be a member of that group, by virtue of some characteristic that all members of the group possess. Prejudice is a negative bias that is often based on 'faulty and inflexible generalization' (Allport, 1954: 9). Discrimination is the further act of distinguishing or differentiating between people on the basis of some personal characteristics, such as age, sex, race, disability, religion, political beliefs or sexual orientation. Discriminatory behavior occurs when a potential or current employee or volunteer is treated less favorably because of some personal attribute, when compared to someone without that attribute. Discrimination can range from subtle favoritism (e.g., a supervisor selects someone more similar than different to himself for a preferred assignment) to overt antagonism (e.g., refusing to work with a colleague who is considered to be different on surface, or deep level characteristics or both), to harassment. Harassment is a behavior 'that is unwanted by [an] individual that affects the dignity of any individual or group of individuals at work' (Lewis, Thornhill & Saunders, 2003: 414). Acts of harassment include not only unwanted physical, written or verbal contact, but also social exclusion. Harassment in the workplace is consistent with bullying (Booth, Fosters, Robson & Welham, 2004). The likelihood of prejudice and discrimination in the workplace is increased when employees or volunteers can be distinguished or differentiated on some personal basis. Research suggests that discrimination is pervasive in sport organizations: women tend to face limited opportunities for advancement in intercollegiate athletics departments, women have more negative work experiences than men, racial minority coaches perceive fewer opportunities for advancement and receive fewer promotions, and gays and lesbians report prejudice and fewer opportunities for advancement in the workplace (Cunningham, 2007).

Diverse individuals who are in the minority in the organization or workgroup are likely to experience more stress in the workplace than others, and are at a disadvantage if their differences are not tolerated. They are less likely to be effective and succeed in the organization when attitudes and behavior different from their own are expected and rewarded. Yet, diversity can also have a negative impact on those who are in the majority in terms of shared surface and deep level attributes. With diversity they may face contrasting and conflicting values and expectations, disrupted communication, and threats to their power and status in the workplace. Diversity comes with benefits and challenges.

The outcome of the diversity challenges may be reduced communication, misunderstanding, ambiguity or confusion, and destructive conflict where consensus is not possible and the conflict becomes more important than the task at hand (Doherty & Chelladurai, 1999). These outcomes can be expected to have a further impact on reduced effort and performance, absenteeism and turnover.

Sport organizations can realize the potential benefits of diversity to the extent that there is diversity in the workplace, it is accepted there, and individuals and workgroups take advantage of differing perspectives that diversity may bring. However, the organization must effectively manage those differences and work to overcome the potential challenges of miscommunication, stereotyping and prejudice, and the uncertainty and anxiety that may cause for all in the organization, not just those who may be in the minority. We turn now to a discussion of strategies to effectively manage diversity.

MANAGING DIVERSITY

The focus of managing diversity is about both creating and optimizing on a diverse workforce. As noted earlier, diversity is likely inevitable in the organization, yet it should also be proactively cultivated. However, there are both benefits and challenges associated with a diverse workforce, with implications for SHRM. We begin by considering legal requirements related to managing diversity, then examine how an organization may capitalize on diversity through an organizational culture that values diversity. Finally, we examine diversity training as a mechanism for meeting an organization's legal requirements as well as developing and strengthening an organizational culture that values diversity.

Legal perspective

In many countries and regions, governments have enacted legislation to ensure the fair treatment of citizens, including employees and volunteers in the workplace. Many of the legal requirements that have led to an increasingly diverse workforce, and which were noted earlier (i.e., civil and human rights legislations), also serve to support and protect organizational employees from discrimination, inequity and harassment. Thus, legislation also serves to manage diversity by protecting people who may be discriminated against on the basis of being different.

Many sport organizations and sport governing bodies have also adopted their own policies that dictate fair and just practices with regard to the treatment of diverse employees. Canadian Interuniversity Sport (CIS), the governing body for interuniversity athletic competition in Canada, has an equity policy which states that it:

> accepts the principles of equity and equality and will ensure that these principles are adhered to in all its activities ... Equity refers to treatment that is fair and just. This definition includes gender, race, ethnicity, language, disability, income and other diversities ... Equality means that all persons enjoy the same status regardless of gender, race, ethnicity, language, disability, income, and other diversities. It means that all persons have equal conditions for realizing their full rights and potential and to benefit from the results.
>
> (Canadian Interuniversity Sport, 2013: 80–29)

All Canadian universities that are part of the CIS must abide by its policies, and demonstrate a commitment towards gender equity – for example, in hiring practices, coaching salaries and support for professional development.

Organizational culture approach

The focus on managing diversity implies that the realization of potentially positive or negative consequences of diversity is a function of how that diversity is managed. We cannot just expect good things to come of differences in the workplace; there are many challenges and potentially negative consequences of diversity as well. Government legislation and organizational policies provide formal guidelines and requirements that help to deal with diversity and the potential challenges it creates. Doherty and Chelladurai (1999) provide a different perspective which is to consider organizational culture as a guiding force for managing diversity.

In Chapter 5, we introduced organizational culture as an underlying system of values, beliefs, and assumptions regarding what is important and how things are done in an organization. These values, beliefs and assumptions are manifested in such organizational processes as communication patterns, decision making, performance appraisal and rewards systems, which reflect what is valued and how things are done, and help to guide employee and volunteer behavior. Thus, Doherty and Chelladurai (1999) argue that an organizational culture that values diversity provides a superior backdrop for the effective management of diversity, in comparison to an organizational culture that values similarity. As noted earlier, employees and volunteers cannot be expected to completely set aside their values, lifestyle preferences and even customs when they join an organization. These things contribute to diversity in the organization. Instead, the challenge to the organization is to accommodate differences and value the diversity they bring to the organization.

An 'organizational culture of diversity' (Doherty & Chelladurai, 1999) is characterized by respect for differences, flexibility, risk acceptance, tolerance of ambiguity, conflict acceptance and equifinality or achieving the same ends by different means. It is manifested in two-way, open communication, performance appraisal based on performance or outcomes rather than style, a flexible and equitable reward system, multilevel decision making and open group membership. In contrast, an 'organizational culture of similarity' (Doherty & Chelladurai, 1999) is characterized by parochialism or ethnocentrism which assumes that there is one best way of doing things, rigidity, risk avoidance, intolerance of ambiguity, conflict avoidance and a 'difference is deficit' perspective. It is manifested in one-way, closed communication, performance appraisal that focuses on style or how things are done rather than how well they are done, an inflexible reward and promotion system, unilateral decision making and closed group membership.

Figure 10.1 presents a theoretical framework that makes several propositions regarding the interactive effect of workplace diversity (on a continuum of high to low) and an organizational culture that values diversity or similarity (Doherty & Chelladurai, 1999). It assumes a strong organizational culture where values and assumptions are widely understood and accepted, and guide member behavior (McKenna & Beech, 2002; see Chapter 5). Cell 1 describes an organization characterized by high diversity and an organizational culture of similarity. In this situation, it is expected that few benefits of diversity may be realized and there is an increased likelihood of negative consequences. The challenges of diversity are

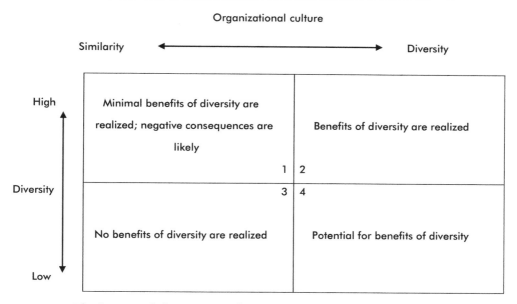

FIGURE 10.1 The impact of diversity as a function of organizational culture (Source: adapted from Doherty & Chelladurai, 1999: 290)

heightened as differences are very present in the organization yet are not tolerated there. As a result, individuals are likely to feel discriminated against; 'time is not taken to overcome the ambiguities associated with ... diversity, and the opportunity for constructive conflict is avoided' (Doherty & Chelladurai, 1999: 290).

Cell 2 describes an organization characterized by high diversity and a culture that values diversity. The benefits of diversity can be realized as individuals feel accepted, and enhanced creativity and constructive conflict can result. In addition, organizations that are more aware and accepting of different points of view become more open to new ideas in general and can be more responsive to their environment than those that have closed and rigid approaches to problem solving (Milliken & Martins, 1996). Cell 3 describes an organization that has little diversity and values similarity. In this situation the potential benefits of diversity cannot be realized, although the challenges of diversity are also less likely to be experienced. Cell 4 describes an organization characterized by low diversity yet an organizational culture that values diversity. In this situation there is potential for the benefits of diversity to be realized if the organization was to become more diverse.

Cunningham (2009, 2011) found support for the positive impact of proactive diversity management that is consistent with a culture that values diversity. Racial diversity in intercollegiate athletic departments was positively associated with organizational performance when those departments were characterized by open communication, strategies intended to capitalize on individual differences, and policies and procedures aimed at preventing problems (Cunningham, 2009). Similarly, Cunningham (2011) found that sexual orientation diversity was positively associated with organizational performance when NCAA athletic departments had a proactive, inclusive diversity culture and performance was inhibited when the organizational culture of those departments was not lesbian, gay, bisexual and transgender

(LGBT) inclusive. To best leverage diversity with LGBT populations Cunningham and Melton (2011) recommend attracting employees who are LGBT to the workplace, and creating and sustaining a proactive and inclusive diversity culture. This could be accomplished by, for example, attendance and employer recruitment at LGBT-specific events and conferences, such as the Gay Games, and ensuring the sport organization is seen as diverse and systemically integrating diversity initiatives throughout the organization.

Indeed, the Doherty and Chelladurai (1999) framework has implications for the effective SHRM of diversity in terms of developing and strengthening an organizational culture that values diversity and increasing diversity in the organization to capitalize on the benefits that may be accrued in this environment. In Chapter 5, we discussed several ways to strengthen or change organizational culture. Briefly, the organization's leaders have an important influence on guiding the direction of organizational culture through what they pay attention to and modeling their own workplace behavior. Organizational culture is influenced through recruitment and selection, where employees or volunteers with certain values and perspectives can help to reinforce or change culture in a desired direction. This is consistent with the notion of proactive hiring to increase diversity discussed earlier. Organizational culture can also be strengthened or changed during the socialization of newcomers and further training and development, where desirable values are presented and reinforced. Diversity training is an opportunity to develop and strengthen an organizational culture of diversity.

Diversity training

The purpose of diversity training is to educate employees and volunteers about diversity-related issues so that they are better able to understand and deal positively with diversity in the workplace. Diversity training comprises awareness training, skill-building or both (Robbins, 1997). Awareness training has the goal of increasing employee knowledge of and sensitivity to diversity and diversity-related issues in the workplace. Skill building has the goal of providing employees with a set of skills to deal effectively with workplace diversity. Diversity training should be included as part of training and development, as described in Chapter 6, and incorporate the principles associated with that process. In this way, diversity training may be viewed as one component of professional development, and received more positively than if it is addressed as an obligation on the part of the organization and its staff to be 're-educated' to be more 'politically correct'.

There are many potential benefits of diversity training (e.g., increased attraction and retention of diverse employees who are bolstered by the organization's commitment to diversity, fostering understanding among diverse individuals and groups, improved worker morale, curbing lawsuits) (Cunningham, 2007, 2012). However, there are also several barriers to its success: sensitive issues such as oppression, prejudice, discrimination and sexual harassment are typically not discussed in open conversation; staff may resist the notion of re-education in political correctness or feel they are being 'blamed' for any negative effects of diversity; and individuals may resist being 'helped' or singled out because they are different. These barriers to success can increase the negative effects of diversity (Cunningham, 2007).

Effective diversity training must be tailored to the particular organization, focusing on issues that are most salient there (e.g., discrimination against women or older workers, intolerance of different perspectives). A preliminary 'needs analysis' should be undertaken to identify the most salient diversity issues in the organization, as well as to confirm who will take part in the training, what information should be addressed, and in what form (Cunningham, 2007, 2012). Some of these considerations must take into account the 'training conditions', including trainees' readiness to learn and support for the training from managers and staff.

Diversity training methods may take a variety of forms, ranging from instructor-led information sessions, to cooperative group meetings, to mixed-gender or mixed-race role play sessions (Cunningham, 2007). Sessions usually begin by illustrating the value of diversity in the workplace, including the benefits that have been noted in this chapter, and increasing awareness of common stereotypes, including how they are formed and the implications of making (often false) generalizations. Diversity training is most effective when it provides an opportunity for individuals to reflect on their own differences, including how those differences may be assets to the organization, and to reflect on 'what it is like' or 'what it would be like' to be treated differently. This approach can enhance individuals' engagement in the training process. The next step is to develop skills to help individuals and workgroups deal effectively with workplace diversity. To be effective, diversity training must focus on the process of attitude change and skills development that is relevant to the needs of the organization (Johns & Saks, 2011). This may include skills for resolving intercultural conflict, team building or a second language. Finally, an effective diversity training program should include a follow-up to assess the content and form of the training itself (e.g., evaluate reactions, knowledge development, short-term behavior), and promote transfer of learning (e.g., ensure a supportive environment for change, reinforce and reward for positive behavior).

Importantly, Doherty, Fink, Inglis and Pastore (2010) concluded that initiatives such as diversity training will only be meaningful and sustained if individuals in the workplace are personally supportive of and even advocate for diversity, resist discrimination and observe institutional commitment to diversity. Relatedly, Cunningham (2012) found that effective transfer of diversity training knowledge, skills and approaches is contingent on employees' motivation for such training, but particularly the perceived integration or alignment of that training with the organization's mission, strategic plan, hiring practices and personnel evaluation.

SUMMARY

Workplace diversity can impact on work outcomes, both positively and negatively. Diversity is based on surface level or demographic differences and deep level or psychological differences. Changing population demographics, especially an aging population and an increasing influx of immigrants to Western nations, has an impact on diversity in sport organizations. Other factors that contribute to workplace diversity include employment-related legislation and practices (e.g., affirmative action), proactive hiring to capitalize on the potential benefits of diversity, changes in the nature of work and changing attitudes that lead to increased awareness of the diversity around us.

The benefits of diversity in the organization include creativity and better quality decisions as a result of different perspectives that challenge traditional ways of doing things. The organization may also benefit from an enhanced reputation as a diversity employer, improved recruiting when people in the workforce see people like themselves in the organization, and greater marketing insights into the needs and habits of diverse customers. Yet, workplace diversity also presents a number of SHRM challenges to the organization. Uncertainty, misunderstanding, ambiguity, confusion, anxiety, poor communication, stereotyping and prejudice, stress, and destructive conflict may result from the interaction of individuals who are different from each other. A further outcome may be reduced effort and performance, absenteeism and turnover.

The potential challenges and benefits of workplace diversity depend on the effective management of that diversity. Legislation exists to protect workers from discrimination based on being different. Organizational culture may be viewed as a strategic mechanism for ensuring that diversity is valued in the workplace, and that supportive organizational processes are in place. The potential benefits of diversity can be expected to be optimized, and the challenges minimized, where an organization has workplace diversity and an 'organizational culture of diversity' which is supportive of and capitalizes on differences.

Diversity training is a strategic program to educate employees and volunteers about diversity-related issues. The intent is to make the participants more aware of differences, including their own, and better prepared to deal with diversity issues in a positive way. Diversity training is one mechanism to develop or strengthen an organizational culture of diversity.

DISCUSSION QUESTIONS

1   Think of an organization where you have worked or volunteered, or with which you are very familiar. Describe the diversity in the organization's workforce (consider surface and deep level characteristics). How does that diversity (or lack of diversity, but rather, similarity) impact how work gets done, and how well it gets done (consider, for example, communication, conflict, creativity)?

2   In groups, discuss some general- and work-related stereotypes based on gender, race and age. Next, discuss stereotypes in sport based on these characteristics. What other stereotypes are there in sport organizations?

3   What deep level differences might be associated with age? Consider the values, expectations, customs and behaviors of different age groups. What implications does this diversity have for the organization and all who work or volunteer there?

4   In groups, discuss affirmative action policies and programs, using real or hypothetical examples. Are you, and your group, for or against affirmative action? Defend your position. Additionally, discuss affirmative action with regard to the parallel strategy of proactive hiring. Are you, and your group, for

or against a joint program of affirmative action and proactive hiring? Defend your position.

5   Refer back to the organization you described in Question 1. Based on the extent of diversity in the organization and your perception of the organizational culture there, where does it fit into the Doherty and Chelladurai (1999) framework in Figure 10.1? What can the organization do, if anything, to improve its management of diversity (e.g., increase diversity, develop or strengthen an organizational culture of diversity)? Discuss particular strategies for making that happen.

6   Identify an organization or type of organization (e.g., professional sports team, community recreation department) of your choice. Design a hypothetical diversity training program for that organization. Consider how you would design a needs analysis, training conditions, content and form of training, and follow-up.

CHAPTER 11

Managing change and future challenges in sport organizations

LEARNING OBJECTIVES

After reading this chapter you will be able to:

- Explain factors driving change in sport organizations
- Describe the human resource (HR) implications of change in the workplace
- Understand how to strategically manage change with respect to HR
- Outline challenges to sport organizations in the future and understand the implications for strategic human resource management (SHRM)

CHAPTER OVERVIEW

This chapter describes the key factors to consider with regard to SHRM when introducing or dealing with change in the sport organization. Planned change is a critical part of an organization's corporate strategy. The strategic corporate issue is the nature of change, while the SHRM issue is the implementation of that change and factors that influence the success of the change initiatives. The nature of change cannot be properly understood without acknowledging the acceptance of or resistance to the change among personnel who have to make it work. Effective human resource management (HRM) is an important part of the successful implementation of strategic organizational change.

There are many factors that drive change in sport and these can come from pressures from either the external environment (e.g., changes to government policy, introduction of competitors into the marketplace, changing patterns of sport participation, aging population) or the internal environment (e.g., decline in membership numbers, financial challenges to overcome, organizational inefficiencies, training needs). Forces that drive different types of change in sport organizations are presented in this chapter. The organizational change process involves the stimulus to take action, identification of the problem and selection of a solution, and finally the implementation of that solution or change initiative which takes the organization from point A to point B. Organizational change is often resisted when employees and volunteers do not share the organization's view about the particular change or about change in general. Humans are creatures of habit and dislike the uncertainty that accompanies any change process. There are several positive strategies that may be used to try to overcome resistance to change and to help people cope with the change in the organization. Key sources of resistance to organizational change and strategies for overcoming that resistance are presented here.

Sport organizations will no doubt experience much change in the next 5–10 years; continuing innovations in technology, the role of social media, changing demographics, together with the next generation's expectations about work and lifestyle, will impact on the way HR is managed and will require organizations to manage the accompanying changes to survive and capitalize on these in order to thrive. We outline some of the likely areas of big change and therefore future SHRM challenges in this chapter.

CHANGE IN SPORT ORGANIZATIONS

It is important to understand the concept of organizational change because: (1) change is inevitable for survival; (2) change is paradoxical in that it is necessary and inevitable, yet stability and predictability are inherently preferred states for organizations and individuals; and (3) successful management of change is essential for organizational effectiveness (Slack & Parent, 2006). The focus of this chapter is on planned change that is systematically developed and implemented vs. day-to-day fluctuations in the organization. Organizational development is a form of planned change and is included within our conceptualization of change.

Types of change

Change may be in the form of products or services that the sport organization offers, production technology, organizational structure and systems (e.g., HR, rewards), or people (Slack & Parent, 2006). Changes to what the organization offers in terms of products or services may be the most common form of change, and may precipitate change in other areas of the organization. For example, when Nike bought Bauer Performance Sports, it added ice hockey skates to its well-established line of running and basketball shoes. This acquisition and change to its product line had further ramifications for the manufacturing, marketing and retail systems of Nike Inc., and resulted in changes to the organization's structure and personnel. On a smaller scale, when a fitness club updates its programs (e.g., eliminating step classes and introducing spin classes), this is likely to have implications for personnel in the club, whether it is no longer employing staff who are not qualified to offer the new programs or providing existing staff with retraining.

Changes in organizational technology are exemplified by the dramatically evolving Internet technology. Sport organizations that are not keeping up with such things as an organization website, electronic retailing, online registration system, social media or live streaming may be considered behind the times and missing a critical mechanism for communicating with staff, volunteers, participants and consumers. Other technological changes include updated production processes, and skills and methods to deliver services. Video replay in sporting contests, computerized scoring in judged sports, computer software that facilitates everything from athlete training to event management, and increasingly sophisticated athlete drug testing are a few examples of technological changes realized in sport.

Changes to organizational structure and systems include modifications to the division of labor or the hierarchy of authority in a sport organization. As a new sport consulting firm grows it may create differentiated units to attend to various aspects of the business – for example, event management, athlete representation, finance and HR departments. Change to an organizational system can be illustrated by the partial or complete revision of a sporting goods retailer's pay structure – for example, with the introduction, or elimination, of a commission-based compensation system (see Chapter 8 for a discussion of rewards systems).

Finally, people changes refer to movement among and modifications within staff and volunteer ranks. People changes may involve hiring, promotion, transfer and dismissal, as personnel come and go or move elsewhere in the organization. Changes within people in the organization may involve at a personal level the development of new skills, values and attitudes in the workplace as a result of training and professional development.

Forces for change

Both internal and external pressures can lead to change in the organization. Internal pressure for change may come from such things as financial challenges or opportunities, operational inefficiencies or disgruntled employees. In order to overcome financial challenges – for example, a sporting goods retailer may eliminate staff, change its pricing structure or sell off part of its stock. In contrast, in order to pursue financial growth opportunities, a community recreation center may add programs, hire additional staff and even consider building or acquiring new sports facility space.

Pressures for change can also be exerted by external stakeholders of the organization and forces in the general environment. Pressure to keep up with competitors, and to better meet the needs of current and prospective customers, maintaining accountability to funding bodies (e.g., government, sponsors), changes in government policy and sport legislative bodies can provide the impetus for strategic organizational change. Sports organizations also face external pressures from the general environment that affect all organizations – for example, changing population demographics, the economy and legislation regarding free trade and human rights. The source, nature and strength of internal and external pressures for organizational change may impact staff and volunteers' reaction to and acceptance of change. For example, a large influx of older adults into the region may require the local swimming center to shift its focus from running learn-to-swim classes for children to offering aqua aerobics and seniors' keep-fit sessions. This type of change is gradual and non-threatening. However, a swimming center that changes from being a local government operated venture offering programs at low cost staffed by instructors with a community service orientation, to a commercial business only running programs with high profit margins with an expectation that staff would engage in sales-type activities might expect some resistance to change from its staff given the significant cultural shift required.

The organizational change process

As the earlier examples suggest, change involves moving from one state of affairs to another, based on various degrees of modification or complete replacement of existing conditions (products, services, technology, structures, systems, people) or the introduction of new conditions. Lewin's (1951) force field model suggests that, before embarking on planned change, an organization is in a state of equilibrium between forces that drive and restrain change. In order to effect change, the driving forces must be strengthened and the restraining forces weakened, so that the organization may 'unfreeze' from its current values, attitudes and ways of doing things, 'change' towards the desired condition, and then 'refreeze' the values, attitudes and practices that support the new condition.

Greiner (1967) elaborates on several stages that an organization goes through in the process of moving from one existing condition to another modified or new condition. A stages model of organizational change helps in recognizing the various pressures and actions throughout the process, and identifying where a breakdown in that process may have occurred. Figure 11.1 presents a simplified illustration of Greiner's stages of organizational change.

Each stage describes the action taken by the organization and (in parentheses) the factors influencing or prompting that action. The role and influence of management and staff is indicated throughout Greiner's (1967) stages model. Top management is prompted to take action by sufficient internal or external pressure, or both (stage 1). Refocusing on what are acknowledged as internal problems or needs (stage 2) is followed by diagnosis of problem areas by individual staff and workgroups or units resulting in the identification of specific problem areas (stage 3). Here the 'problem' is used broadly to refer to a dilemma or challenge faced by the organization. Successful organizational change involves staff in the diagnosis and identification of problem areas as it sends the message that their input is valued by the top management (Greiner, 1967). This is also the case at the next stage where potential solutions are identified and a preferred course of action is selected (stage 4); again, the involvement of staff can enhance the creativity and practicality of alternative solutions (as they are the ones adopting the change) and increase their commitment to the change process. The final stages, 5 and 6, involve evaluating the impact of small, incremental modifications as the specific organizational change(s) is introduced on a small scale at first, then expanded until the change is implemented in its entirety and, presumably, accepted.

Greiner's (1967) model is not perfect as it assumes a smooth, sequential process that does not account for incomplete or partial change (Slack & Parent, 2006). However, it is useful for understanding key steps in the change process, and the potential role and influence of staff at various stages. The importance of involving staff in the change process is consistent with the notion of creating positive employee relations presented in Chapter 9. It is also consistent with managing resistance to change that is manifested when people's views about change differ from the organization's and, at a basic level, when people prefer stability and predictability over the disruption and uncertainty that is inherent in organizational change. Resistance (restraining forces) must be overcome if the organization is to successfully unfreeze from its current conditions, change to its desired conditions, and refreeze into a state of equilibrium (Lewin, 1951). We turn now to a discussion of resistance to change, and managing that resistance.

RESISTANCE TO CHANGE

Organizational change is a critical SHRM issue in large part because of the expected internal resistance to change. Change may be resisted by external stakeholders as well; however, our discussion focuses on the internal workplace. As a restraining force (Lewin, 1951), resistance can affect how efficiently, and completely, the planned change has been implemented. Humans are creatures of habit and so we inherently prefer stability and

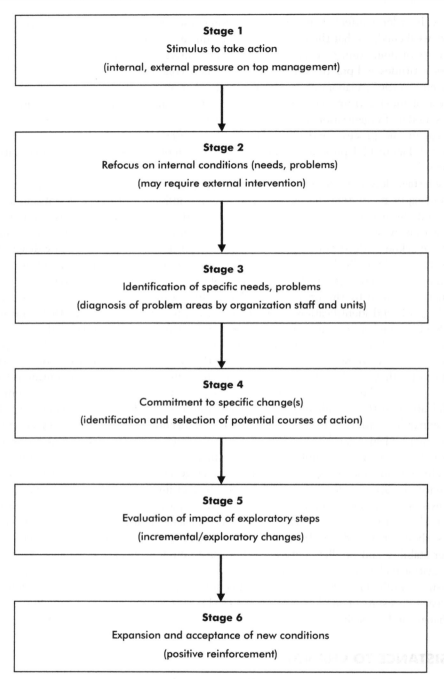

FIGURE 11.1 Stages of action (and factors influencing that action) in the organizational change process (Greiner, 1967)

certainty (Langton, Robbins & Judge, 2010). As such, change can be uncomfortable because it challenges established routines and practices. Of course, people will also resist change if they do not agree with the need, form or consequences of the planned change. Slack and Parent (2006) identify four major sources of resistance to change (consider these with respect to some of the types of changes noted earlier), as follows.

- *Self-interest*: people are focused on their own self-interests in the organization. As a result, change may be resisted if, for example, it threatens one's power or influence and expertise in the organization, if it results in reduced resources allocated to one's program or department, it compromises future job security and income or challenges an individual's values and beliefs.
- *Lack of trust*: the uncertainty associated with change may breed mistrust between management and staff or between staff who do and do not support the change. This mistrust is likely to cause resistance to change. If there is already a certain level of mistrust in the organization, change may heighten that situation and add to the resistance.
- *Differing perceptions of outcomes*: individuals may not value or give much weight to the purported need for change and the anticipated benefits or they may not feel that the anticipated benefits will be realized at all. As a result, they will resist change as a needless effort that will only create uncertainty and anxiety in the organization.
- *Cost of change*: change may be resisted because of the anticipated costs, in terms of time, money and effort, to implement the change, particularly if it is felt that the costs outweigh the benefits.

The expression of resistance to change may be overt or implicit, and it may be immediate or deferred (Langton et al., 2010). Resistance is expressed immediately in direct response to the announcement (or rumor) of change. Deferred resistance may be played out over time and continue, or be postponed to, well after the change has been implemented. Overt reactions include voicing complaints, writing letters, engaging in a work slowdown or even threatening to strike. Implicit resistance is more subtle and may be difficult to link to the proposed change – for example, loss of motivation, absenteeism, poor performance or reduced loyalty.

The case in Box 11.1 describes an example of organizational change and the resistance to it, which had a significant impact on the time it took for the change to be implemented.

MANAGING RESISTANCE TO CHANGE

Coping with change

Assuming that individuals prefer stability and certainty, and dislike the anxiety and stress caused by resistance to organizational change, we may expect that they will make every effort to cope with change. Coping is defined as a conscious effort to use one's resources to deal positively with a stressful circumstance(s) (Ashford, 1988). Understanding the psychological coping process can help organizations to support their workforce in dealing with change. Later in this chapter, we consider several strategies for helping personnel to overcome any resistance they may feel and to cope with the new organizational conditions.

BOX 11.1

The adoption of an anti-doping policy in an elite sport organization

Until six Finnish cross country skiers tested positive for blood doping at the 2001 World Championships in Lahti, Finland – the 'Lahti scandal' (Hanstad, 2008: 379) – the International Ski Federation (FIS) had what were considered to be relatively lax anti-doping policies and testing. This particular incident was a critical catalyst for change within the FIS, which had been pressured by various internal and external stakeholders over the previous two decades to increase its commitment to fighting what was believed to be widespread doping within the sport at the international level. Those pressures had, however, been countered by some individuals in the organization who either denied or ignored the issues. Some examples of resistance to adopt stronger anti-doping policies by the FIS included the following.

The FIS president from 1951 to 1998 neglected to make anti-doping a high profile issue within the FIS during his term, despite several incidents of high profile positive tests among cross country skiers in the 1980s and 1990s and its increasing attention across the international amateur sport world.

In the 1980s and 1990s, the majority of FIS Council members were representing other sports including ski jumping and alpine skiing, and did not have a primary interest in cross country skiing, the issues it was facing or the assignment of resources to deal with them.

The Chairman of the FIS Medical Committee, hailing from the strong cross country ski nation of Austria, failed to inform the FIS Council of tests, instituted in 1996/97, that revealed upper limit hemoglobin levels which 'indicated the probable use of doping' (Hanstad, 2008: 387).

The FIS Cross Country Ski Race Director claimed that he allowed a Finnish skier with an abnormally high hemoglobin level to participate in the 2001 Lahti championships in order to avoid the bad publicity that would inevitably result from such a ban.

Information from Hanstad (2008)

For discussion

1   Describe the resistance various individuals in the FIS were experiencing, and expressing, with regard to pressures to adopt more rigorous anti-doping policies.

2   Think about other examples of where there has been resistance to change in an organization. This might involve strategy or structural change, changes required by external reviews/pressure (e.g. to issues of ethics, integrity or discrimination) or adaption to a new technology. What were the main reasons for the resistance? Did the change go ahead? If yes, what were the key actions that supported the change? If no, why was the status quo retained?

According to Carnall (2007), employees and volunteers will go through a 'cycle of coping' with change – one that can have important implications for their self-esteem, motivation and performance. In general, when first presented with a proposal for change, individuals may experience *denial* that any change is necessary. Through this denial they may feel a heightened sense of self-esteem as they reflect on their attachment to the current way of doing things. Subsequently, individuals may experience *defense* as preliminary discussions take place about the nature and form of the change. This resistance can manifest itself in lowered self-esteem, motivation and performance as individuals feel threatened by the impending change. This resistance may continue as more concrete plans take shape and are presented in the organization.

The next stage in the coping cycle involves, eventually, *discarding* old attitudes and ways of doing things as individuals realize that the planned change is necessary and inevitable. This stage is consistent with 'unfreezing' the organization from its existing state (Lewin, 1951), and coincides with some improvement in self-esteem as individuals let go of 'the old way' and prepare to move on. Motivation and performance may continue to be suppressed as individuals experience uncertainty regarding what is expected in the transition from old to new. Next, individuals will experience *adaptation* by coming to terms with the new way(s) of doing things. This is consistent with the 'change' phase of Lewin's model. While individuals' self-esteem and motivation can be expected to increase with their greater understanding of and comfort with new conditions, performance may still lag behind, particularly where new skills are required. The final stage in the coping cycle is *internalization*, where the change is well understood and accepted, and the organization 'refreezes' to a state of equilibrium (Lewin, 1951). Increased self-esteem, motivation and performance can be expected as individuals have adopted the new conditions and acquired the knowledge and skills to perform in the new environment.

Strategies

There are several ways to overcome resistance in the organization (Langton et al., 2010; Slack & Parent, 2006). These strategies are intended to address the various types of resistance noted above.

1 *Communication and education*: resistance to change can result from a lack of information or misinformation about the need for change, nature of the change and anticipated consequences. Effective communication of thorough, accurate and timely information about the change process is necessary for managing resistance to change. Information can be shared through various methods of communication, depending on the volume and complexity of the information and whether feedback is desired – for example, memos or reports, individual, workgroup, departmental- or organization-wide staff meetings or workshops. Communication and education is an effective strategy for reducing resistance to change, assuming that inadequate information is the cause of resistance, and there is mutual trust and credibility in the management–employee relationship.

2 *Participation*: consistent with the employee relations approach advocated in Chapter 9, direct involvement in the change process, particularly in decision making, can be an effective way to generate commitment to the change, as well as taking advantage of

the knowledge and creativity of the personnel who will be directly associated with that change. Staff and volunteer participation in the change process, from the early planning stages (Greiner, 1967), is particularly important for those individuals who are or may be expected to be the most vocal opponents of the (or any) change. The trade-off of reduced resistance, increased commitment and greater quality decisions is the potentially heavy time cost to individuals and the organization for the meaningful involvement of staff and volunteers in the change process.

3   *Change teams*: groups formed specifically to facilitate communication, education, and participation of staff and volunteers in the change process can be very effective mechanisms for managing resistance in the organization. A change team (or multiple teams) may be, for example, a task force, transition team or an interdepartmental committee of employee representatives. Change teams are charged with participating in the change process on behalf of their colleagues, communicating with those colleagues about what is happening along the way (providing their perspective, or formal information from management or both), assisting with any training that is required as a result of the change, and providing counselling to staff and volunteers as requested. The participation of change teams is likely more efficient than the involvement of the full organizational workforce, and may be more effective in terms of compiling the information and bringing it to their peers.

4   *Idea champions*: individuals who are very committed to the notion of change in general, and the proposed organizational change in particular, are effective idea champions. They must be knowledgeable and well respected in the organization in order to play a key role in getting people involved in the change process and helping to counter any resistance. Idea champions may be identified by the organization and co-opted to serve that role, or they may emerge informally based on their commitment and knowledge of the change. Either way, they may be 'one of the most effective weapons in the battle for change' (Daft, 1992: 273, in Slack & Parent, 2006).

5   *Facilitation and support*: change teams, and the organization itself, can provide support to help staff and volunteers cope with the change process. A supportive atmosphere can help individuals deal with the anxiety and stress resulting from the uncertainty associated with change, which may lead to resistance. Employee counseling or therapy, skills training and even a short-paid leave of absence may facilitate the adjustment process, although there is no guarantee that these potentially costly efforts will lower resistance to change. They are most likely to be effective with personnel who need some help moving on to the 'discarding' and 'adaptation' stages of the coping cycle (Carnall, 2007).

6   *Negotiation*: another, perhaps last resort, strategy for overcoming resistance to change is through exchanging something of value in return for compliance with the planned change. This negotiation or bargaining tactic may be necessary when resistance comes from a powerful individual or group in the organization. For example, when several Canadian national sport organizations relocated from Ottawa (the capital of the country) to Toronto, Ontario (the *corporate* capital of the country), senior staff members were offered a pay increase and housing allowance to encourage them to accept the change.

Several of these strategies for managing resistance to change may be used in combination as the organization deems appropriate and necessary. The more traditional practices of manipulation (e.g., distorting or providing false information about change that makes it seem more attractive to employees, splitting, and therefore weakening, dissenting groups or covertly influencing powerful resistors) and coercion (e.g., threatening demotion, transfer or dismissal) for managing resistance by completely bypassing it are not consistent with the SHRM approach.

BOX 11.2

The adoption of an anti-doping policy in an elite sport organization continued

For discussion: Looking back at the case of change, or stalled change, in the FIS anti-doping policies (see Box 11.1), and considering the strategies noted above, what could the FIS (or at least those in support of change to more rigorous policies) have done to reduce resistance to the adoption of a stronger stance?

Continuing with the case: As noted, the Lahti scandal of 2001 (see Box 11.1) impelled the FIS to take action. The recently installed FIS president (in the third year of his term) took charge and 'reorganized the anti-doping activity without any influence from others within the FIS'; Council members 'were just told that this was the way it was' (Hanstad, 2008: 389). In addition, the Lahti scandal was likely a wake-up call to Council members representing other skiing sports and the possibility of being tarnished with the same brush. The result was a more interested and supportive Council with regard to the president's anti-doping initiatives. Other support came from the recently established (1999) World Anti-Doping Agency (WADA), which the FIS welcomed to provide expertise on cleaning up the sport of cross country skiing. To this day, the FIS continues to work with WADA and the IOC to promote drug free sport.

For discussion: Describe the strategies that were eventually used to overcome resistance to the FIS' anti-doping efforts.

Our discussion to this point has identified change as a strategic corporate issue that has critical implications for effective HRM to ensure its successful implementation in the organization. We turn now to a discussion of several challenges that will present internal and external pressures for change in sport organizations in the near future.

CHALLENGES FOR HRM

Contemporary sport organizations, like organizations in many other industries, need to deal with challenges and opportunities associated with globalization, technology and telecommunication advances, diversity and other workforce trends, demands for work/life balance, as well as trends in the nature of work (Langton et al., 2010). Perhaps particular to the sport industry, there is increasing interaction between sport and other forms of cultural engagement – for example, professional sport and celebrity, and fashion and music. The development of the Olympic Winter Games, for example, has been driven by concepts such as the X Games where sport, fashion and music merge to produce a holistic product that is different from sport in isolation – issues will emerge over the next 10 to 20 years that we cannot even contemplate today.

In addition to simply having a sense of what is going on around one's organization, environmental scanning is a systematic way for a sport organization, or organizations within a particular sector of the sport industry (e.g., fitness clubs, community recreation centers, professional sport leagues), to consider future challenges and their implications for the management of human resources. This can be done in steps (Bartlett & McKinney, 2003): (1) identify various sectors of influence in the organization's environment (e.g., economy, demographics, technology, market trends); (2) determine a time horizon upon which to focus (e.g., five to ten years, longer); (3) examine the environmental sectors for the given time period; (4) infer effects of the anticipated environmental change (how will it affect the organization; what will the organization need to do to respond); and (5) identify future organizational needs with respect to HR (e.g., training, career planning). Some of the challenges that currently face sport organizations or are escalating are outlined in the next section of this chapter.

Globalization

Globalization refers to 'growth of trade and investment, accompanied by the growth in international businesses and the integration of economies around the world' (Punnett, 2009: 6). While sport may still be delivered in local markets its reach and context is increasingly global, multi-faceted and complex. Regional priorities are often either influenced or overshadowed by a global economic perspective. Major sport events such as the Olympic Games and FIFA World Cup have faced major opposition and community backlash associated with the significant financial and social costs of these events to hosting cities and countries. In recent years the safety and security measures required by the event owners have escalated dramatically and led to changes in the associated HR requirements including more rigorous levels of security checks of employees and volunteers, through to an ever expanding security related workforce. Many sport organizations now think more globally when recruiting staff, from coaches through to CEOs. Local market restrictions are being removed and replaced by free trade agreements, and sport businesses are exporting expertise through franchises, partnerships and virtual operations. Global trends, competition for leisure time and new models of sport consumption are increasingly impacting and influencing local demand and the SHRM thinking, requirements and processes.

A sport organization's extent of globalization may be represented through a range of indicators such as the amount of foreign investment in the sport (e.g., the number of non-UK owners of football teams in the English Premier League) and the growing presence of multinational sport companies (e.g., Dorna Sports in Spain, UK and Japan). Satellite dishes in the world's most remote areas bring the sport product to audiences anywhere and anytime, and there is intense competition to buy the media rights to broadcast sport in and beyond national boundaries. Global telecommunication has opened up sports markets (e.g., the use of eBay and Amazon for match tickets and all types of sporting merchandize means that you can purchase via the Internet from wherever you are in the world). These changes have significant implications for workers and organizations as 'backroom' support services may be located in the country with the best access to the required human resource/labor pool (and wage structure). Many of the large multinational sport clothing apparel manufacturers and sport teams are a case in point as their production base shifts to low wage countries such as Indonesia and Cambodia to protect profit margins. For example, the Dallas Cowboys were in the news in 2012 for using sweatshop labor to manufacture apparel overseas and were criticized for violations of their own employee code of conduct in those factories (Fainaru-Wada & Gubar, 2012). In 2013, the college-logo apparel companies of Russell Athletic, Adidas, Knights Apparel and Top of the World signed a Bangladesh Safety Accord, an agreement between unions and brands to work towards creating safe workplaces.

Sport organizations that move or expand production or sales overseas to reduce costs or to develop synergies with local and regional market requirements need to ensure that their HRM policies and practices are appropriate to the host country conditions and requirements. This may necessitate adjusting job specifications and requirements, employment contracts, reward structures and performance management systems to meet local conditions. When moving into developing countries there may also be a need to increase the amount of training and development offered to staff. This includes training for both managerial staff from the organization's home country, who need to learn about the culture in which they will be working, and training for local employees to ensure they are orientated to and prepared for the requirements and expectations of working for the host organization. For example, many professional sports are establishing Asian affiliate leagues, which may require further development of sport business skills and knowledge in the local workforce.

There is an expanding array of jobs in the sport sector and many of these require a skilled and technologically savvy workforce. It is also anticipated that with global expansion there will be an increasing number of people who may be working for an organization, but who will not be physically working *in* the organization. Johns and Gratton (2013) suggest that there have been three waves of change in the last 30 year for knowledge work employees: first, as freelancers working via home computers; second, as global employees using mobile technologies and global teams; and third, through community and shared spaces that have been initiated to ameliorate worker isolation and drive collaboration. Managing virtual employees and teams requires a skill set that encompasses dealing with logistical, cultural and communication aspects that can be complex in these types of work arrangements. In their book on sport leadership Borland, Kane and Burton (2015) discuss the specific challenges associated with leading virtual teams.

New ways of working, such as via telecommuting or video conferencing, together with decreasing numbers of people with 'permanent' contracts of employment and the proliferation of other types of work arrangements such as part-time and temporary work, have begun to challenge traditional industrial relations approaches to accommodate different types of employment contracts, and different types of pay systems to reward performance and skills. This requires flexible, adaptive HRM policies and practices that can be responsive to change and transformation and capture creativity and innovation in the search for better processes, and improved products and services across borders.

Globalization of the sport workforce is not just about paid workers; it is also relevant to sport volunteers, especially for global events. For example, the Athens Olympic Games organizers recruited Games time volunteers from 201 countries, including 10 per cent Greeks abroad and 23 per cent of non-Greek origin, and they processed some 41,500 applications from overseas (Atkinson, 2004). The 2008 Beijing Olympic Organizing Committee recruited significant numbers of volunteers from outside China to assist with the delivery of the Games as part of a specific HR strategy of attracting a global volunteer base. London 2012 reported that more than 240,000 people applied to volunteer, with 86,000 interviewed before the final selection of approximately 70,000 volunteers for the Games, many of whom came from outside of England (International Olympic Committee, 2013c). There are also a number of sport for development volunteer and internship programs. The Canadian Sport Leadership Corps (CSLC) International Internship Programme, run through Commonwealth Games Canada, involves an 8-month international placement with National Olympic and Paralympic Committees, National Sport Councils, Government Ministries, National Sports Organizations, Non-Governmental Organizations, community-based organizations and educational institutions in Africa and the Caribbean (Commonwealth Games Association of Canada, 2011). The recruitment, training and deployment of an international cadre of volunteers clearly has numerous HR implications and requires a systematic process to handle matters such as cultural context, different languages and visa requirements.

Increasing diversity in the workplace

Effectively managing a diverse body of talent can bring innovative ideas, perspectives and views to the sport organization. The challenge is to capitalize on the potential of workplace diversity as a strategic organizational asset and to value diversity as an opportunity. As the organizational workforce becomes increasingly diverse, supporting this diversity is a way of attracting and retaining talent. As more and more organizations become global through market expansion, either physically or virtually, there is a necessity to employ diverse talents to understand the various niches of the markets in which they operate.

As discussed in previous chapters in this book, one critical demographic issue is the ability of an organization to deal with the challenge of an aging workforce. The projections of an aging population and the associated retirements will create potential gaps and result in a loss of critical expertise, both for employees and managers. In dealing with this issue it is also paramount to address negative attitudes towards older workers to ensure that there is no age discrimination in HRM practices. Due to this demographic shift, recruitment of younger persons and the organization's ability to retain key personnel is of increasing importance. This includes: tackling the barrier of people's perceptions and attitudes about the worth of older workers; exploring new recruitment options, and developing a reputation as an active recruiter and good employer of older workers; utilizing older workers as trainers/mentors, allowing for transfer of knowledge and corporate memory; and bringing in flexible working arrangements to facilitate the retention of experienced workers such as allowing phased-in retirement, long-term care insurance, pre-retirement planning, health and wellness programs and comprehensive medical coverage.

Technology and big data

An increasing array of technological developments will continue to be highly influential and will impact all aspects of the sport industry, including spectator sport, participant sport, sport events and the sporting goods industry. Work performed in sport organizations is increasingly tied to providing information and knowledge production and capitalizing on new technologies. Increasing compliance requirements and the thirst for information means that sport organizations are constantly collecting and providing data on their participants, customers and sponsors. The introduction of customer relationship marketing that draws on consumer data and preference and information-based marketing and communication initiatives has changed the nature of business for many sport organizations. There is also tracking technology that collects information on athlete performance. This output provides the basis for sport analytics and performance-based measurements and the vast range of applications therewith. Associated entrepreneurial sport businesses are springing up in the areas of digital platforms, social media, equipment technology, new apps and so on, all providing opportunities for enhanced access and better performance. The sport product is being complemented by online delivery modes, via podcasts, and discussed on blogs and played in virtual situations. We need to become accustomed to dealing with creative and innovative work. This shift is shaping the skill, knowledge and mindsets for future sport organization workers and will also lead to different work practices and reward structures for employees.

The growth of data analysis and statistics to track every player movement, fan experiences and patterns of purchasing behavior and attendance will be an expanding area of employment. For example, an advertisement for a data analyst in a leading company that provides digital software and services to the grassroots sporting community likely requires applicants to be proficient in data analysis, expert in MS Excel and advanced SQL querying and data manipulation, understand Google Analytics and other web reporting tools, and be able to generate specific sport data. Big data is also being used to make HR decisions. Data generated via psychometric tests (refer to Chapter 4 re selection methods) have long been used in recruitment, as have climate surveys to assess employee job satisfaction and engagement, and 360s for performance; however, there is a new use of data in HR. Many high-tech companies (e.g., Amazon, Google) embrace 'data-driven' management. Currently, only a small number of organizations have the capability to perform 'predictive analytics' and understand the drivers of performance and retention, use statistics to decide who to hire or analyze how pay correlates to performance. The challenge is to move from just collecting and reporting data to really using it. Bersin, O'Leonard and Wang-Audia (2013) report that it is critical to get project managers who can combine data and business, and people who can translate data finding into a program or solution that drives business change. High performing analytics teams should have business understanding, consulting skills, data visualization, data management, statistics and executive support – a wide-ranging set of capabilities.

BOX 11.3

Discussion question

In groups discuss/debate the most impactful technologies in sport/organizations in the past 5–10 years.

Now describe the SHRM implications (planning, recruiting/selecting, orienting, motivating and so on) for the organizations that are managing those changes.

Work/life issues and ways of organizing work

Quality of work life encompasses good salaries and benefits, adequately defined tasks, a healthy organizational environment, supportive and efficient leadership, high motivation and continuous feedback. It means providing rewards for productive contributions such as psychological effort, communication and interaction, and creates the psychological state necessary for the employee to produce quality work for the organization in return. It also now implies ensuring personnel have the work/life balance they desire between work and life commitments, and which will presumably ensure they are most productive when at work (Ivancevich, 2010). This increasingly involves looking to non-traditional ways to better meet employees' and volunteers' professional and personal needs, through flexible working arrangements. Initiatives may include: guaranteed part-time work for employees aged 55 years and over, lifestyle leave, career breaks to pursue personal development or family commitments, job sharing, flextime work schedule (e.g., longer days in a shorter week), telecommuting and flexible work childcare policies. Dixon and colleagues have undertaken a program of research examining the nature of work/life conflict in sport, especially for female coaches. They found that work hours and travel required, and an expectation to be 'in the office', were the most critical contributors to the work/life conflict experienced by women coaches who were also mothers (Dixon & Bruening, 2007). Another study revealed that perceived organizational support that is associated with various benefits provided to employees reduced coaches' sense of work/life conflict (Dixon & Sagas, 2007). Together, this work serves to highlight the challenge of supporting staff through flexible working arrangements yet ensuring the organization's goals are being met.

As noted in relation to globalization, traditionally structured jobs and work practices are being replaced by new work practices such as facilitating high-performing and virtual teams, telecommuting, video conferencing, flexible work patterns and more diverse and integrated work. Work is moving from being done during a standard eight-hour day to being completed at any time, and at any place, to the extent that workers are becoming suppliers for various activities and even different companies at the same time. The notion of a single job for life, exclusive and full time, is being redefined in the digital age. New forms of reward structures focus on how the employee delivers on strategy and results, and on being innovative and creative. These will all impact on HR issues such as motivation, leadership, training and development of high-performance cohesive work teams.

Volunteer and paid staff relationships

A working relationship between volunteers and paid staff continues to evolve in non-profit voluntary sport organizations. While sport organizations in other sectors may also rely on volunteers to carry out their activities, volunteer participation is a defining feature of voluntary sport organizations (Cuskelly, Hoye & Auld, 2006). Community, provincial or state and national level amateur sport organizations are the most common examples of voluntary sport organizations. While these organizations are governed and primarily run by volunteer personnel (e.g., board of directors, committee members, coaches), there is a continuing incidence of hiring paid staff to help deal with the increasing complexity and sophistication of organized sport (Cuskelly et al., 2006). The so-called 'professionalization' of amateur sport is a function of hiring paid 'professional' staff, as well as the adoption of more sophisticated management practices to increase organizational effectiveness.

While a voluntary sport organization can undoubtedly benefit from the assistance provided by paid staff, this depends on an effective working relationship between the paid staff and volunteers. This relationship is particularly critical at the management level. Typically, staff are hired and supervised by a volunteer management committee or board of directors, and have a non-voting role with that group. The board sets policy and staff implements it. Issues tend to revolve around the distribution of power and influence in decision making between these volunteer boards and staff (Cuskelly et al., 2006). The relationship is also inherently constrained by the regular turnover of committee and board members as a result of the organization's constitutional election and appointments process (Cuskelly et al., 2006).

Both effective management *by* volunteers (such as with a board of directors) and management *of* volunteers (e.g., those in supporting roles such as coaching, fundraising, program delivery) depends on an organizational culture that values and supports volunteerism, and an organization that recognizes the strategic role of volunteers alongside paid staff (and vice versa) in the achievement of the organization's goals. Their respective expectations and orientations to work must be effectively managed (aligned). As Netting, Nelson, Borders and Huber (2004) note, perhaps typical assumptions that volunteers are not well versed in the facts, paid staff are more valuable because they get paid, volunteers need to be spoon-fed, staff do not really know what is going on in the real world, and staff work for pay but volunteers work for good, need to be quashed. This may require some cultural realignment within an organization. With the increasing complexity of the environment and operations of voluntary sport organizations (e.g., Nichols, Taylor, James, King, Holmes & Garrett, 2003), continuing professionalization of voluntary sport organizations, including the involvement of paid staff, is an SHRM challenge.

Emerging nations

In many developing countries, and in those that have experienced regime change such as post-communist countries, the level of 'professionalization' in the management of sport is not well advanced. Bayle and Robinson (2007) suggest that sport organization performance is linked to a number of HRM-related aspects displayed as forms and levels of professionalization, which basically relates to the degree to which the organization deploys paid staff and contemporary or leading edge management practices. They identified four stages in professionalization ranging from stage 1, where there is some recruitment of administrative support staff, through to stage 4, which is characterized by full professionalization throughout the organization. Many sports in emerging economies are grappling with how to build human resources and improve their human resource functions. In describing the challenges found in Croatian sport, Jerkunica, Gabrić and Bratinčević (2010) note the importance of HRM and better education of sport personnel in improving the sport system. The practice of making political appointments in sport positions and the widespread nepotism involved has meant there is a dearth of knowledge and professional qualities needed to perform responsible functions in sport. Nesić, Fratrić and Ilić (2011) similarly note the immediate need for better training programs and education for sport managers in Serbia.

SHRM into the future

Sport organizations are increasingly focusing on human capital investment through the training and exchange of coaches, administrators and managers. For example, many International Sport Federations have formal coach exchange programs, and the IOC and FIFA provide funding to national bodies to build coaching and management capacity through training and exchange. While not all sport organizations strategically position and develop their human resources, those that have moved in this direction emphasize the collaboration facilitated between managers, employees, volunteers, customers, strategic partners and members of community organizations in order to be more effective in managing the organization's human resources. The ways in which effective SHRM can be achieved have been discussed in this book in some detail.

The HRM function involves a partnership of the leadership team of the organization and the HR team, managers, employees and volunteers. HRM was historically concerned with the short-term, operational aspects of personnel management. In contemporary sport organizations, human resources are much more broadly conceptualized and thus are increasingly involved in the longer-term, strategic directions of the organization.

SHRM involves understanding the strategic direction of the sport organization, including appreciating the product or service, its customers and how it is positioned competitively in the marketplace. The process of linking human resources to the broader, long-term needs of organizations is the essence of SHRM (Jackson & Schuler, 2000; Storey, 2001). Organizational performance improves when recruiting and selection systems are consistent with its competitive strategy; reward systems reflect successful strategy implementation in performance appraisals; and employee compensation, and training and development strategies align with performance management systems and business objectives (Huselid & Becker, 2011). SHRM also requires innovative approaches and solutions to improve productivity and the quality of work life while complying with government and legislative requirements in an environment of high uncertainty and change, and intense global competition. Managing human resources through strategy implementation is often about change. The responsibility of managing the change process, both at the individual and the organizational level is a significant HRM role. As sport organizations grapple with new technologies, structures, processes and cultures, HRM will accordingly facilitate organizational change and ensure flexibility and adaptability. This means being aware of anticipated changes to the external environment, and working to ensure that the right skills and competencies are available at the appropriate time.

While large sport organizations may employ HR specialists and generalists, many sport organizations will not have individuals with special expertise in human resources – that is, people with specialized and technical knowledge of HR issues, laws, policies and practices. In these cases the responsibilities of HR will fall to the employees and managers to deal with. Sport organizations will choose to allocate responsibility for HR activities in many different ways; however, whatever the approach, good HR management will link HR activities to strategy and help the sport organization achieve competitive advantage, effective operations, motivated and satisfied employees and volunteers.

SUMMARY

Organizational change is inevitable, yet paradoxical because of our innate desire for stability and a critical issue for SHRM. There are innumerable examples of planned organizational change in the ever-changing sport industry. Sport organizations face internal (e.g., financial challenges, inefficiencies, training needs) and external forces (e.g., government policy, consumers, competitors, sport governing bodies) that pressure them to make changes for growth and for survival. In simple terms, the process of organizational change involves 'unfreezing' current conditions, moving to the desired state and 'refreezing' those new conditions. However, the process may be hindered by too strong restraining forces in the form of staff and volunteer resistance to that change. Resistance occurs because of the perceived threat of change to one's own self-interests in the organization (e.g., one's power, expertise, resource allocations, job security), mistrust of management and others who support the change, differing perceptions about the expected outcomes of the change, and the cost in terms of time, money, and effort to implement the change. To overcome resistance and help people cope with change in the organization, strategies are directed towards educating staff and volunteers about change, involving them in the change process, and providing additional support through change teams, idea champions, and various organizational measures such as counseling, therapy and retraining. Negotiating or bargaining for compliance on the part of resistors may not have the lasting effect that is desired.

DISCUSSION QUESTIONS

1   Building on information provided in the chapter, describe other examples of product or service changes, technology changes, structure and system changes and people changes in sport organizations. Discuss what prompted each of these changes.

2   Think of an organizational change initiative with which you are most familiar. What type of change was it? What prompted the change (what internal and/ or external pressures influenced the organization)? Describe any internal (employee, volunteer) resistance to the change, and how the organization managed that resistance. Was the change process successful? If not, where did the breakdown occur? (Consider Greiner's stages of organizational change in Figure 11.1.)

3   Building on information provided in the chapter, discuss further the potential advantages and disadvantages of each of the strategies for managing resistance to change.

4   Consider each of the SHRM challenges introduced in this chapter. Elaborate, where you can, on examples of each in sport in general, or in a particular sport organization with which you are most familiar (e.g., what else do you know

about volunteer–staff relationships in sport?). What are some of the key SHRM issues associated with each challenge? As a manager, how would you deal with these issues? (Reflect back on relevant chapters in the text to frame your answer.) *Suggestion to instructors: Students could form groups and each group addresses one of the challenges listed here.*

5 What do you think is the greatest SHRM challenge for sport organizations in the future, and why? Describe how this challenge may lead to change in the organization. What is the nature of that change? What are the implications of that change for HRM? Consider the steps in environmental scanning to help work through this discussion.

6 Globalization continues to be a challenge facing sport organizations, both those that have already expanded to markets in other countries, and those that are considering it. Such expansion often involves the assignment of employees in the organization's home country to work and live in another country. You may know someone who has done this. List key factors to consider in a cross-cultural training program for expatriates who are moving to a developing country (e.g., in South America, Asia, Africa) to manage a sport organization's expanding operations. What information do the expatriates need to acquire? How can this be done?

7 Drawing on the material in various chapters in the book (e.g., HR planning, recruitment, organizational culture, motivation, diversity management), discuss the possible advantages and disadvantages of 'virtual teams' that use computer technology to connect workgroup members who are physically separated, whether across a city, a country or the world.

BOOK SUMMARY

Human resource management is becoming increasingly involved with strategic planning and the development of means by which people can work proactively towards the achievement of organizational objectives. Employees and volunteers are no longer just an organizational resource; they provide the basis for competitive advantage and organizational sustainability. It is people who shape such intangibles, as the organization's image or reputation, organizational culture, customer service, creativity and innovation, competitiveness and the basis for dealing with the changing sport landscape over the next 5–10 years. Recognition of this shift is found in the changing nomenclature of HR departments to titles such as: 'people and culture', 'performance and people' and 'people capital and breakout'. This is a change from a function-orientated to a process-orientated culture, from an organization that offers services to a concern for the organization's intellectual capital and its ultimate productivity.

Employees and volunteers are integral to the development and execution of the organization's values, policies and goals. Therefore, they need to be engaged through a range of participative programs, assisted to achieve their needs and aspirations, and receive appropriate rewards and recognition. Achievement of organizational objectives occurs through the contributions of the people directly linked with the final results. Recruitment and selection processes should validly identify and attract people with the requisite characteristics and talents. Training and development processes should generate results for the organization and the employee or volunteer. Reward systems should be capable of motivating and supporting efforts to achieve desired goals, results and related issues.

Good SHRM addresses the need for competitiveness in a changing global marketplace and the importance of employee and volunteer contributions of internal partners to attract clients and achieve results. The SHRM approaches, practices and trends identified in this book reflect the capacity people have for developing and creating value and how to develop and support that capacity for the success of the organization. An organization's competitiveness based on its employees and volunteers is what SHRM is all about.

References

Acosta, R.V. & Carpenter, L.J. (2005). *Title IX*. Champaign, IL: Human Kinetics.

Acosta, R.V. & Carpenter, L.J. (2012). Women in intercollegiate sport: A longitudinal, national study thirty-five year update 1977–2012. Retrieved 14 April 2014, from http://acostacarpenter.org/AcostaCarpenter2012.pdf

Adams, J.S. (1965). Inequity in social exchange. In *Advances in Experimental Psychology*, Vol. 2, pp. 267–299 (Berkowitz, L., ed.). New York: Academic Press.

Adidas Group (n.d.). Employer of choice approach. Retrieved 9 April 2014, from http://www.adidas-group.com/en/sustainability/employees/employee-choice-approach/

Adler, N.J. (1997). *International Dimensions of Organizational Behaviour* (3rd edn). Cincinnati, OH: South-Western College Publishing.

Allen, D.G. (2006). Do organizational socialization tactics influence newcomer embeddedness and turnover? *Journal of Management*, 32(2), 237–246.

Allport, G.W. (1954). *The Nature of Prejudice*. Cambridge, MA: Addison-Wesley.

Andrews, K. (2006). Australia's cultural diversity set to remain. Retrieved 9 May 2007, from http://www.minister.immi.gov.au/media/media-releases/2006/v06017.htm

Aon Hewitt & Associates (2013). Best Employer 2.0 – Asia 2013 study participation. Retrieved 10 December 2013, from http://www.aon.com/apac/human-resources/thought-leadership/talent-organization/best-employers/participate.jsp

Appelbaum, E., Bailey, T., Berg, P. & Kalleberg, A.L. (2000). *Manufacturing advantage. Why high-performance work systems pay off*. Ithaca, NY: ILR Press.

Armstrong, M. (2006). *A Handbook of Human Resource Management Practice* (10th edn). London: Kogan Page.

Armstrong, M. & Baron, A. (1998). *Performance Management: The New Realities*. London: Institute of Personnel and Development.

Arthur, W., Bennett, W., Edens, P.S. & Bell, S.T. (2003). Effectiveness of training in organizations: A meta-analysis of design and evaluation features. *Journal of Applied Psychology*, 88(2), 234–245.

Ashford, S.J. (1988). Individual strategies for coping with stress during organizational transitions. *Journal of Applied Behavioural Science*, 24(1), 19–36.

Ashford, S.J. & Black, J.S. (1996). Proactivity during organizational entry: The role of desire for control. *Journal of Applied Psychology*, 81(2), 199–214.

Ashforth, B.E. & Saks, A.M. (1996). Socialization tactics: Longitudinal effects on newcomer adjustment. *Academy of Management Journal*, 39(1), 149–178.

Ashforth, B.E., Sluss, D.M. & Saks, A.M. (2007). Socialization tactics, proactive behaviour, and newcomer learning: Integrating socialization models. *Journal of Vocational Behavior, 70*, 447–462.

Asmuß, B. (2008). Performance Appraisal Interviews Preference Organization in Assessment Sequences. *Journal of Business Communication*, 45(4), 408–429.

Atkinson, M. (2004). Travel notes for parliament. Adelaide: South Australia Parliament.

Australian Football League Players' Association (2012). 2012 Development & Wellbeing Report. Retrieved 4 February 2014, from https://secure.ausport.gov.au/__data/assets/pdf_file/0003/524307/AFL-Player-Wellbeing-Report-2012.pdf

Australian Government (2013). State and Territory migration summary report. Retrieved 2 June 2014, from https://www.immi.gov.au/media/publications/statistics/immigration-update/state-territory-summary-dec-2013.pdf

Australian Sports Commission (2000). Volunteer management program retaining volunteers. Retrieved 12 May 2014, from http://www.ausport.gov.au/__data/assets/pdf_file/0012/150033/Retaining_Volunteers.pdf

Australian Sports Commission (2014a). Factsheet – Orientation and training of volunteers Retrieved 12 May 2014, from http://www.ausport.gov.au/participating/volunteers/resources/publications_and_fact_sheets/factsheet_-_orientation_and_training_of_volunteers

Australian Sports Commission (2014b). Factsheet – Recognising volunteers. Retrieved 12 May 2014, from http://www.ausport.gov.au/participating/volunteers/resources/publications_and_fact_sheets/factsheet_-_recognising_volunteers

Australian Sports Commission (2014c). Factsheet – Rights and responsibilities of volunteers. Retrieved 17 May 2014, from http://www.ausport.gov.au/participating/volunteers/resources/publications_and_fact_sheets/factsheet_-_rights_and_responsibilities_of_volunteers

Barney, J. (1991). Firms resources and sustained competitive advantage. *Journal of Management, 17*(1), 99–120.

Barrick, M.R., Dustin, S.L., Giluk, T.L., Stewart, G.L., Shaffer, J.A. & Swider, B.W. (2012). Candidate characteristics driving initial impressions during rapport building: Implications for employment interview validity. *Journal of Occupational and Organizational Psychology, 85*(2), 330–352.

Bartlett, K.R. & McKinney, W.R. (2003). A study of external environmental scanning for strategic human resource management in public park and recreation agencies. *Journal of Park and Recreation Administration, 21*(2), 1–21.

Baruch, Y., Wheeler, K. & Zhao, X. (2004). Performance-related pay in Chinese professional sports. *International Journal of Human Resource Management, 15*(1), 245–259.

Bauer, T.N., Bodner, T., Erdogan, B., Truxillo, D.M. & Tucker, J.S. (2007). Newcomer adjustment during organizational socialization: A meta-analytic review of antecedents, outcomes, and methods. *Journal of Applied Psychology, 92*(3), 707–721.

Bayle, E. & Robinson, L. (2007). A framework for understanding the performance of national governing bodies of sport. *European Sport Management Quarterly, 7*(3), 249–268.

Becker, B.E. & Huselid, M.A. (1992). The incentive effects of tournament compensation systems. *Administrative Science Quarterly, 37*(2), 336–350.

Beer, M., Spector, B., Lawrence, P., Quinn, M.D. & Walton, R. (1985). *Human Resource Management: A General Manager's Perspective*. Glencoe, IL: Free Press.

Bernthal, P. & Wellins, R. (2006). Trends in leader development and succession HR. *Human Resource Planning, 29*(2), 31–41.

Bersin, J., O'Leonard, K. & Wang-Audia, W. (2013). High-impact talent analytics: Building a world-class HR measurement and analytics function. Retrieved 14 May 2014, from http://www.bersin.com/Practice/Detail.aspx?id=16909

Beyer, J.M. & Hannah, D.R. (2002). Building on the past: Enacting established personal identities in a new work setting. *Organization Science, 13*(6), 636–652.

Black, J.A. & Boal, K.B. (1994). Strategic resources: Traits, configurations and paths to sustainable competitive advantage. *Strategic Management Journal, 15*, 131–148.

Booth, N., Fosters, S., Robson, C. & Welham, J. (2004). *Managing a Diverse Workforce*. London: LexisNexis.

Borland, J.F., Kane, G.M. & Burton, L.J. (2015). *Sport Leadership in the 21st Century*. Burlington, MA: Jones & Barlett Learning.

Bower, G.G. (2009). Effective mentoring relationships with women in sport: Results of a meta-ethnography. *Advancing Women in Leadership, 29*(3). Retrieved from http://www.advancingwomen.com/awl/Vol29_2009/Dr_Glena_Bower.pdf

Boyatzis, R. (1999). The financial impact of competencies in leadership and management of consulting firms (Working Paper). Cleveland, OH: Department of Organizational Behavior, Case Western Reserve University.

Boxall, P. & Macky, K. (2009). Research and theory on high-performance work systems: progressing the high-involvement stream. *Human Resource Management Journal, 19,* 3–23.

Brannen, P. (1983). *Authority and Participation in Industry.* London: Batsford Academic.

Breuer, C., Wicker, P. & von Hanau, T. (2012). Consequences of the decrease in volunteers among German sports clubs: is there a substitute for voluntary work? *International Journal of Sport Policy and Politics, 4*(2),173–186.

Brown, P. (2010). The power of HR outsourcing. *Strategic HR Review, 9*(6), 27–32.

Buswell, J. (2004). Sport and leisure service encounter. In *Sport and Leisure Operations Management* (McMahon-Beattie, U. & Yeoman, I., eds). Oxon: CABI Publishing.

Byham, W.C. (2001). *Targeted Selection.* Pittsburgh, PA: Development Dimensions International Inc.

Cable, D.M. & Parsons, C.K. (2001). Socialization tactics and person-organization fit. *Personnel Psychology, 54*(1), 1–23.

Campion, M.A. (1988). Interdisciplinary approaches to job design: A constructive replication with extensions. *Journal of Applied Psychology, 73*(3), 467–481.

Campion, M.A., Medsker, G.J. & Higgs, A.C. (1993). Relations between work group characteristics and effectiveness: Implications for designing effective work groups. *Personnel Psychology, 46,* 823–847.

Canadian Association for the Advancement of Women and Sport and Physical Activity (2013). Women on boards. Retrieved 11 December 2013, from http://www.caaws.ca/leadership/women-on-boards/

Canadian Centre for Occupational Health and Safety (2006). Hazard control: OSH answers. Retrieved 15 May 2014, from http://www.ccohs.ca/oshanswers/hsprograms/hazard_control.html

Canadian Centre for Occupational Health and Safety (2008). Job safety analysis: OSH answers. Retrieved 15 May 2014, from http://www.ccohs.ca/oshanswers/hsprograms/job-haz.html

Canadian Centre for Occupational Health and Safety (2009). Hazard and risk: OSH answers. Retrieved 15 May 2014, from http://www.ccohs.ca/oshanswers/hsprograms/hazard_risk.html

Canadian Interuniversity Sport (2013). Policies and procedures 80 – Administration. Retrieved 17 April 2014, from http://static.psbin.com/b/8/rpq156smytsqxk/14_Policy_80.50-80.100.pdf

Carmeli, A. & Tishler, A. (2004). The relationships between intangible organizational elements and performance. *Strategic Management Journal, 25*(13), 1257–1278.

Carnall, C.A. (2007). *Managing Change in Organizations* (5th edn). Harlow: Prentice-Hall.

Carr, J.C., Pearson, A.W., Vest, M.J. & Boyar, S.L. (2006). Prior occupational experience, anticipatory socialization, and employee retention. *Journal of Management, 32*(3), 343–359.

Cascio, W. (1996). Managing for maximum performance. *HR Monthly,* September, 10–13.

Chapman, A. (2005). Exit interviews. Retrieved 10 April 2007, from http://www.businessballs.com/exitinterviews.htm

Chass, M. (1994). Players' next step is a legal challenge. *The New York Times,* December 24, C26.

Chelladurai, P. (2005). *Managing Organizations for Sport and Physical Activity: A Systems Perspective* (2nd edn). Scottsdale, AZ: Holcomb Hathaway.

Chelladurai, P. (2006). *Human Resource Management in Sport and Recreation* (2nd edn). Champaign, IL: Human Kinetics.

Chelladurai, P. & Madella, A. (2006). *Human Resource Management in Olympic Sport Organizations.* Champaign, IL: Human Kinetics.

Choi, Y.S., Martin, J.J. & Park, M. (2008). Organizational culture and job satisfaction in Korean professional baseball organizations. *International Journal of Applied Sports Sciences, 20*(2), 59–77.

Claringbould, I., Knoppers, A. & Elling, A. (2004). Exclusionary practices in sport journalism. *Sex Roles, 51,* 709–718.

Coaching Association of Canada (2006). Request for proposal: Engaging new Canadians in coaching and the National Coaching Certification Program (NCCP). Retrieved 9 May 2007, from http://www.coach.ca/eng/links/documents/RFPNCCPJune06.pdf

Commonwealth Games Association of Canada (2011). Beyond the Podium programs. Retrieved 14 May 2014, from http://www.commonwealthgames.ca/beyond-the-podium/programs.html

Conlon, R. (2011). The role of the board and the CEO in ensuring business continuity (senior manager succession management). *Human Resource Management International Digest, 19*(3) Retrieved 17 April 2014, from http://www.emeraldinsight.com/doi/full/10.1108/hrmid.2011.04419cad.006.

Council Directive (2000). Council Directive 2000/43/EC of 29 June 2000 implementing the principle of equal treatment between persons irrespective of racial or ethnic origin. Retrieved 17 April 2014, from http://eur-lex.europa.eu/LexUriServ/LexUriServ.do?uri=CELEX:32000L0043:en:HTML

Covell, D. & Walker, S. (2013). *Managing Sport Organizations: Responsibility for Performance* (3rd edn). Abingdon, NY: Routledge.

Cropanzano, R. & Greenberg, J. (2001). Progress in organizational justice: Tunnelling through the maze. In *Organizational Psychology and Development*, pp. 243–298 (Cooper, C.L. & Robertson, I.T., eds). Chichester: Wiley.

Cunningham, G. (2007). *Diversity in Sport Organizations*. Scottsdale, AZ: Holcomb Hathaway.

Cunningham, G.B. (2009). The moderating effect of diversity strategy on the relationship between racial diversity and organizational performance. *Journal of Applied Social Psychology, 39*(6), 1445–1460.

Cunningham, G.B. (2011). The LGBT advantage: Examining the relationship among sexual orientation diversity, diversity strategy, and performance. *Sport Management Review, 14*(4), 453–461.

Cunningham, G.B. (2012). Diversity training in intercollegiate athletics. *Journal of Sport Management, 26*(5), 391–403.

Cunningham, G.B. & Melton, E.N. (2011). The benefits of sexual orientation diversity in sport organizations. *Journal of Homosexuality, 58*(5), 647–663.

Cuskelly, G., Hoye, R. & Auld, C. (2006). *Working with Volunteers in Sport: Theory and Practice*. London: Routledge.

Cuskelly, G., Taylor, T., Hoye, R. & Darcy, S. (2006). Volunteer management practices and volunteer retention: A human resource management approach. *Sports Management Review, 9*(2), 141–163.

Daft, R.L. (1992). *Organization Theory and Design* (4th edn). St. Paul, MN: South-Western.

Das, B. (1999). Development of a comprehensive industrial work design model. *Human Factors and Ergonomics in Manufacturing, 9*(4), 393–411.

Dawson, A., Wenner, K., Phillips, P., Gastin, P. & Salmon, J. (2013). *Profiling the Australian Coaching Workforce*. Burwood, VIC: C-EES. Retrieved 17 April 2014, from https://www.deakin.edu.au/news/2013/Aus%20Coaching%20Workforce%20full%20report_web.pdf

De Cieri, H., Kramar, R., Noe, R., Hollenbeck, J., Gerhart, B. & Wright, P. (2005). *Human Resource Management in Australia. Strategy-People-Performance* (2nd edn). Sydney: McGraw-Hill.

De Knop, P., Van Hoecke, J. & De Bosscher, V. (2004). Quality management in sports clubs. *Sport Management Review, 7*(1), 57–78.

Dickson, T.J., Benson, A.M., Blackman, D.A. & Terwiel, A.F. (2013). It's all about the Games! 2010 Vancouver Olympic and Paralympic Winter Games Volunteers. *Event Management, 17*(1), 77–92.

Dipboye, R.L., Macan, T. & Shahani-Denning, C. (2012). Chapter 15. The Selection Interview from the Interviewer and Applicant Perspectives: Can't Have One without the Other. In *The Oxford Handbook of Personnel Assessment and Selection*, pp. 323–352 (Neal Schmitt, ed.). Oxford: Oxford University Press.

Dixon, M.A. & Bruening, J.E. (2007). Work–family conflict in coaching I: A top-down perspective. *Journal of Sport Management, 21*, 377–406.

Dixon, M.A. & Sagas, M. (2007). The relationship between organizational support, work-family conflict, and the job-life satisfaction of university coaches. *Research Quarterly for Exercise and Sport, 78*(3), 236–247.

Doherty, A. (1998). Managing our human resources: A review of organizational behaviour in sport. *Sport Management Review, 1*, 1–24.

Doherty, A. (2003). *A Study of the Volunteers of the 2001 Alliance London Jeux du Canada Games*. London, ON: University of Western Ontario.

Doherty, A. (2005a). *A Profile of Community Sport Volunteers*. Toronto: Parks and Recreation Ontario and the Sport Alliance of Ontario.

Doherty, A. (2005b). *Volunteer Management in Community Sport Clubs: A Study of Volunteers' Perceptions*. Toronto: Parks and Recreation Ontario and the Sport Alliance of Ontario.

Doherty, A. & Chelladurai, P. (1999). Managing cultural diversity in sport organizations: A theoretical perspective. *Journal of Sport Management, 13*(4), 280–297.

Doherty, A., Fink, J., Inglis, S. & Pastore, D. (2010). Understanding a culture of diversity through frameworks of power and change. *Sport Management Review, 13*(4), 368–381.

Driscoll, M.P. (1994). *Psychology of Learning for Instruction*. Needham Heights, MA: Allyn and Bacon.

Drucker, P.F. (1995). *Managing in a Time of Great Change*. New York: Truman Valley.

Eddy, E., D'Abate, C, Tannenbaum, S., Givens-Skeaton, S. & Robinson, G. (2006). Key characteristics of effective and ineffective developmental interactions. *Human Resource Development Quarterly, 17*(1), 59–84.

Egli, B., Schlesinger, T. & Nagel, S. (2014). Expectation-based types of volunteers in Swiss sports clubs. *Managing Leisure*. DOI: 10.1080/13606719.2014.885714. Retrieved 20 May 2014.

ESPN (2014a). ESPN Inc. Fact Sheet. Retrieved 7 November 2013, from *http://espnmediazone.com/us/espn-inc-fact-sheet/*

ESPN (2014b). ESPN Careers: Working at ESPN. Retrieved 7 November 2013, from *http://espncareers.com/working-here/default.aspx*

ESPN (2014c). Corporate culture at ESPN. Retrieved 7 November 2013, from *http://espncareers.com/working-here/corporate-culture.aspx*

ESPN (2014d). Diversity at ESPN. Retrieved 7 November 2013, from *http://espncareers.com/working-here/diversity-resource-group.aspx*

ESPN (2014e). ESPN employee resource groups. Retrieved 7 November 2013, from *http://espncareers.com/working-here/diversity.aspx*

European Women and Sport (2014). European women and sport programmes. Retrieved 11 December 2013, from http://www.ews-online.org/en/menu_main/european-women-and-sport-programmes

Fainaru-Wada, M. & Gubar, J. (2012 January 9). The unseen faces of sports apparel. Retrieved 15 May 2014, from http://espn.go.com/espn/otl/story/_/id/7435424/dallas-cowboys-dip-sports-apparel-business-comes-allegations-sweatshop-labor

Fédération Internationale de Football Association (2001). Extraordinary FIFA Congress ratifies resolution against racism. Retrieved 3 June 2014, from http://www.fifa.com/aboutfifa/organisation/bodies/news/newsid=78421/

Feldman, D.C. (1976). A contingency theory of socialization. *Administrative Science Quarterly, 21*(3), 433–452.

Ferkins, L., Shilbury, D. & McDonald, G. (2005). The role of the board in building strategic capability: Towards an integrated model of sport governance research. *Sport Management Review, 8*(3), 195–225.

Folger, R. & Cropanzano, R. (1998). *Organizational Justice and Human Resource Management*. Thousand Oaks, CA: Sage.

Forbes (2012). The best companies to work for in 2013. Retrieved 9 February 2014, from http://www.forbes.com/sites/jacquelynsmith/2012/12/12/the-best-companies-to-work-for-in-2013/

Forbes (2013, 23 January). Corporations can learn a lot about diversity management from the NFL. Retrieved 17 April 2014, from http://www.forbes.com/sites/glennllopis/2013/01/23/corporations-can-learn-a-lot-about-diversity-management-from-the-nfl/

Fombrum, C., Tichy, N. & Devanna, M.A. (1984). *Strategic Human Resource Management*. New York: Wiley.

Gagne, R. & Driscoll, M. (1988). *Essentials of Learning for Instruction* (2nd edn). Englewood Cliffs, NJ: Prentice-Hall.

Gallant, H., Remick, L.Z. & Resnick, B.M. (2005). Labor relations in professional sports. In *The Management of Sport: Its Foundation and Application* (4th edn). pp. 301–332 (Parkhouse, B.L., ed.). New York: McGraw-Hill.

Gallo, J. (2006). Byears shows new-look mystics what a difference a player makes mystics. *Washington Post Sunday*. Retrieved 28 May 2006, from http://www.washingtonpost.com/wpdyn/content/article/2006/05/27/AR2006052700911.html

Gatewood, R.D., Field, H.S. & Barrick, M.R. (2011). *Human Resource Selection* (7th edn). Mason, OH: South-Western, Cengage.

Gerrard, B. (2005). A resource-utilization model of organizational efficiency in professional sports teams. *Journal of Sport Management, 19*, 143–169.

GHK (2010). Final report on volunteering in the European Union. Retrieved 10 December 2013, from http://ec.europa.eu/citizenship/pdf/doc1018_en.pdf

Goldstein, I. & Ford, J. (2002). *Training in Organizations: Needs Assessment, Development and Evaluation* (4th edn). Belmont, CA: Wadsworth.

Goleman, D. (1998). *Working with Emotional Intelligence.* New York: Bantam

Goodman, D., French, P. E. & Battaglio, R. P. (2013). Determinants of local government workforce planning. *The American Review of Public Administration* 1–18 (online).

Government of Canada (2013). Progressive discipline. Retrieved 20 May 2014, from http://www.labour.gc.ca/eng/standards_equity/st/pubs_st/discipline.shtml

Gratton, L. & Truss, C. (2003). The three-dimensional people strategy: Putting human resources policies into action. *Academy of Management Executive, 17*(3), 74–86.

Greenberg, J. (1987). A taxonomy of organizational justice theories. *Academy of Management Review, 12*(1), 9–22.

Greenberg, J. & Baron, R. (2008). *Behavior in Organizations* (9th edn). Upper Saddle River, NJ: Prentice Hall.

Greiner, L.E. (1967). Patterns of organization change. *Harvard Business Review, 45*(3), 119–130.

Griffeth, R.W. & Hom, P.W. (2001). *Retaining Valued Employees.* Thousand Oaks, CA: Sage.

Griffiths, M. & Armour, K. (2012). Mentoring as a formalized learning strategy with community sports volunteers. *Mentoring & Tutoring: Partnership in Learning, 20*(1), 151–173.

Guest, D. (1987). Human resource management and industrial relations. *Journal of Management Studies, 24*(5), 503–521.

Hackman, J.R. & Oldham, G.R. (1975). Development of the job diagnostic survey. *Journal of Applied Psychology, 60*, 159–170.

Hackman, J.R. & Oldham, G.R. (1980). *Work Design.* Reading, MA: Addison-Wesley.

Hafeez, K. & Aburawi, I. (2013). Planning human resource requirements to meet target customer service levels. *International Journal of Quality and Service Sciences, 5*(2), 230–252.

Hall, D.T. (1976). *Careers in Organizations.* Pacific Palisades, CA: Goodyear.

Hanstad, D.V. (2008). Drug scandal and organizational change within the International Ski Federation: A figurational approach. *European Sport Management Quarterly, 8*(4), 379–398.

Hargrove, R. (2002). *Masterful Coaching: Extraordinary Results by Impacting People and the Way They Think and Work Together.* San Francisco, CA: Jossey-Bass.

Harrison, D.A., Price, K.H. & Bell, M.P. (1998). Beyond relational demography: Time and the effects of surface- and deep-level diversity on work group cohesion. *Academy of Management Journal, 41*(1), 96–107.

Hatch, M.J. & Schultz, M. (1997). Relations between organizational culture, identity and image. *European Journal of Marketing, 31*(5/6), 356–365.

Herzberg, F. (1968). One more time: How do you motivate people? *Harvard Business Review, 46*(1), 53–62.

Higgins, M.C. & Kram, K.E. (2001). Reconceptualizing mentoring at work: A developmental network perspective. *Academy of Management Review, 26*(2), 264–288.

Hofacre, S. & Branvold, S. (1995). Baseball front office careers: Expectations and realities. *Journal of Sport Management, 9*(2), 173–181.

Hornby, L. (2012). Comparing the CBAs. Retrieved 14 May 2014, from http://www.torontosun. com/2012/08/26/comparing-the-cbas

Hoye, R., Smith, A., Westerbeek, H., Stewart, B. & Nicholson, M. (2005). *Sport Management: Principles and Application*. Oxford: Elsevier.

Huselid, M. A. & Becker, B. E. (2011). Bridging micro and macro domains: Workforce differentiation and strategic human resource management. *Journal of Management, 37*(2), 421–428.

International Olympic Committee (2006, February). Women in sport leadership: Evaluation of the 10–20 per cent objectives (women representation in the IOC). Retrieved 9 May 2007, from http://multimedia.olympic.org/pdf/en_report_98.pdf

International Olympic Committee (2013a). Final Report of the IOC Coordination Commission: Games of the XXX Olympiad, London 2012. Retrieved 11 October 2013, from http://www.olympic.org/Documents/Games_London_2012/Final%20Cocom%20Report%20London%202012%20EN.pdf

International Olympic Committee (2013b). Relieve Vancouver 2010. Retrieved 10 October 2013, from http://www.olympic.org/content/archive/olympic-games-old/all-past-olympic-games/winter/vancouver-2010-old/calendar/re-live-vancouver-2010---day-11/

International Olympic Committee (2013c). Volunteers helping to make the Games happen. Retrieved 10 October 2013, from http://www.olympic.org/news/volunteers-helping-to-make-the-games-happen/168630

International Olympic Committee (2013d). Factsheet – Women in the Olympic movement update – October 2013. Retrieved 17 April 2014, from http://www.olympic.org/Documents/Reference_documents_Factsheets/Women_in_Olympic_Movement.pdf

Ivancevich, J.M. (2010). *Human Resource Management* (11th edn). New York: McGraw-Hill/Irwin.

Jackson, S.E., May, K.E. & Whitney, K. (1995). Understanding the dynamics of diversity in decision-making teams. In *Team Decision-Making Effectiveness in Organizations*, pp. 204–261 (Guzzo, R.A. & Salas, E., eds). San Francisco, CA: Jossey-Bass.

Jackson, S.E. & Schuler, R.E. (2000). *Managing Human Resources: A Partnership Perspective* (7th edn). Cincinnati, OH: South-Western College Publishing.

Jaques, E. (1961). *Equitable Payment*. New York: John Wiley and Sons.

Jerkunica, A., Gabrić, A. & Bratinčević, T. (2010). Introductory view on issues concerning human resources management in Croatian sports. *Sport Science, 3*(1), 75–78.

Jiang, K., Lepak, D.P., Hu, Kia, & Baer, J.C. (2012).How does human resource management influence organizational outcomes? A meta-analytic investigation of mediating mechanisms. *Academy of Management Journal, 55*(6), 1264–1294.

Johns, G. & Saks, A.M. (2011). *Organizational Behaviour: Understanding and Managing Life at Work* (8th edn). Toronto: Pearson.

Johns, T. & Gratton, L. (2013). The third wave of virtual work. Harvard Business Review Magazine (January–February). Retrieved 15 May 2014, from http://hbr.org/2013/01/the-third-wave-of-virtual-work/ar/1

Jones, R.L., Harris, R. & Miles, A. (2009). Mentoring in sports coaching: A review of the literature. *Physical Education and Sport Pedagogy, 14*(3), 267–284.

Jones, D.C., Kalmi, P. & Kauhanen, A. (2010). How does employee involvement stack up? The effects of human resource management policies on performance in a retail firm. *Industrial Relations, 49*, 1–21.

Kabanoff, B. (1991). Equity, equality, power, and conflict. *Academy of Management Review, 16*(2), 416–441.

Kammeyer-Mueller, J.D. & Wanberg, C.R. (2003). Unwrapping the organizational entry process: Disentangling multiple antecedents and their pathways to adjustment. *Journal of Applied Psychology, 88*(5), 779–794.

Kaplan, R.S. & Norton, D.P. (1996). Using the balanced scorecard as a strategic management system. *Harvard Business Review, 74*(1), 75–85.

Kelly, M. (2004). A biographical interpretation of women's journeys through athletic leadership: Pre and post title ix legislation. Unpublished Ph.D. Dissertation, University of Maryland.

Kim, M.S. (2004). Influence of individual difference factors on volunteer willingness to be trained. Unpublished Ph.D. Dissertation, The Ohio State University.

Kim, M., Chelladurai, P. & Trail, G.T. (2007). A model of volunteer retention in youth sport. *Journal of Sport Management, 21,* 151–171.

Kim, M., Zhang, J.J. & Connaughton, D. (2010). Modification of the Volunteer Functions Inventory for application in youth sports. *Sport Management Review 13,* 25–38.

Kim, T-Y., Cable, D.M. & Kim, S-P. (2005). Socialization tactics, employee proactivity, and person–organization fit. *Journal of Applied Psychology, 90*(2), 232–241.

Koskia, P. (2012). Finnish sports club as a mirror of society. *International Journal of Sport Policy and Politics, 4*(2), 257–275.

Kovach, K.A., Hamilton, N.G. & Meserole, M. (1997). Leveling the playing field. *Business and Economic Review, 44*(1), 12–18.

Kristof-Brown, A.L., Zimmerman, R.D. & Johnson, E.C. (2005). Consequences of individuals' fit at work: A meta-analysis of person-job, person-organization, person-group, and person-supervisor fit. *Personnel Psychology, 58,* 281–342.

Lado, A. & Wilson, M.C. (1994). Human resource systems and sustained competitive advantage: A competency-based perspective. *Academy of Management Review, 19*(4), 699–727.

Langton, N., Robbins, S.P. & Judge, T.A. (2010). *Organizational behaviour: Concepts, controversies, applications* (5th Can. edn). Toronto: Pearson.

Lapchik, R. (2008). *The 2008 Racial and Gender Report Card of the Associated Press Sports Editors.* Orlando, FL: The Institute for Diversity and Ethics in Sport/The University of Central Florida.

Lee, S.K.J. & Yu, K. (2004). Corporate culture and organizational performance. *Journal of Managerial Psychology, 19*(4), 340–359.

Legge, K. (1995). *Human Resource Management: Rhetorics and Realities.* London: Macmillan.

Lepak, D.P. & Shaw, J.D. (2008). Strategic HRM in North America: looking to the future. *The International Journal of Human Resource Management, 19*(8), 1486–1499.

Lewin, K. (1951). *Field Theory in Social Science.* New York: Harper and Row.

Lewis, M. (2003). *Moneyball: The Art of Winning an Unfair Game.* New York: W.W. Norton.

Lewis, P., Thornhill, A. & Saunders, M. (2003). *Employee Relations: Understanding the Employment Relationship.* London: Prentice-Hall.

Lok, P. & Crawford, J. (1999). The relationship between commitment and organizational culture, subculture, leadership style and job satisfaction in organizational change and development. *Leadership and Organization Development, 20*(7), 365–376.

London, M. (2003). *Job Feedback Giving, Seeking, and Using Feedback for Performance Improvement* (2nd edn). Mahwah, NJ: Lawrence Erlbaum Associates.

MacIntosh, E. & Doherty, A. (2005). Leader intentions and employee perceptions of organizational culture in a private fitness corporation. *European Sport Management Quarterly, 5*(1), 1–22.

MacIntosh, E. & Doherty, A. (2007a). Inside the Canadian fitness industry: Development of a conceptual framework of organizational culture (Working paper). London, Ontario: The University of Western Ontario.

MacIntosh, E. & Doherty, A. (2007b). Extending the scope of organizational culture: The external perception of an internal phenomenon. *Sport Management Review, 10*(1), 45–64.

MacIntosh, E. & Doherty, A. (2010). The influence of organizational culture on job satisfaction and intention to leave. *Sport Management Review, 13*(2), 106–117.

MacIntosh, E. & Walker, M. (2012). Chronicling the transient nature of fitness employees: An organizational culture perspective. *Journal of Sport Management, 26,* 113–126.

MacLean, J. (2001). *Performance Appraisal for Sport and Recreation Managers.* Champaign, IL: Human Kinetics.

MacLean, J. & Chelladurai, P. (1995). Dimensions of coaching performance: Development of a scale. *Journal of Sport Management, 9*(2), 194–207.

Magnay, J. (2010, 30 September). Commonwealth Games 2010: Indians burn effigy of Games chief executive Mike Hooper. *The Telegraph.* Retrieved 10 October 2013, from http://www.telegraph.

co.uk/sport/othersports/commonwealthgames/8034158/Commonwealth-Games-2010-Indians-burn-effigy-of-Games-chief-executive-Mike-Hooper.html

Major League Baseball Players Association (2012). *2012–2016 basic agreement.* Retrieved 14 May 2014, from http://mlb.mlb.com/pa/pdf/cba_english.pdf

Makover, B. (2003). *Examining the employee–customer chain in the fitness industry.* Unpublished Ph.D. Dissertation, Florida State University.

Malenfant, E.C., Lebel, A. & Martel, L. (2010). *Projections of the diversity of the Canadian population, 2006 to 2031.* Retrieved 14 April 2014, from http://www.statcan.gc.ca/pub/91-551-x/91-551-x2010001-eng.htm

Martin, J.J. (1992). *Cultures in Organizations: Three Perspectives.* New York: Oxford University Press.

Maslow, A.H. (1943). A theory of human motivation. *Psychological Review, 50*, 370–396.

Mayer, R.E. (1982). Learning. In *Encyclopedia of Educational Research*, pp. 1040–1058 (Mitzel, H.E., ed.). New York: Free Press.

McClelland, D. (1961). *The Achieving Society.* Princeton, NJ: Van Nostrand.

McGraw, P. (2002). The HR function in local and overseas firms: Evidence from the PricewaterhouseCoopers-Cranfield HR Project (1999). *Asia Pacific Journal of Human Resources, 40*(2), 1–24.

McGregor, D. (1957). An uneasy look at performance appraisal. *Harvard Business Review, 35*(3), 89–94.

McKenna, E. & Beech, N. (2002). *Human Resource Management: A Concise Analysis.* London: Prentice-Hall.

McShane, S.L. & Steen, S.L. (2012). *Canadian Organizational Behaviour* (8th edn). Toronto: McGraw-Hill Ryerson.

Meglino, B.M. & Ravlin, E.C. (1998). Individual values in organizations: Concepts, controversies, and research. *Journal of Management, 24*(3), 351–390.

Meyer, H.H., Kay, E. & French, J.R.P. (1965). Split roles in performance appraisal. *Harvard Business Review, 43*(1), 123–129.

Milkovich, G.T., Newman, J.M. & Gerhart, B. (2011). *Compensation* (10th edn). New York: McGraw-Hill Irwin.

Millar, P. & Stevens, J. (2012). Management training and national sport organization managers: Examining the impact of training on individual and organizational performances. *Sport Management Review, 15*(3), 288–303.

Milliken, F.J. & Martins, L.L. (1996). Searching for common threads: Understanding the multiple effects of diversity in organizational groups. *Academy of Management Review, 21*(2), 402–433.

Mitchell, T.R. & Daniels, D. (2003). Motivation. In *Handbook of Psychology, Vol. 12, Industrial and Organizational Psychology* (Borman, W.C., Ilgen, D.R. & Klimoski, R.J., eds). Hoboken, NJ: John Wiley and Sons.

Moore, N. & Levermore, R. (2012). English professional football clubs: Can business parameters of small and medium-sized enterprises be applied? *Sport, Business and Management: An International Journal, 2*(3), 196–209.

National Audit Office (2012). *The London 2012 Olympic Games and Paralympic Games: post-Games review.* Retrieved 11 October 2013, from http://www.nao.org.uk/wp-content/uploads/2012/12/1213794.pdf

National Basketball Players Association (2012). *CBA 101.* Retrieved 14 May 2014, from http://www.nba.com/media/CBA101_9.12.pdf

National Hockey League Players' Association (2013). *Collective bargaining agreement.* Retrieved 14 May 2014, from http://www.nhlpa.com/inside-nhlpa/collective-bargaining-agreement

Nesić, M., Fratrić, F. & Ilić, D. (2011). Education of sports managers in the context of the Bologna process. *Research in Kinesiology, 39*(2), 221–226.

Netting, F.E., Nelson, H.W., Borders, K. & Huber, R. (2004). Volunteer and paid staff relationships: Implications for social work administration. *Administration in Social Work, 28*(3/4), 69–89.

Neufeind, M., Güntert, S.T. & Wehner, T. (2013). The impact of job design on event volunteers' future engagement: insights from the European Football Championship 2008. *European Sport Management Quarterly, 13*(5), 537–556.

New South Wales Department of Sport and Recreation (n.d.) Office of Sport and Recreation. Retrieved 8 April 2007, from http://www.dsr.nsw.gov.au/industry/index.asp

Neville, S. (2013, 19 July). 2,000 Sports Direct staff to receive £100,000 bonus after record profits. *The Guardian*. Retrieved from http://www.theguardian.com/business/2013/jul/18/sports-direct-staff-bonus-profits

Nichols, G., Padmore, J., Taylor, P. & Barrett, D. (2012). The relationship between types of sports club and English government policy to grow participation. *International Journal of Sport Policy and Politics*, 4(2), 187–200.

Nichols, G., Taylor, P., James, M., King, L., Holmes, K. & Garrett, R. (2003). Pressures on sports volunteers arising from partnerships with the central government. *Loisir et Societe/Society and Leisure*, 26(2), 419–430.

Nonaka, I. & Takeuchi, H. (1995). *The Knowledge Creating Company: How Japanese Companies Create the Dynamics of Innovation*. New York: University Press.

North America's National Hockey League Players' Association (2013). Collective bargaining agreement. Retrieved 14 May 2014, from http://cdn.agilitycms.com/nhlpacom/PDF/NHL_NHLPA_2013_CBA.pdf

Ontario Ministry of Labour (2013a). Termination of employment. Retrieved 20 May 2014, from http://www.labour.gov.on.ca/english/es/pubs/guide/termination.php

Ontario Ministry of Labour (2013b). Severance pay. Retrieved 20 May 2014, from http://www.labour.gov.on.ca/english/es/pubs/guide/severance.php

Ormrod, J.E. (1999). *Human Learning* (3rd edn). Sydney, NSW: Prentice-Hall Australia.

Østerlund, K. (2013). Managing voluntary sport organizations to facilitate volunteer recruitment. *European Sport Management Quarterly*, 13(2), 143–165.

Park, S. & Kim, M. (2013). Development of a hierarchical model of sport volunteers' organizational commitment. *European Sport Management Quarterly*, 13(1), 94–109.

Parks, J. & Parra, L. (1994). Job satisfaction of sport management alumnae/i. *Journal of Sport Management*, 8(1), 49–56.

Pederson, P.M., Lim, C.H., Osborne, B. & Whisenant, W. (2009). An examination of the perceptions of sexual harassment by sport print media professionals. *Journal of Sport Management, 23*, 335–360.

Pfeffer, J. (1998). *The Human Equation: Building Profits by Putting People First*. Boston: Harvard Business School Press.

Porter, M.E. (1979). How competitive forces shape strategy. *Harvard Business Review*, 57(2), 137–145.

Prahalad, C.K. & Hamel, G. (1990). The core competence of the corporation. *Harvard Business Review*, 68(3), 79–91.

Pulakos, E. & Schmitt, N. (1995). Experience-based and situational questions: Studies of validity. *Personnel Psychology*, 48(2), 289–309.

Punnett, B.J. (2009). *International Perspectives on Organizational Behaviour and Human Resource Management* (2nd edn). Armonk, NY: M.E. Sharpe.

Randstad USA (2013). Company culture and reputation important in attracting company employees. Retrieved 10 December 2013, from http://www.randstadusa.com/about-randstad/press-room/company-culture-and-reputation-important-in-attracting-potential-employees

Rhodes, C. & Fletcher, S. (2013). Coaching and mentoring for self-efficacious leadership in schools. *International Journal of Mentoring and Coaching in Education*, 2(1), 47–63.

Ringuet-Riot, C., Cuskelly, G., Auld, C. & Zakus, D. H. (2014). Volunteer roles, involvement and commitment in voluntary sport organizations: evidence of core and peripheral volunteers. *Sport in Society*, 17(1), 116–133.

Robbins, S.P. (1997). *Organizational Behaviour: Concepts, Controversies, and Applications* (6th edn). Englewood Cliffs, NJ: Prentice-Hall.

Robbins, S.P. & Langton, N. (2004). *Fundamentals of Organizational Behaviour* (2nd Can. edn). Toronto: Pearson.

Rodgers, R. & Hunter, J. (1991). Impact of management by objectives on organizational productivity. *Journal of Applied Psychology*, 76(2), 322–326.

Rothwell, W.J. (2011). Replacement planning: a starting point for succession planning and talent management. *International Journal of Training & Development, 15*(1), 87–99.

Rousseau, D.M. (2001). Schema, promise and mutuality: The building blocks of the psychological contract. *Journal of Occupational and Organizational Psychology, 74*(4), 511–541.

Ruddick, G. (2013, 6 August). Sports Direct staff cash in with £112m bonus. *The Telegraph.* Retrieved from http://www.telegraph.co.uk/finance/newsbysector/retailandconsumer/10226755/Sports-Direct-staff-cash-in-with-112m-bonus.html

Running Room (2014a). About John Stanton. Retrieved 24 April 2014, from http://www.runningroom.com/hm/inside.php?id=3035

Running Room (2014b). History. Retrieved 24 April 2014, from http://www.runningroom.com/hm/inside.php?lang=1&id=3036

Sackmann, S. (2001). Cultural complexity in organizations: The value and limitations of qualitative methodology and approaches. In *International Handbook of Organizational Culture and Climate,* pp. 143–163 (Cooper, C.L., Cartwright, S. & Earley, P.C., eds). New York: John Wiley and Sons.

Saks, A.M. & Ashforth, B.E. (1997). Organizational socialization: Making sense of the past and present as a prologue for the future. *Journal of Vocational Behaviour, 51*(2), 234–279.

Salas, E., Tannenbaum, S.I., Kraiger, K. & Smith-Jentsch, K.A. (2012). The science of training and development in organizations: What matters in practice. *Psychological Science in the Public Interest, 13*(2), 74–101.

Schein, E.H. (1985). *Organizational Culture and Leadership.* San Francisco, CA: Jossey Bass.

Schmidt, F.L. & Hunter, J.E. (1983). Individual differences in productivity: An empirical test of estimates derived from studies of selection procedure utility. *Journal of Applied Psychology, 68*(3), 407–414.

Schoonover, S.C. (2011). Best practices in implementing succession planning. Retrieved 12 February 2014, from http://www.schoonover.com/userfiles/Succession%20Planning%20Best%20Practices.pdf

Schuler, R.S., Jackson, S.E. & Tarique, I. (2011). Global talent management and global talent challenges: Strategic opportunities for IHRM. *Journal of World Business, 46*(4), 506–516.

Seippel, Ø. (2002). Volunteers and professionals in Norwegian sport organizations. *Voluntas: International Journal of Voluntary and Nonprofit Organizations, 13*(3), 253–269.

Senge, P. (1990). *The Dance of Change: The Challenges of Sustaining Momentum in Learning Organizations.* New York: Doubleday.

Sheridan, J.E. (1992). Organizational culture and employee retention. *Academy of Management Journal, 35*(5), 1036–1056.

Silverthorne, C. (2004). The impact of organizational culture and person–organization fit on organizational commitment and job satisfaction in Taiwan. *Leadership and Organization Development Journal, 25*(7/8), 592–599.

Skirstad, B. & Chelladurai, P (2011). For 'love' and money: a sports club's innovative response to multiple logics. *Journal of Sport Management, 25*(4), 339–353.

Slack, T. & Parent, M.M. (2006). *Understanding Sport Organizations: The Application of Organization Theory* (2nd edn). Champaign, IL: Human Kinetics.

Smart, D.L. & Wolfe, R.A. (2000). Examining sustainable competitive advantage in intercollegiate athletics: A resource-based view. *Journal of Sport Management, 14,* 133–153.

Smith, A. & Shilbury, D. (2004). Mapping cultural dimensions in Australian sporting organizations. *Sport Management Review, 7*(2), 133–165.

Smucker, M.K. & Kent, A. (2004a). The influence of referent selection on pay, promotion, supervision, work, and co-worker satisfaction across three distinct sport industry segments. *International Sports Journal, 8*(1), 27–43.

Smucker, M.K. & Kent, A. (2004b). Job satisfaction and referent comparisons in the sport industry. *International Journal of Sport Management and Marketing, 5*(3), 262–280.

Sochi 2014 Organizing Committee (2013). Volunteers Sochi 2014. Retrieved 10 October 2013, from http://vol.sochi2014.com/en/

Social Media Influence (2013, 29 October). Social media spotlight: recruitment through Facebook? This sports brand proves it can be done. Retrieved 30 May 2013, from http://socialmediainfluence.

com/2012/10/29/social-media-spotlight-recruitment-through-facebook-this-sports-brand-proves-it-can-be-done/

Sport Chalet (2014a). About us. Retrieved 19 May 2014, from http://www.sportchalet.com/category/about+us.do

Sport Chalet (2014b). Benefits. Retrieved 19 May 2014, from http://jobs.sportchalet.com/benefits

Stone, R.J. (2010). *Managing Human Resources*. Queensland: John Wiley & Sons Australia.

Storey, J. (2001). *Human Resource Management: A Critical Text* (2nd edn). London: Thomson Learning.

Suffield, L. (2005). *Labour Relations*. Toronto: Pearson Education Canada.

Summer Universiade in Kazan Executive Directorate (2014). Students and teachers of IEML thanked for their contribution to Universiade. Retrieved 10 October 2013, from http://www.kazan2013.com/en/news_items/10843

Sutherland, K. (2013, 22 May). Social media puts HR ethics under the spotlight. Retrieved 30 May 2013, from http://monash.edu/news/show/social-media-puts-hr-ethics-under-the-spotlight

Talent Management (2014). ESPN: The right plays on talent. Retrieved 7 November 2013, from http://talentmgt.com/articles/view/espn_the_right_plays_on_talent/6

Taylor, T., Darcy, S., Hoye, R. & Cuskelly, G. (2006). Using psychological contract theory to explore issues in effective volunteer management. *European Sport Management Quarterly*, 6(2), 123–148.

Taylor, T. & Ho, C. (2005). Global human resource management influences on local sport organisations. *International Journal of Sport Management and Marketing*, 1(1/2), 110–126.

Taylor, T. & McGraw, P. (2006). Exploring human resource management practices in non-profit sport organisations. *Sport Management Review*, 9(3), 229–251.

Tichy, N., Fombrum, C. & Devanna, M.A. (1982). Strategic human resource management. *Sloan Management Review*, 23(2), 47–61.

Time Inc. (2014). Fortune best companies 2014. Retrieved 2 June 2014, from http://fortune.com/best-companies/google-1/

Tomlinson, A. (2014). The supreme leader sails on: leadership, ethics and governance in FIFA. *Sport in Society: Cultures, Commerce, Media, Politics*, DOI: 10.1080/17430437.2013.856590.

Torrington, D. (1989). Human resource management and the personnel function. In *New Perspectives on Human Resource Management*, pp. 56–66 (Storey, J., ed.). London: Routledge.

Torrington, D. & Hall, L. (1998). *Human Resource Management* (4th edn). London: Prentice-Hall.

Torrington, D., Hall, L. & Taylor, S. (2002) *Human Resource Management* (5th edn). Harlow: Pearson Education Limited.

Tosi, H.L., Mero, N.P. & Rizzo, J.R. (2000). *Managing Organizational Behaviour* (4th edn). Maiden, MA: Blackwell Publishers Inc.

Uggerslev, K.L., Fassina, N.E. & Kraichy, D. (2012). Recruiting through the stages: A meta-analytic test of predictors of applicant attraction at different stages of the recruiting process. *Personnel Psychology*, 65(3), 597–660.

UK Sport (2014). UK Sport – The UK's high performance sports agency. Retrieved 15 October 2013, from https://www.uksport.gov.uk

Union of European Football Associations (2014). Volunteers playing a vital role – UEFA. Retrieved 10 October 2013, from http://m.uefa.com/news/1829448/

United Nations (2013). World population prospects: The 2012 revision. Retrieved 17 April 2014, from http://esa.un.org/unpd/wpp/Documentation/pdf/WPP2012_HIGHLIGHTS.pdf

van der Linden, D., te Nijenhuis, J. & Bakker, A.B. (2010). The general factor of personality: A meta-analysis of Big Five intercorrelations and a criterion-related validity study. *Journal of Research in Personality*, 44(3), 315–327.

Van der Wagen, L. (2007). *Human Resource Management for Events*. Oxford: Butterworth-Heinemann.

Van Maanen, J. (1976). Breaking in: Socialization to work. In *Handbook of Work, Organization, and Society*, pp. 67–130 (Dubin, R., ed.). Chicago, IL: Rand-McNally.

Van Maanen, J. & Schein, E. (1979). Towards a theory of organizational socialization. In *Research in Organizational Behavior*, pp. 209–264 (Staw, B.M., ed.). Greenwich, CT: JAI Press.

Volunteer Canada (2006). The Canadian code for volunteer involvement. Ottawa: Volunteer Canada.

Vos, S., Breesch, D., Késenne, S., Lagae, W., Hoecke, J.V., Vanreusel, B. & Scheerder, J. (2012). The value of human resources in non–public sports providers: the importance of volunteers in non–profit sports clubs versus professionals in for–profit fitness and health clubs. *International Journal of Sport Management and Marketing*, *11*(1), 3–25.

Vroom, V.H. (1964). *Work and Motivation*. New York: Wiley.

Wanous, J.P. & Colella, A. (1989). Organizational entry research: Current status and future directions. In *Research in Personnel and Human Resources Management*, Vol. 7, pp. 59–120 (Ferris, G.R. & Rowlands, K.M., eds). Greenwich, CT: JAI Press.

Ward, D. (1996). Workforce demand forecasting techniques. *Human Resource Planning*, *19*(1), 54–55.

Warner, S., Tingle, J. K. & Kellett, P. (2013). Officiating attrition: The experiences of former referees via a sport development lens. *Journal of Sport Management*, *27*(4), 316–328.

Watson, T. (1977). *The Personnel Managers: A Study in the Sociology of Work and Industry*. London: Routledge and Keegan Paul.

Watt, B., Bennett, A. & Taylor, T. (2004). Career planning and development. In *Human Resources Guide*, pp. 371–384 (Redden, J. & Martin, G., eds). Sydney: CCH Australia Ltd.

Weaver, M. & Chelladurai, P. (2002). Mentoring in intercollegiate athletic administration. *Journal of Sport Management*, *16*(2), 96–116.

Weingarden, S. (2008). Top Choice – A case study in succession management. Retrieved 10 February 2014, from http://www.shrm.org/Education/hreducation/Documents/Top%20Choice%20Instructor%20Manual.pdf

Weinstein, D. (2012). The psychology of behaviorally-focused résumés on applicant selection: Are your hiring managers really hiring the 'right' people for the 'right' jobs? *Business Horizons*, *55*(1), 53–63.

Welty Peachey, J.W., Lyras, A., Cohen, A., Bruening, J.E. & Cunningham, G.B. (2013). Exploring the motives and retention factors of sport-for-development volunteers. *Nonprofit and Voluntary Sector Quarterly*, DOI: 10.1177/0899764013501579.

Whitmore, J. (2004). *Coaching for Performance: Growing People, Performance, and Purpose* (3rd edn). London: Nicholas Brealey Publishing.

Wolfe, R., Wright, P.M. & Smart, D.L. (2006). Radical HRM innovation and competitive advantage: The moneyball story. *Human Resource Management Journal*, *45*(1), 111–145.

Worman, D. (2005). Is there a business case for diversity? *Personnel Today*, 17 May, 27–28.

Wright, P.M. & McMahon, G.C. (1992). Theoretical perspective for strategic human resource management. *Journal of Management*, *18*(2), 295–320.

YMCA (2012). Discover your passion: Explore a career at the Y. Retrieved 1 May 2014, from http://www.ymca.net/career-opportunities/y-careers.pdf

Zeng, J.B. (2011). An investigation and research on the employment expectations and current situation of P.E. majors in China – A case study of 11 normal universities in East-China area. *Journal of Beijing Sport University*, *33*(2). Retrieved 23 August 2014, from http://en.cnki.com.cn/Article_en/CJFDTOTAL-BJTD201102030.htm

Zhang, L. & Gowan, M.A. (2012). Corporate social responsibility, applicants' individual traits, and organizational attraction: A person–organization fit perspective. *Journal Of Business & Psychology*, *27*(3), 345–362.

Zhao, S., Smith, R. & Campbell, M. (2012). Trends in succession management in Asia: HR perspectives across three countries, Center for Creative Leadership. Retrieved 12 February 2014, from http://www.ccl.org/leadership/pdf/research/TrendsSuccessionMgmtAsia.pdf

Index